Until his death in 2018, **Ira Berlin** was one of the preeminent historians of American slavery. He was the author of *Many Thousands Gone, Generations of Captivity,* and *Slaves Without Masters* (published by The New Press). He co-edited *Families and Freedom* (with Leslie S. Rowland) and *Slavery in New York* (with Leslie M. Harris), both published by The New Press. His books have won the Frederick Douglass Prize, the Los Angeles Times Book Prize, and the Gilder Lehrman Lincoln Prize, among many other awards.

Marc Favreau is the Executive Editor and Director of Programs of The New Press. He is the editor of *A People's History of World War II: The World's Most Destructive Conflict, as Told by the People Who Lived Through It* (The New Press). He lives in New York City and Martha's Vineyard, Massachusetts.

Steven F. Miller is a co-editor of the Freedmen and Southern Society Project and a co-editor (with Ira Berlin, Barbara J. Fields, Joseph P. Reidy, and Leslie S. Rowland) of *Free at Last: A Documentary History of Slavery, Freedom, and the Civil War* (The New Press).

Annette Gordon-Reed is the Carl M. Loeb University Professor at Harvard and the winner of sixteen book prizes, including the Pulitzer Prize for History in 2009 and the National Book Award in 2008 for *The Hemingses of Monticello.* She divides her time between New York City and Cambridge, Massachusetts.

REMEMBERING SLAVERY

AFRICAN AMERICANS
TALK ABOUT THEIR PERSONAL
EXPERIENCES OF SLAVERY

AND

EMANCIPATION

EDITED BY

IRA BERLIN, MARC FAVREAU,
AND STEVEN F. MILLER

NEW YORK
LONDON

Requests for permission to reproduce selections from this book
should be made through our website: https://thenewpress.com/contact.

The publisher of *Weevils in the Wheat: Interviews with Virginia Ex-Slaves* by
Charles L. Perdue Jr., Thomas E. Barden, and Robert K. Phillips (Charlottesville,
Va., 1994) has generously given permission to use extended quotations from this
copyrighted work. Reprinted with permission of the University Press of Virginia.

The portrait on the cover is of Fannie Moore, a resident of Asheville, North Carolina.
Ms. Moore's interview appears on pages 132–34.

"Mother to Son," from *The Collected Poems of Langston Hughes*, copyrighted by the
estate of Langston Hughes, reprinted by permission of Alfred A. Knopf, Inc.

The photographs of former slaves are from "U.S. WPA Record: Ex-Slave Narratives" in
the collection of the Manuscript Division of the Library of Congress.

Published in the United States by The New Press, New York, 2021
Distributed by Two Rivers Distribution

ISBN 978-1-62097-028-7 (pb)
ISBN 978-1-62097-044-7 (ebook)
CIP data available.

The New Press publishes books that promote and enrich public discussion
and understanding of the issues vital to our democracy and to a more equitable world.
These books are made possible by the enthusiasm of our readers; the support of a
committed group of donors, large and small; the collaboration of our many partners in
the independent media and the not-for-profit sector; booksellers, who often hand-sell
New Press books; librarians; and above all by our authors.

Printed in the United States of America

2 4 6 8 10 9 7 5 3 1

CONTENTS

Editors' Note

When *Remembering Slavery* was first prepared for publication, the text was part of a broader multimedia project involving different partners, notably the Library of Congress and Smithsonian Productions. The core of the project was a collection of remarkable early recordings of the voices of formerly enslaved people, which had been digitized in the 1990s and made audible and accessible for the first time. These recordings were combined with selections from the Slave Narratives from the Federal Writers project to produce the book and its companion radio documentary. In a format that is difficult to imagine today, the book was originally published with a set of audio cassette tapes; later editions included two compact discs. This new edition of *Remembering Slavery* reproduces the original text of the first edition, and includes references to these audio components (which for obvious reason no longer accompany the book). Readers interested in hearing the original recordings of interviews with formerly enslaved people can access them at the Library of Congress: www.loc.gov/collections/voices -remembering-slavery/about-this-collection. They remain historically important and are also immensely stirring.

Foreword to the 2021 Edition

One of the many deep tragedies of American slavery is the anonymity that was forced upon the vast majority of the people who lived under the strictures of that system. Denied education—except in the rarest circumstances—and kept outside of legal marriage, property ownership, and the capacity to contract, the overwhelming majority of enslaved people left no documents that could tell us about their lives. Instead, we are left to the self-serving records of the people who enslaved them or to analyzing documents related to court cases—civil and criminal—over which the enslaved had only minimal, if any, influence. So the thoughts, feelings, and words of the people most directly affected by the myriad day-to-day cruelties of an institution that treated human beings like property are underrepresented in the historical record.

But as the recollections in this volume show, however the legal system defined them, whatever those who enslaved them thought and said about them, enslaved African Americans were human. Their humanity shines through clearly and unmistakably in these pages as they speak about their families, their attempts to carry on under the oppression of chattel slavery, their religious views, and their assessments of the people who oppressed them and of other enslaved people. The deep wrong visited upon them—the word "wrong" does not begin to do justice to the magnitude of slavery—comes through with equal clarity in the descriptions of their lives.

The twenty-fifth anniversary of the appearance of *Remembering Slavery*, first published in 1996, falls in the midst of what has been touted as a twenty-first-century American "reckoning" with the problem of race. Concerns about police brutality against people of color, voter suppression, the rise of White nationalist groups, and other racially related issues have led to soul searching at nearly all levels of society. The term "white supremacy" has gained currency as Americans try to come to terms with the confusing dynamics of the country's racial situation that seems at once to be improving, sliding backwards, and remaining static. While the status of Black Americans has, by some metrics, improved much since the end of the Civil Rights Era of the 1960s, with greater access to education, the expansion of the Black middle class, and the development of an elected leadership class, serious problems persist. Black wealth stubbornly remains just a fraction of that of White wealth. The life expectancy of Black males is lower than that of any other group in the country. Black women are three times more likely to die in childbirth than White women. During the COVID-19 pandemic of 2020–2021, Blacks experienced the highest death rate. It appears that starting from behind, in a system that has yet to totally rid itself of the racial inequalities built into its structure, has hampered Blacks' efforts to achieve the full measure of the rights that the Declaration of Independence proclaimed as universal: namely the rights to life, liberty, and the pursuit of happiness.

Quite naturally, people look to history for clues about how we have arrived at our present state. There is no doubt that America's system of racially based slavery, which existed nearly three centuries, has helped shape American attitudes about race, and has contributed to some of the problems noted above. The specific laws of slavery, and the laws that operationalized the institution through the general laws of property, trusts and estates, contract and criminal law created a template for how to think about race, enacting White supremacy at every turn. Even after slavery's end, the logic of those laws and customs carried over, and were the impetus for the rules of legalized racial segregation—Jim Crow—that lasted until the mid 1960s. One can truly say that the United States has existed as a legally free and equal society just over a half a century, after passage of the Voting Rights Act in 1965.

There is no better way to think about an important part of the past that has helped shape our present than by looking at, and thinking about, the institution of slavery through the eyes of the enslaved. The recollections of slavery that appear in this volume tell this story in the most intimate way.

Very significantly, what we see here is not only the story of slavery. We see the construction of a racial hierarchy. The laws designed to set the contours of the peculiar institution also set forth how people of African descent could be treated in America—as if they were naturally inferior to Whites and could never truly be equal members of the American community. Racially based slavery, therefore, even defined the lives of the minority of Blacks who were free. Even outside of slavery, these people were to be treated as second-class Americans.

It is important to note that the laws, and the customs that grew up along with the laws, not only affected Black people, they affected Whites as well—as the stories told in *Remembering Slavery* reveal. After all, the enslaved and the enslavers existed in dynamic relationship to one another. Unlike actual property, enslaved people could talk back, they could make plans, and they reacted to things done to them. Importantly, they had reactions that enslavers had to ignore or rationalize away—crying upon the loss of loved ones through death or sale, anger at mistreatment or obvious unfairness. In the face of their humanity, enslavers constructed narratives about Black people that justified their enslavement, narratives that survived the end of slavery.

Like all marginalized people who lived under the power of others, enslaved people had to study and know the people who controlled their lives. It was actually more important for them to know the ways and whims of their enslavers than it was for their enslavers to know them. Lacking structured power, the enslaved were left to using whatever leverage they had, which was most often very little, to ameliorate their circumstances as best they could. They had to learn how far they could go with one White person, and how they could not go far with another. Tellingly, these recollections show that enslaved people were well aware of their true value to those who enslaved them. Anne Clark, born and enslaved in Mississippi, was adamant about what the end of slavery meant in the South: "You know, the white folks hated to give us up worse thing in the world," she declared.

One cannot read these stories without asking, "What would motivate people to treat other human beings in the manner described in these anecdotes?" The word "property" is key. Property was at the heart of the Anglo-American system of law. The chance to acquire it was one of the main reasons Europeans came to North America, leaving behind a country where few had the opportunities to obtain property. Owning property was associated with independence and, perhaps, the chance to amass wealth. Those who possessed it, according to the ideal, could be self-sufficient and could have the right to vote and participate in the running of the society. As for the property itself, owners had the right to control, use, and dispose of their property as they saw fit.

With the development of slavery, and the concept of property in people, the attributes associated with the ownership of things—land and personal items—were transferred to ownership of persons of African descent, with the tragic results displayed in these pages. Enslavers used their human property for labor in the fields, homes, and in factories. They leased them out. They used them for sexual pleasure. They disposed of them through gift and sale. Enslavers controlled their human property through corporal punishment and other forms of torture. These recollections make clear that slavery apologists' claim that, because the enslaved were property and were thus valuable, they were not mistreated, was untrue.

Perhaps the most frightening aspect of being considered an item of property was the knowledge that one's owners had the right to dispose of one's person as they saw fit. The truly heartbreaking passages in these recollections are from the enslaved, like Betty Simmons of Alabama, Texas, who were sold away from family members "never" to see them any "more in [this] world." The recollections make plain that the threat of sale was a more potent tool for maintaining control than the ubiquitous whip or other physical punishments that were meted out to the enslaved, male and female alike. The descriptions in these memoirs of families torn apart when an enslaver died and his or her property in land and enslaved people was divided among heirs, or of when people sold families apart to gain extra money, bring the horror of slavery home in the most visceral way. The bonds of family and community, connections that could be severed upon the whim of others, were extremely important. They were, in a sense, all the enslaved had in the world. Enslavers knew this well, and often used it to exercise control over the people they held in bondage.

We owe the existence of these extraordinary memoirs to the Federal Writers Project, working under the auspices of the Works Progress Administration. Otherwise unemployed writer/interviewers fanned out across the states of the Old South between 1936 and 1938, gathering the memories of formerly enslaved people. Although these interviews should be seen as the treasures they are, they should be read with some caution. Some of the people in charge of gathering the information had very specific ideas about how the people interviewed were to sound. The interviewers were encouraged to use the universal dialect attributed to Black Americans rather than writing in Standard English. As a result, enslaved people from Texas to Virginia sound exactly the same, even though accents in these various southern locales would not have been exactly the same. Often, the renditions sound like caricatures, putting distance between reader and speaker that need not have been there. It is highly unlikely that had they been interviewing White southerners, who would also have had accents, that they would have insisted on rendering every one of their words the way they spoke them. What should have been important was the substance of what the people were saying, not how they were saying it. The push for some notion of "authenticity," when that is not sought for Whites who had what may be seen as idiosyncratic speech patterns, reinforced the notion of Blacks as "the other" and Whites as "normal" or "standard." As a result, readers must work through what are almost certainly imperfect and inaccurate renderings of Black speech to get to the very important things the interviewees were saying. That work should be done, but the WPA interviewers did the enslaved no favors.

As the memory of slavery recedes further and further from view, and as we continue to grapple with the subject of race in the United States, *Remembering Slavery* will remain an important guide to the how and why of the country's racial predicament. One important way to pay homage to the people whose suffering and oppression helped build the American nation is to listen carefully to what they had to say about their lives. It is a debt that we owe them.

—Annette Gordon-Reed
April 2021

FOREWORD

Racial slavery has shaped virtually every aspect of our nation's history. Slavery provided one of the essential legs upon which modern capitalism was built. Slavery shaped the development of the American political structure, from its peculiar form of federalism to the astonishing, and continuing, disproportional influence of Southern legislators. Today's various racial constructions—whiteness, blackness, and an Other category that persistently renders nonwhites and nonblacks invisible—are obviously rooted in the history of slavery and Jim Crow.

Enslaved Africans and their descendants were and are assigned the impossible role of maintaining stable American race relations. Slaves were instructed on pain of injury not to protest an unhealthy relationship fixed by whites for the benefit of whites. Remarkably, slaves did not obey. They managed to bring on the Civil War; in the process, they destroyed the system of slavery and delivered a more fully realized American democracy.

Those heroic people are the generation most represented in this important book-and-CD set. Daughters and sons of Africa, these children who bore the mark of the lash wanted free universal education for everyone, the right to vote for everyone, the right to own and work their land, the right to build communities, worship, and love each other without the threat of mob violence. The architects of a new nation . . . these are the people the Federal Writers' Project and others sought to restore to history during the 1930s and early 1940s. And these are the souls Ira Berlin, Marc Favreau, and Steven F. Miller want us to remember.

Those ex-slaves who lived to tell their stories do not all speak in one voice, nor do they share one big collective memory. The interviews do represent one of the few bodies of slave thought in which black slaves described the conditions they faced, their oppressions, their resistance. But some of the passages will frustrate readers interested only in dramatic cases of brutality or heroic acts of defiance. Alongside the tragic we find stories of "happy darkies" who virtually pine for the days of slavery, as well as detailed, moving descriptions of the day-to-day violence inflicted on the very young and very old.

Stories like the latter were told at considerable risk. As Wes Brady put it in his interview, "Some white folks might want to put me back in slavery if I tells how we was used in slavery time, but you asks me for the truth." Readers must remember that when these interviews were being conducted, the stench of "strange fruit" still lingered in the Southern countryside where many of the informants still resided. In 1935 alone there were fifteen recorded lynchings, for which no one was prosecuted. Prisons and jails were populated with African Americans whose only crime was insolence, the most infamous case involving nine young men falsely accused of raping two white women near Scottsboro, Alabama.

The ex-slaves had reason to be scared. Readers must also keep in mind that what the elderly informants remembered about the old times was being filtered through their present struggle to endure the Great Depression. They spoke with their heads and their stomachs. "We was happy," recalled Felix Haywood. "We got our lickings, but just the same we get our fill of biscuits every time the white folks had 'em. Nobody knew how it was to lack food."

But fear and Depression hunger alone do not explain the complicated character of their recollections. Slavery was a painful period, an era African Americans had been trying to forget since Reconstruction. Consider that many black churches worked hard to eliminate the "ol' spirituals" as a way of removing all vestiges of slavery from their cultural memory. The worst of the informants' slavery experiences may have been purged from their minds.

In any case, the moments of pleasure and happiness that the ex-slaves *did* remember never celebrate the master class or endorse the system of slavery. Even as slaves, black people struggled to own their own lives; they turned the quarters and yards and woods into places of quiet contemplation or hideaway dens for party people. Later they recalled those good times and even expressed sympathy and kindness for their keepers. How could they not? How on earth could so many people held in bondage have survived slavery without humor, joy, love, good times, healthy relationships, a sense of self-worth?

If all of these disparate stories and diverse voices embody one single theme, it is humanity. Together the narratives reinforce the incredible ability of African Americans to maintain their dignity and self-worth, to offer the rest of the world a model of humanity that could emancipate "free" people the world over, including their own masters, the overseers, and even the "paddy rollers" dispatched to hunt down runaways. The smartest slaveholders must have come to appreciate black humanity and its capacity for love and forgiveness—for those qualities are precisely what spared the lives of the "masters" and their families. It is our recognition of the ex-slaves' humanity that enables us to discard the false dichotomies of "Sambo" and "rebel" and see these amazing black survivors as complicated human beings.

Robin D. G. Kelley

PREFACE

Remembering Slavery is a short book with a long history. First among its many progenitors is André Schiffrin, publisher of The New Press. In 1995, Schiffrin and Ralph Eubanks, director of publications at the Library of Congress, initiated a project to make available a book-and-tapes version of the audio recordings of former slaves dating from the late 1930s and 1940s. A year later, Schiffrin invited Ira Berlin of the University of Maryland to lead the project; Berlin in turn enlisted Marc Favreau, then beginning graduate studies at the university, to join him. Together they began the laborious process of transcribing and annotating the tapes at the Library of Congress, which had been copied from the primitive aluminum disks that had originally stored the former slaves' reminiscences. In this work they found indispensable the extraordinarily detailed transcriptions crafted by linguists Guy Bailey, Natalie Maynor, and Patricia Cukor-Avila. Professor Bailey, now a dean at the University of Texas, San Antonio, generously granted permission to use these transcriptions and offered his own expertise in interpreting him. For that we would like to thank him.

Coincidentally, Jacquie Gales Webb, the series producer of Smithsonian Productions (the broadcasting and audio reproduction arm of the Smithsonian Institution), had embarked on a similar project using the recorded ex-slave interviews. With the aid of the institution's talented technicians, the Smithsonian group had retransferred the collection from the original source disks at the Library of Congress and performed audio restoration. Not only were the remastered tapes easier on the ear, they also permitted more complete and accurate text transcriptions. The Smithsonian had been working with the Institute of Language and Culture in Montgomery, Alabama, which under the leadership of Project Director Kathie Farnell had received a planning grant from the National Endowment for the Humanities to develop a radio documentary based on the interviews and had independently gathered many of the linguists and social historians interested in the audio transcripts.

In 1997, the two groups who had been working independently found each other. Steven F. Miller, one of the consultants for the Smithsonian project, joined Berlin and Favreau on the book project, and the two teams struck an active collaboration, coordinated by Joe Wood of The New Press. The projects jointly agreed to supplement the recorded ex-slave interviews with the transcribed interviews with former slaves gathered in the late 1930s by the Federal Writers' Project. This book and the two-part radio documentary of the same title are the fruits of this collaboration. Our aim has been to create two distinct, but complementary works. Their subjects are closely related and their contents overlap somewhat, but each contains considerable material that is not available in the other. (A transcript of the radio documentary appears as an appendix.)

An undertaking such as this, involving artists, scholars, and technicians from four different institutions, is rife with possibilities for confusion and even gridlock. That it ran smoothly and on time is a testament to the staffs at Smithsonian Productions, The New Press, and the Institute of Language and Culture. At Smithsonian Productions, we wish to thank Paul Johnson, director; Wesley Horner, executive producer, Martha Knouss, marketing manager, and particularly Jacquie Gales Webb. Technical wizards John Tyler, audio production manager, and Todd Hulslander, production engineer, performed the remastering of the recorded interviews. At The New Press, Joe Wood helped to shape an idea into a manuscript; and Diane Wachtell, associate director, Grace Farrell, managing editor, Fran Forte, production manager, and Greg Carter, editorial assistant, helped transform the manuscript into a book. Kathie Farnell of the Institute of Language and Culture was instrumental in coordinating the various components of an enterprise that grew larger and more complicated as time went on.

Both the book and the radio documentary have benefited from the scholars who served as consultants: Guy Bailey; Richard Bailey of Montgomery, Alabama; Alwyn Barr of Texas Tech University; Jeutonne P. Brewer of the University of North Carolina, Greensboro; Horace Huntley of the Birmingham Civil Rights Institute; and Robert McElvaine of Millsaps College. Their criticisms and suggestions have been enormously helpful. Alan Jabbour, director of the American Folklife Center at the Library of Congress, and Joe Hickerson, the center's head of acquisitions, generously explicated the complex history of the Slave Narrative Collection after its accession to the Library. We would especially like to thank Jeutonne Brewer, who shared her unrivaled knowledge of the making and preservation of the recorded interviews and offered sensible suggestions about presenting them to an audience of general readers.

Like all modern scholars of slavery, we are indebted to the pioneering work of George P. Rawick and his associates, Ken Lawrence and Jan Hillegas, who brought into print the typescripts of the ex-slave narratives collected by the Federal Writers' Project. Thanks are due as well to Charles L. Perdue, Jr., Thomas E. Barden, and Robert K. Phillips. Excerpts from their volume, *Weevils in the Wheat: Interviews with Virginia Ex-Slaves*, appear herein with the generous permission of the University Press of Virginia.

In the radio documentary, the written words of former slaves were brought to life by the voices of Debbie Allen, Clifton Davis, Louis Gossett, Jr., James Earl Jones, Melba Moore, Esther Rolle, Jedda Jones, John Sawyer, and host Tonea Stewart. Composer Bryant Pugh provided the extraordinary musical accompaniment.

The radio programs are supported by grants from the National Endowment for the Humanities, the Corporation for Public Broadcasting, the Southern Humanities Media Fund, and the Alabama Humanities Council.

Ira Berlin

Marc Favreau

Steven F. Miller

College Park, Maryland

INTRODUCTION: SLAVERY AS MEMORY AND HISTORY

The struggle over slavery's memory has been almost as intense as the struggle over slavery itself. For many, the memory of slavery in the United States was too important to be left to the black men and women who experienced it directly. The stakes were too great. The American nation had invested much in slavery, maintaining it for more than two centuries and destroying it in a bloody Civil War that took nearly one million lives and destroyed billions of dollars in property. Indeed, its demise elevated slavery's importance and intensified the struggle over how it should be remembered by posterity. Northerners who fought and won the war at great cost incorporated the abolitionists' perspective into their understanding of American nationality: slavery was evil, a great blot that had to be excised to realize the full promise of the Declaration of Independence. At first, even some white Southerners— former slaveholders among them—accepted this view, conceding that slavery had burdened the South as it had burdened the nation and declaring themselves glad to be rid of it. But during the late nineteenth century, after attempts to reconstruct the nation on the basis of equality collapsed and demands for sectional reconciliation mounted, the portrayal of slavery changed. White Northerners and white Southerners began to depict slavery as a benign and even benevolent institution, echoing themes from the planters' defense of the antebellum order. They contrasted the violence and enmity of the postwar period with the supposed tranquility of slave times, when happy slaves frolicked in the service of indulgent masters. Such views, popularized in the stories of Joel Chandler Harris and the songs of Stephen Foster, became pervasive during the first third of the twentieth century.

Against this new romanticized representation of slavery stood the men and women who had survived the institution. Frederick Douglass and other members of the old abolitionist generation railed against the rehabilitation of slavery's reputation, testifying from personal experience to its ugly power. But as death shrank their numbers, the old opponents of slavery could rarely be heard outside the black community. Their frail and distant voices were generally ignored, if heard at all, by the majority of white Americans.

Still, the men and women who survived slavery had much to tell. And as the first generation of black people born in freedom came of age, fears that the slave experience would be lost forever troubled some scholars, particularly those at African-American colleges for whom the new portrayal of slavery was an anathema. At Fisk University in Nashville, Southern University in Baton Rouge, and Kentucky State University in Frankfort, historians initiated projects to interview former slaves. Their accounts, published privately or in the recently established *Journal of Negro History* during the 1920s, had little impact on the larger historical profession. White historians either discounted the validity of these accounts or saw them as peripheral to what they believed to be slavery's larger meaning in American life—its role in the coming of the Civil War. According to historian Ulrich B. Phillips, whose view of slavery as a benign institution dominated the field, the "asseverations of politicians, pamphleteers, and aged survivors" were hopelessly tainted, unfit to use even as a "supplement" to other, superior sources. By and large, the ex-slave narratives of the 1920s languished in the archives unread.

While ignored by historians, the narratives impressed folklorists, whose discipline gained new visibility in the 1930s. The Great Depression forced scholars, like all Americans, to reconsider the experience of the American people. In the study of history, as in many other disciplines, the emphasis was on the common folk, their language, song, art, and stories. The New Deal's Federal Writers' Project—one of several efforts to employ artists, musicians, and actors—gloried in the celebration of everyday Americans. Among its tasks was the collection of first-hand biographies of ordinary American people.

To this end, a special section of the Federal Writers' Project directed first by John A. Lomax, then by Benjamin A. Botkin, and finally by Sterling A. Brown, took up the task that black scholars had begun in the 1920s. Lawrence Reddick of Kentucky State University, who in 1935 had expanded his earlier work into the Ohio Valley under the auspices of Federal Emergency Relief Administration, bridged the work of black scholars and the new, more expansive federal effort. Between 1936 and 1938, project-sponsored interviewers in seventeen states collected the reminiscences of thousands of former slaves. In the process, they produced tens of thousands of pages of typescripts. In some cases, photographs of the interviewees and their families accompanied the documentation. Although the project was terminated before its completion, by the end of the decade some of the interviews were finding their way into print. In 1939, control of the Federal Writers' Project passed from the federal government to the states, and in October of that year the interviews were deposited at the Library of Congress in Washington. There Benjamin Botkin and his staff began evaluating and indexing the interviews, and two years later the "Slave Narratives: A Folk History of Slavery in the United States from Interviews with Former Slaves" was placed in the Library's manuscript room.

Even before the Federal Writers' Project had expanded and extended Reddick's work in the Ohio Valley, another group of scholars had begun to record the words and songs of former slaves. Burdened by primitive recording equipment and the lack of precedents to guide them, these pioneering men and women—who included John and Ruby Lomax and John's son Alan, Zora Neal Hurston, Roscoe Lewis, and John Henry Faulk—journeyed through the South trying to capture the voices of men and women who had experienced slavery. John Lomax, who had just been appointed honorary curator of the Library of Congress's Archive of Folk Song, led the effort; his and his son's work inspired Faulk, who was then beginning his graduate studies at the University of Texas. Others, working separately, followed the same course, often in consultation with Lomax and sometimes with the aid of Rosenwald fellowships. It would be Faulk, whose work extended into the early 1940s, who would eventually make the most important recordings of former slaves. His acetate discs would be deposited in the Library of Congress, where they were incorporated into the Archive of Folk Song, and in the University of Texas Library in Austin.

Historians of slavery continued to ignore this rich trove of evidence, although its existence became well known with the 1945 publication of Benjamin Botkin's *Lay My Burden Down*, the first of many anthologies drawn from the Federal Writers' Project narratives. Indeed, soon after the appearance of Botkin's volume, the Library of Congress microfilmed its collection to increase availability. Still, most historians treated the narratives with disdain. Some scholars condemned them as tainted by the unreliable memories of elderly informants, most of whom had been children at the time of slavery's demise; others questioned the statistical representativeness of the informants, who equaled roughly 2 percent of the ex-slave population in 1930 and, of course, only a tiny fraction of the slave population in 1860. Thus, through the 1950s, the slave narratives gathered dust in federal depositories, and many of those in state archives and private hands may have been destroyed or lost forever.

Beginning in the 1960s, though, stoked by the Civil Rights movement, a growing interest in slavery as the root cause of America's racial dilemma reawakened interest in the narratives. Concerned with slavery less as a cause of the Civil War than as the primary experience of millions of Americans, historians pored over the narratives as a means of gaining access to the slaves' voices. In 1972, when George P. Rawick compiled and published nineteen volumes of the Library of Congress's transcripts under the title *The American Slave: A Composite Autobiography*, he saw as his "primary reason . . . to make it possible to gain a perspective on the slave experience in North America from those who had been slaves." True to Rawick's promise, *The American Slave* immediately sparked a thorough rethinking of African-American captivity and underlay major reinterpretations of slavery by John W. Blassingame, Eugene D. Genovese, Herbert G. Gutman, Lawrence Levine, Leon F. Litwack, Albert J. Raboteau, Thomas L. Webber, and Rawick himself. Meanwhile, new collections of narratives were uncovered in state and local archives and brought to print. In 1977, when Rawick published a second series of twelve volumes drawn from state archives as well as the Library of Congress, the number of narratives in print reached 3,500. Another ten volumes followed over the next two years, including the interviews compiled at Fisk University in the 1920s. Archivists and historians, searching out long-lost transcripts, published compilations reflecting the experience of slaves in particular states. From these volumes came yet others assembled for classroom use. The narratives, once dismissed as historical ephemera, had moved to the center of the study of slavery. By 1979, according to one historiographic review, the narratives were "as widely used as any other single source of data on American slavery."

The new scholars of slavery remained skeptical of the narratives' value, but for different reasons than their predecessors. Whereas Phillips had feared that the narratives would cast doubt on benevolent views of slavery, the revisionists worried that the narratives would foster just such a view of a kindly institution. They observed that the interviewers—nearly all of whom were white Southerners—had tended to select the most obsequious informants, "good Negroes" in the euphemism of the day. Noting that most of those interviewed were old and impoverished in a rigidly segregated society, slavery's new historians suspected that ex-slaves had told not what had actually happened but what their interviewers wanted to hear. After all, many of the interviewers were descended from the same people who had once owned the former slaves and their parents. Moreover, they were employed by a government agency, which led some interviewees to believe that the interviewers might help them obtain pensions, relief, or other benefits.

The interviewers themselves, of course, approached their work with their own beliefs and assumptions about slavery and its aftermath. Like most Americans, they generally accepted the notion that the Civil War had been a tragedy, Reconstruction a great mistake, and slavery as much an ordeal for white people as for black people. Even when the interviewers were sympathetic to the slaves' plight, they frequently patronized their subjects, calling them "uncle" and "aunt" and asking leading questions about sensitive issues of race relations, both historical and contemporary, that informants likely feared to answer straightforwardly. By their person and their approach, such interviewers evoked carefully hedged responses. Black men and women, drawing on a tradition that reached back into slavery, answered in a way that obliged the interviewer. Some interviewees preferred not to dredge up painful memories, much less share them with a white interviewer. Others answered in vague generalities that owed at least as much to their suspicions about the questioners as to the dimness of their recollections. A common pattern was to characterize their own treatment under slavery as benign, while describing that of neighboring slaves as brutal. Although such testimony reflected the fact that master–slave relations varied greatly from place to place, the transference in which former slaves attributed to their neighbors that which had actually happened to them revealed both the complexity of contemporary race relations and the manner in which former slaves believed it necessary to cloak their experiences.

As scholars closely inspected the narratives and the records of the Federal Writers' Project, other problems emerged. They discovered that in preparing what project editors called "ex-slave stories," many interviewers edited the informants' words, eliminating references they found indelicate, implausible, personally objectionable, or ideologically offensive. Moreover, interviewers often altered the dialect as well as the words of their informant—sometimes to make them conform to popular caricatures of "authentic" black speech, sometimes to make them conform to standard English. In any case, the narratives were rarely verbatim transcriptions. As a rule, they were reconstructions of conversations based on notes taken by the interviewer. Most of the narratives might best be considered fair summaries. A few were little more than fabrications, far more indicative of the historical memory and racial attitudes of white Southerners in the 1930s than of the lives of black slaves of the 1850s.

But, for all these and other problems, the corpus of narratives had great historic value. Many of the interviews—particularly those taken by sympathetic interviewers—evoked compelling remembrances of slavery of the sort it is impossible to fabricate. Former slaves were often eager to tell their tales, even to the most condescending of interviewers. Some had lost their fear of retaliation, prefacing their remarks with a warning that their interviewer might not like what they had to say, but they had to speak their minds. Although some interviewers may have dismissed their accounts—a few went so far as to record their displeasure or dissent in footnotes to their transcripts or memos to their superiors—many accepted them. The age of the former slaves, and the respect traditionally granted elderly people in Southern society, often provided an opportunity for slaves to speak openly and forcefully. Moreover, the administrators of the Federal Writers' Project, aware of how the former slaves' testimony was being adulterated, issued directives against such revisions, which restrained some of the more zealous editors and curbed the more outlandish dialect renderings.

Viewed from this perspective, the narratives were like every other historical source: they had strengths and weaknesses. If they were in some respects tainted, so too were other sources of slavery—including the records produced by slaveholders and their white supporters. The historian's task was, as always, to employ them in ways that maximized their utility. The best scholars of slavery have used them critically and cautiously, carefully evaluating the quality of each narrative, verifying the ex-slaves's memory against other sources, and sometimes even sifting through multiple versions of the same interview. Thus, the narratives, have become subject to all the requirements of any other historical source.

While the typescript narratives, readily available in print, became a standard source for the study of slavery, historians gave little attention to the sound recordings of the ex-slaves. During the 1960s, the Archive of Folk

Song at the Library of Congress transferred its recordings from the fragile aluminum and acetate discs to ten-inch tape reels, but the sound remained scratchy and often inaudible; not until the mid 1980s did they attract a group of linguists interested in the evolution of African-American English. Led by Guy Bailey, Natalie Maynor, and Patricia Cukor-Avila, they began to transcribe the sound recordings and, in 1991, their book, *The Emergence of Black English: Text and Commentary*, presented detailed transcriptions of the tapes. Other scholars, most notably Jeutonne P. Brewer of the University of North Carolina, Greensboro, have since developed improved versions.

Linguists found in the recordings an extraordinarily rich opportunity to study the development of Black English Vernacular. Viewing the recordings as primary texts, they not only discovered new ways of understanding the transformation of language in the African-American community but also developed new standards to measure how faithful Federal Writer's Project interviewers had been to their subjects' words. Moreover, during the 1990s, new techniques of digitizing or "remastering" the old aluminum and acetate discs has made a fuller rendition possible and, in some cases, made intelligible material that had previously been incomprehensible. In so doing, they raised new questions about the written typescripts and gave new importance to the voice recordings.

The recordings, like the typescripts, are problematic as historical sources. Their small number made it impossible to view them as statistically representative. While the interviewers, some of them the nation's most experienced folklorists, demonstrated great sensitivity in questioning aged former slaves, they admitted having difficulty gaining access to informants, since white authorities often viewed them as outside agitators. Harassed and threatened, weighted down with bulky and unwieldy equipment, the recorders had limited range. Moreover, since they worked outside the guidelines of the Federal Writers' Project, they had no particular reason or mandate for focusing on slavery, and their informants often preferred to talk about other matters. Indeed, the recordings tell more about the life after emancipation than before it.

Nonetheless, the recorded interviews had great value. The immediacy of the voices of men and women who had experienced enslavement provided listeners a link to a world of slaves and slaveowners—a world often relegated to the distant past. Through the medium of the spoken word, the slaves' memory exploded out of the archives into the here and now.

Understanding the memories that former slaves brought to freedom is enriched by an understanding of slavery's long history. In 1865, when the defeat of the Confederacy and the ratification of the Thirteen Amendment ended slavery in the United States, black people had been captives for almost two hundred and fifty years. Slavery had its origins in violent usurpation: from the beginning, when the first Africans were dragged across the Atlantic, slavery rested on the most extreme forms of coercion. Murders, beatings, mutilations, and humiliations—both petty and great—were an essential, not an incidental, part of chattel bondage. Across the centuries, the history of slavery could be written as a tale of maniacal sadism by the frenzied slaveowners who lashed, traumatized, raped, and killed their slaves, for the list of lurid tales is endless.

But slavery's brutality inhered less in brutish and sadistic outbursts than in the routine, systematic violence slaveowners found necessary to reduce men and women to things. The commonplace, if relentless, character of the violence implicit in slavery revealed itself when Robert "King" Carter, the largest slaveholder in colonial Virginia, calmly petitioned and received permission from the local court to lop off the toes of his runaways; or when William Byrd, the founder of one of America's great families, forced a slave who wet his bed to drink a "pint of piss"; or when Thomas Jefferson carefully calculated that the greatest punishment he could inflict upon an incorrigible fugitive was to sell him away from his kin.

Violence called forth powerful resistance. Slavery's heroes and heroines should no more be forgotten than should the adversity they confronted. While it is easy to celebrate those who stood up to the bullies and faced—or beat—them down, such as Frederick Douglass in his classic confrontation with the slavebreaker Covey, it is equally important to appreciate the silent, everyday heroics of the men and women who stoically took the slaveholders' worst and quietly educated their children to take back piecemeal what the "masters" had appropriated at once. In short, men and women recognizing their inability to overthrow slavery, taught their children how to survive until their moment arrived.

But slavery was more complicated than the sad duet of domination and resistance. New World slavery did not originate in a conspiracy to dishonor, shame, or brutalize Africans—although it did all of those things. The design of the American captivity of African peoples was the extraction of labor. This struggle over labor—which made some people rich and powerful, while degrading and denying the very humanity of others—shaped the history of slavery.

Because slavery was a matter of contested power, it was an ever-changing institution. The lives of slaves were different in 1619, when the first Africans marched down the gangplank at Jamestown, than in 1700, when the Plantation Revolution began; and so, as well, than in 1800, when African-Americans began their Great Migration westward across the Appalachians, or in 1861, when the Civil War began the slaves' long-awaited exodus from bondage. While this long history shaped the memories that black people carried from bondage, the last decades of enslavement figured most prominently for those freed in the great Civil War.

Slavery's last years were among its most complex. At the beginning of the nineteenth century, the great mass of slaves lived along the Atlantic seaboard, cultivated tobacco or rice, and practiced a variety of religious faiths derived from Africa. On the eve of emancipation, most slaves resided in the interior of the South, grew cotton or sugar cane, and professed some variant of Christianity. These massive demographic, economic, and cultural changes combined to reweave the fabric of African-American society. At no time in slavery's two-hundred-and-fifty year history in mainland North America was change greater than in the half century prior to the Civil War.

First and perhaps most important of these transformations was the movement of slaves from the eastern seaboard to the interior of the South. In 1810, more than 80 percent of the slave population resided between the Delaware and Savannah rivers in Maryland, Virginia, and the Carolinas. By the beginning of the Civil War, only one-third of the slave population lived in Maryland, Virginia, and North and South Carolina. Most slaves resided in the lower South—Georgia, Alabama, Mississippi, Louisiana, and the states and territories to the west. Indeed, the slave population was growing fastest on the Arkansas and Texas frontier.

Within the Lower South, slaves were even more concentrated. A ribbon of rich soil that stretched from Georgia to Mississippi—the so-called Black Belt, named for the color of the soil and the people who worked it—became a primary site of African-American life in slavery. A second concentration of slaves could be found along the Mississippi River, especially between Memphis and New Orleans. Although slaves in the Black Belt and Mississippi Valley never predominated to the extent they had in lowcountry Carolina during the eighteenth century—where slaves composed more than 90 percent of the population—they nevertheless made up a substantial majority in these areas.

The movement of some million slaves from the seaboard to the Black Belt and the river bottoms of the interior deeply disrupted the civilization that black people had established in the aftermath of their forced exodus from Africa. During nearly two centuries of settlement along the seaboard, African and African-American slaves had created complex communities, linked by ties of kinship and friendship and resting upon a foundation of shared values and beliefs. Those communities became increasing self-contained with the closing of the trans-Atlantic slave trade, which had ended in the Lower South by constitutional mandate in 1808 and a generation earlier in the Upper South. The westward movement of plantation culture—whether it was driven by individual owners who accompanied their slaves or by professional slave traders—tore that society asunder, exiling hundreds of thousands from their birthplace and traumatizing those who remained. Families and sometimes whole communities dissolved under the pressure of this Second Great Migration.

Changes founded on the seaboard resonated in the interior. Generally, it was the young who were the first to be sent west, since frontier planters needed the muscle of young men and women to clear the land as well as their reproductive capacity to ensure a steadily expanding labor force. On the frontier, slaves—disproportionately children—reconstructed African-American life from the memories of the older seaboard civilization, much as their ancestors had earlier fashioned their lives on the western side of the Atlantic from memories of Africa.

Still, in many ways, the Second Great Migration differed from the first, not only dwarfing it in size but also presenting a distinctive demographic outline. The forced trans-Atlantic migration had been heavily weighted toward men, while men and women moved to the interior of the South in roughly equal numbers. Additionally, Africans who arrived in mainland North America in the seventeenth and eighteenth centuries had differed from one another linguistically and culturally, speaking a variety of languages, practicing a host of different customs, and articulating a variety of different beliefs. They knew little of their owners' language or culture, and what they knew, they knew imperfectly. In the nineteenth century, by contrast, African-Americans who were carried into the interior of the South spoke the same language and shared many elements of an evolving American culture. Differences between African-Americans originating in the Chesapeake and the Carolina lowcountry paled in comparison to differences between Africans derived from the Senegambia and Angola. And if Africans had hardly known anything of the Europeans who had enslaved them, African-Americans knew the ways of their owners all too well.

Whatever the differences between the trans-Atlantic and the trans-Appalachian migrations, the process of cultural reconstruction was similar. Families had to be reconstituted, leadership reasserted, and culture refashioned in new circumstances so that a new generation—one that would know its parents' homeland only through dim recollections—could be tutored in the ways of the elders. In many ways, the memory of Virginia and Carolina—kept alive by the continued influx of newcomers to the west—became as important for black people in the nineteenth-century Black Belt as the memory of Africa had been for black people in the seventeenth- and eighteenth-century seaboard.

The forcible relocation of thousands of African-Americans from the seaboard states also reshaped the lives of those left behind. Slaves who lived under the ever-present threat of sale "down the river" or "to the cotton country" were forced to adjust their hopes and expectations to the relentless reality of the westward movement; in so doing, they reformulated African-American life. Few enslaved parents could expect to nurture their children to maturity, see their grandchildren grow up, or succor their own parents in their last years. Slavery played havoc with African-American family life in the new frontier and the old settlements.

Whatever the effects of the Second Great Migration on Southern slave society at its terminal points, the movement west was neither direct nor linear. Those who traveled west with their owners in family groups or entire plantation populations—rather than with traders in coffles of strangers—enjoyed a measure of security. This was a short-lived consolation, though: few pioneering owners stayed in one spot for long in their search for cheap and fertile land. This process was fueled in part by the Indian removals and government land sales first in Georgia, then in Alabama and Mississippi, and finally in Arkansas and Texas. With little cash and few ties to reliable sources of credit, aspiring planters were vulnerable to the wild swings of a boom-or-bust economy. When catastrophe struck, slaves were ruined with their owners. But even in the best of times, slaves might be sold or traded anywhere along the way, as each stop provided the occasion for yet another division. Separated from friends only recently acquired, many transplanted slaves were forced once again to reconstruct their lives. Among such men, women, and children, for whom transiency was the only certainty, the task of reestablishing shattered ties of kinship and friendship was continual.

The number of slaveholders grew steadily as plantation society marched west. Most newly minted masters and mistresses owned only a few slaves, but most slaves lived on plantations—conventionally defined in the United States as a unit of agricultural production with twenty or more resident slaves. More than one quarter of the slave population—some one million slaves in 1850—dwelled on great plantations with fifty or more slaves. In the states of the Lower South, where the plantations were concentrated, this proportion exceeded one third. Thus, although slaves could be found in a variety of different venues—towns and cities, farmsteads and mill runs, iron forges and turpentine camps—the plantation surpassed all as the locus of nineteenth-century African-American life in slavery.

The plantation was many things, a unit of production and the site of a community, but for slaves plantation life meant work—unrelentingly hard work that began at sunup, paused only slightly at sundown, and frequently continued long into the night. Most plantation slaves engaged in the meanest sort of labor, and they derived few tangible benefits from it. But the same work could also be a source of personal satisfaction and, ultimately, of political self-assertion. The act of creation, which even the most onerous and exploitative labor entailed, allowed slaves to affirm the humanity that chattel bondage denied. By producing something where once there was nothing, slaves discredited the masters' shibboleth that they were simply property, countered the daily humiliations that tested their self-esteem, and laid claim—if only symbolic claim—to the fruits of their labor for themselves and their posterity.

Labor became the terrain on which slaves and their owners battled for the wealth that the slaves produced. The conflict took many forms, involving the organization of labor, the pace of work, the division of labor, and the composition of the labor force. If slaveowners wielded the lash—for slavery never ceased to rest upon brute force—slaves employed an array of weapons of their own, feigning ignorance, slowing the pace, maiming animals, breaking tools, disappearing at critical moments, and, as a last resort, confronting slave owners directly and violently.

The character of these workplace struggles rested, to a considerable degree, on the productive processes themselves, which differed throughout the South. Here, too, much changed between the colonial and the antebellum periods, as many slaveholders abandoned the great staples of the colonial era and introduced new ones. During the seventeenth and eighteenth centuries, most plantation slaves grew tobacco and rice, with indigo being a secondary crop in lowcountry Carolina and in Louisiana. While the cultivation of tobacco and rice remained important in the nineteenth-century South—indigo fell to the vagaries of international politics and trade—the crops that plantation slaves grew changed. The American government's purchase of Louisiana during the first decade of the nineteenth century placed a major sugar-producing area within the bounds of the United States. Many planters, particularly in the Upper South, grew less tobacco and expanded cereal production. They introduced new crops such as hemp, and new varieties of older ones such as bright-leafed tobacco, all the while diversifying their output by combining traditional crops with dairying and herding.

Each of the great staples had evolved a particular regimen, which both reflected and shaped the demography, economy, and society of the region in which it was grown. Around the Chesapeake, for example, slaves grew tobacco on independent satellite farms called "quarters," which were organized around a single large estate. At the home quarter, resident planters presided over what observers characterized as small villages with the Great House nestled among artisan shops, barns, an ice house, laundry, and occasionally even a small infirmary—buildings denominated, with a nice sense of the plantation's social order, as "dependencies." Rice, on the other hand, was produced on larger unitary plantations carved out the swamps of the South Carolina and Georgia lowlands. Production was directed by planters residing in Savannah, Charleston, or the lesser rice ports rather than on site, through a long chain of command at the base of which stood slave foremen or "drivers." In southern Louisiana, sugar production presented yet another spatial and organizational schema. Estates encompassed both agricultural production and industrial processing—the fields in which the cane was grown and the mill in which it was transformed into sugar and molasses. Farm and factory surrounded the Great House, whose owner typically also spent much time in a New Orleans or Natchez townhouse.

The diverse economic geography of plantation life reflected an equally diverse occupational structure, managerial hierarchy, and work regimen. Although sugar was grown by large gangs of field hands supervised by white overseers, it required a small army of slave artisans to process the cane, pack the sugar and molasses into hogsheads, and transport them by wagon and boat. Rice planters, operating from their urban command posts, eschewed gang labor and instead organized fieldwork by the "task," thereby allowing slaves to set the pace of their labor and giving them a small measure of time to work independently for their own benefit. Tobacco planters, preoccupied with care of the broad-leafed weed—the tedious process of worming, topping, suckering, and priming through the summer until the mature plant was cut, stripped, cured, and packed in hogsheads in the winter—organized their slaves in closely supervised squads rather than gang-sized units.

The organization of tobacco, rice, and sugar production—as well as that of wheat and other small grains—had been established in the eighteenth century. But it did not remain unaltered in the new era. Alert to agricultural reform, planters throughout the South introduced new tools, experimented with new work regimens, and inaugurated new systems of management in an effort to squeeze more profit from their slaves' labor. The introduction of new technology, new methods, and new systems of supervision set in motion new conflicts between slave owners and slaves, keeping the plantation in perpetual turmoil.

Yet no tool or method had as powerful an effect on nineteenth-century slave life as the changes set in motion by the Cotton Revolution. Few mainland slaves grew cotton prior to American independence. This changed dramatically in the last decade of the eighteenth century, as the first stirring of the Industrial Revolution increased demand for the fiber. Along the Georgia and Carolina coast, planters quickly expanded production of long-staple cotton, whose smooth black seeds were easily separated by hand from its luxuriant, silky strands. But this variety grew well only in the unique environs of the lowcountry South Carolina and

Georgia, and attempts to expand production of a short-staple variety were hindered by the difficulty of removing its sticky green seeds from the fiber. Once that obstacle was overcome by the invention of a mechanical "gin," though, production soared, and cotton cultivation spread quickly to the uplands east of the Appalachians and then across the mountains to the newly opened territories of Tennessee, Alabama, and Mississippi. By 1820, cotton production had moved west into the interior of the South, sinking its deepest roots in the Black Belt.

The creation of the vast empire of cotton was the work of a generation of slaves, who cleared the land, broke the soil, "chopped" (or thinned out) the young cotton plants, picked the tufts of fiber from the prickly bolls, separated the seeds from the fiber, packed the fiber into bales, and sent it off to manufacture in Europe or the North. In 1800, the South produced less than one hundred thousand bales of cotton; sixty years later, cotton production stood at over four million bales—the vast majority of which was grown by slaves. On the eve of the Civil War, some three million slaves—three-quarters of the Southern slave population— were directly involved in the production of cotton.

Because cotton was grown almost everywhere in the Lower South, and parts of the Upper South as well, and because its cultivation occupied the vast majority of slaves, its special requirements and seasonal rhythms shaped the development of slave culture. Its most distinguishing characteristic was utter simplicity of production and the general absence of supporting crafts. Unlike sugar, whose production was equally industrial and agricultural, or even tobacco and rice, cotton, once ginned, required almost no refining or special handling. Virtually imperishable so long as it was kept dry, cotton needed no packing in barrels or housing in specially designed barns or sheds. Squeezed into bales by a simple mechanical process, it could sit under a tarpaulin on a plantation landing or in an urban warehouse for months or even years. Consequently, the occupational structure of the cotton plantation lacked the diversity and complexity of estates devoted to tobacco, rice, or sugar. With the exception of a blacksmith or carpenter on a great plantation, virtually all slaves were field hands who did pretty much the same work. The slave coopers, wheelwrights, harness-makers, and tanners who serviced the plantation economy during the eighteenth century, and whose presence was so visible on the great sugar estates in the nineteenth century, were almost totally absent from cotton plantations. Cotton planters sometimes promoted a particularly adept slave to the head of a work gang in the hope that he or she would set a fast pace; or sometimes they distinguished between field workers who plowed and those who hoed. In general, though, the uniformity of the processes associated with planting, cultivating, and harvesting cotton reduced the significance of such a division of labor to differences of age and sex. The movement from seaboard to the interior, from tobacco and rice to cotton, occasioned a sharp decline of skilled slaves.

Moreover, since there was no special urgency in moving cotton to market and since the Lower South was a particularly well-watered region with plantations often located by a river or bayou, wagoners—along with blacksmiths, wheelwrights, harness-makers, and tanners who served them—were also much reduced in number. As boatmen and wagoners disappeared from the plantation roster, the number of slaves who regularly traversed the countryside and thereby gained knowledge of the world beyond the plantation also declined.

The growth of cotton culture also reduced the proportion of slaves—almost always men—in managerial positions. In the eighteenth century, urban-based rice planters relied upon drivers to mediate between themselves and their plantation slaves. In the Chesapeake, tobacco planters frequently placed trusted slaves in charge of individual quarters. Indeed, many quarters took the name of the slave foreman. While slave drivers and foremen continued to reign in the older plantation areas, they were far less common in the cotton South, where the white overseer became a plantation fixture. Thus, as cotton came to dominate Southern agriculture, the prospects for social mobility, like those for geographical mobility, declined.

The Cotton Revolution altered slave life in still other ways. Slaveholding planters seized control of rich soils of the Black Belt and the river basins, relegated yeoman farmers to the margins, and dominated the production of the staple. However, cotton plantations rarely grew so large, or became so profitable, as to support the quasi-absenteeism of either rice or sugar production, where slaveowners maintained an urban residence at least part of the year. Only a few cotton planters could afford to single out more than one or two adult slaves for special duties in the house. Indeed, most house servants were children. Those adults who worked in and around the Big House often labored in the field part of the time; or if they did not, they had kinfolks and friends who did. The distance between house and field in the cotton South was small—physically and socially—and slaves moved easily between the Big House and the quarter.

The few slave men and women who had a permanent place in the Big House as cooks and carriage drivers, seamstresses and valets, housekeepers and gardeners had little opportunity to pass their special place in the plantation hierarchy to their children. Such a hereditary class had begun to emerge in the seaboard South during the late eighteenth century, as planters elaborated their great estates. The movement west severed these lines of occupational descent, and the advent of cotton culture stymied their reformation. The absence of a hereditary retinue of house servants or a corps of body servants in the cotton South, like the absence of a large number of plantation-based tradesmen and managers, promoted solidarity within the slave community, creating an intraplantation unity that was unique among the plantation slaves of the New World.

With the resident planter as its beau ideal, life on the plantation became increasingly insular during the nineteenth century. Planters sealed the borders of their estates and claimed the right to regulate visitors to the quarter. They denounced marriages outside of the plantation "family" and became chary about slaves traveling off the plantation for any reason. Such practices had been common in the eighteenth-century seaboard South and continued into the nineteenth century in the Upper South, where the small size of agricultural units made visiting and interplantation marriages a necessity. To curb the mobility of their slaves, some planters constructed their labor force in a manner calculated to provide every marriageable hand a partner within the estate. A few even purchased slaves for this reason. Planters were never entirely successful in closing their estates to the outside world, as patterns of sociability and the necessity of production continued to breach the barriers they tried to create. Nonetheless, plantation borders became considerably less permeable in the nineteenth century than they had been in the eighteenth, and slave society became more insular as a result. If relocation from one estate to another became an increasingly common experience, once relocated the slaves' acquaintance with the world outside their residence shrank.

Within the boundaries of the plantation, Southerners—both black and white—came to identify themselves with the land, its singular beauty, and its ancient mysteries. Although the reality of Southern life belied this image of ageless stability, slaveholding planters found much to like in this seeming timelessness. From it, they inferred an immutable relationship between subordinate and superior.

Planters understood this relationship in terms of the patriarchal ideal. Emphasizing that their slaves, like their wives and children, were fed and clothed out of the household larder, slaveholders celebrated their special responsibility for the workers they owned, whom they often called "family." Planters draped themselves in the cloak of paterfamilias and consigned their slaves to an eternal childhood, often denominating them "girls" and "boys" until age had transformed them into "uncles" and "aunts." The slaveholders' assault fell particularly heavily on slave men: equating manhood with control over an independent household, the masters of the great plantation contested their right to choose a wife, discipline their children, and care for their aged parents, thus relegating slave men to a lesser roles within their own families.

The incorporation of slaves into what planters called their "family, white and black" enhanced the slaveholders' sense of responsibility for their slaves and encouraged the owners to improve the material circumstances of plantation life. Slaves were generally better fed and housed in the nineteenth century than they had been in the seventeenth and eighteenth. Along with these material improvements, however, came a deepening intrusion into the private portions of life in the quarter. Aspects of slave life that slaveholders had largely ignored during the eighteenth-century—everything from child-rearing to religious practices—came under intense scrutiny during the nineteenth, as owners became increasingly self-conscious about their patriarchal responsibilities. Still, like all ideologues, slaveholders violated their own principles when it suited their purposes; and, like all paternalists, slaveholders tended to emphasize their subordinates' responsibility to them rather than their responsibility to their subordinates. Indeed, the paternalist ideology provided slaveholders with a powerful justification for their systematic expropriation of the slaves' labor.

Slaves viewed relations with their owners from a different perspective. Though subject to their owners' overwhelming power, slaves struggled to increase their independence in all areas of their lives, asserting that in every way they were full human beings. They pressed for nothing more relentlessly than control over their own labor, the denial of which constituted the very essence of chattel slavery. Conceding what they could not alter or deny, slaves worked without direct compensation but claimed a right to a predictable portion of what they produced. They expected their owners to feed, clothe, and house them in accordance with customary usage. Challenging their owners to meet their paternalist ideal, slaves insisted that "good masters" provided well materially for their slaves; but, while they welcomed the regular allotment of rations and played their part in the charade surrounding Christmas gifting, they did not rest satisfied with the dole.

Through a continuous process of contest and negotiation with slaveholders—often playing on the slaveholders' recognition of their humanity implicit in paternal ideology—slaves established the right to control a portion of their lives. When permitted to do so, they used small grants of free time to cultivate gardens, hunt, and fish; raise poultry, pigs, and cattle; make baskets, weave clothes, and practice other handicrafts; hire themselves to neighboring farmers and artisans; and receive payments for overwork. Although the property they accumulated had no legal standing, it gained recognition in practice. The slaves' self-directed economic activities—what historians have called "the slaves' economy"—fostered a vision of an independent life, even though the opportunity to realize the vision would not come until after emancipation.

The Second Great Migration and the Cotton Revolution threatened to unravel the customs that had been established through a long process of hard bargaining and continuous struggle. Access to gardens and provision grounds, free Sundays and half Saturdays, the right to visit friends, market produce, and keep small earnings from work done outside the owners' ken were all put at risk by the creation of a new plantation order.

Slaveholders used the new circumstance of life and labor in the interior and the isolation of transplanted slaves to ratchet up labor demands. They increased time spent in the field and expanded the stint or the task for which slaves were responsible, reduced the slaves's free time and cut the number of holidays, denied the right to travel off the plantation, and constricted the slaves' internal economy. Although the new circumstances of the interior sometimes offered slaves new opportunities to limit the authority of the owner, generally it was the master who gained from starting afresh. Indeed, many slaveholders saw in the movement west an opportunity to liquidate the limits slaves had set and to begin plantation life anew. Customary practices established in years of hard bargaining withered in the shadow of the Second Great Migration and dissolved in the heat of the Cotton Revolution.

Against the slaveholders' assault, slaves drew upon their memory of the past and an array of institutions they had created for their own benefit. The most important of these was the African-American family. Since the early eighteenth century, African and African-American slaves in mainland North America had been a population growing by natural increase, with births exceeding deaths. Slaveowners, who were often marginal to the larger Atlantic plantation system, seized upon the prospect of this self-reproducing labor force and turned from the trans-Atlantic slave trade to natural growth as a source of labor. By the late eighteenth century, the growth of an indigenous African-American slave population allowed mainland slaveholders to close the African trade or acquiesce to the 1808 Constitutional mandate to end it.

Playing upon the slaveholders' dependence on the slaves' natural increase, slaves struggled for control of the reproductive processes. They asserted the right to choose their marriage partner and control the birthing process. Slave women, or elderly "grannies," served as midwives; only rarely, and then in dire emergencies, did slaveholders and their agents usher slave infants into the world. Slaves challenged their owners' right to name their children, so that while a slaveholder might claim symbolic paternity for the entire plantation family, many children were named after their natural fathers and mothers and only a few named after their owners.

During the nineteenth century, the hallmark of the slave's domestic life was a nuclear family enmeshed in a dense network of kin relationships. Courting and sexual activity between young slave men and women began in their late teens. Sometimes these relations begot children, but Southern slaves generally did not marry until their early twenties, when they settled down in long-term monogamous relationships, which generally lasted until disruption by sale or death. Although women bore primary responsibility for child care, the slave family was not a matriarchy, and men played an important and visible role in supporting their households, raising children, and, on occasion, protecting wives and children from the overwhelming power of the master and his underlings.

A web of distinctive customs and beliefs sustained those lifelong relations and separated the family life of African-American slaves from that of other Southerners. For example, nineteenth-century slaves rarely married blood relatives. Indeed, marriage between slaves as distantly connected as second cousins was so unusual as to suggest the existence of a powerful proscription that some scholars have traced back to Africa. Such endogamy distinguished slaves from their owners (as well as from propertied free people of color) who regularly married within much closer blood relations. Indeed, cousin marriage was one of the distinguishing features of the domestic life of the planter class.

Although usually known to their owners by only a single name, most slaves in fact had surnames or, as they called them, "titles," which they maintained clandestinely. Titles stretched back to Africa on occasion, but more commonly slaves reached for the most distant genealogical marker they could identify, perhaps the name of their forebears' first owner. Slave surnames, although derived from the owning class, distinguished the slaves who adopted them from their present owner and established—at least in their own eyes—a separate lineage, heritage, and identity that contested the masters' claims to rule a "family, white and black."

Slaves nurtured these generational connections in violation of laws that denied their existence. Slaves who had accumulated small amounts of property covertly developed their own system of inheritance, whereby one generation of slaves gave the next "a start." These inheritance practices differed from place to place, but they became more deeply entrenched as slaves elaborated their internal economies. Although the property passed from generation to generation was often nothing more than a few sticks of furniture, some cookware and tools, or a few barnyard animals, generational exchanges had deep emotive and psychological meaning. And they were not without material significance.

Scarcely less important than the family was the slaves' religion. Whereas the dense network of kinship that knit together the slave community in the nineteenth century had evolved along lines established in the seventeenth and eighteenth centuries, the religion of the quarter emerged from a new set of circumstances. Prior to American independence, most slaves knew little of Christianity, and most slaveholders were indifferent if not hostile to their slaves imbibing the teaching of Jesus. Despite the efforts of missionary organizations, few slaves converted to Christianity, and most remained unchurched. However, a series of evangelical awakenings that began prior to the American Revolution and continued into the nineteenth century changed that radically. To the evangelicals, nothing more fully validated the power of God's grace than the conversion of the lowly slave. Indeed, some evangelical Christians not only welcomed slaves into the fold as brothers and sisters in Christ but also openly criticized slavery and, on occasion, accepted the leadership of black preachers and ministers.

The egalitarianism of these evangelical revivals waned in the late eighteenth century and had been all but extinguished among slaveholders by the first decade of the nineteenth century. Nevertheless, many slaveholders remained committed to converting their slaves—not so much as Christian egalitarians seeking a unity in Christ but as Christian stewards bringing their God to heathens and slaveholding paternalists bringing their civilization to savages. That the promise of a better life in the afterworld might make for greater subordination of slaves in the present made this new missionary spirit that much more compelling to some members of the slaveholding class. Drawing upon the Pauline dictum that slaves should obey their masters, slaveholders built plantation chapels, invited itinerant ministers to preach to their slaves, and—donning the paternalist mantle—sometimes led their slaves in prayer and Bible catechism.

For their part, slaves were increasingly receptive to the possibility of joining their owner's church. For some, it assured a Sabbath respite from labor and an occasion for fellowship with other slaves from neighboring plantations. But it also was an opportunity to practice a religion which, by the story of Moses, promised liberation from earthly bondage and, by the story of Jesus, promised eternal redemption and divine justice, in which the good would be rewarded and the wicked punished.

During the nineteenth century, tens of thousands of slaves converted to Christianity, and many thousands more were born into a faith their eighteenth-century forebears either had not known or had consciously rejected. In its polity, the slaves' new religion did not differ markedly from that of their owners. Most slaves subscribed to Baptist, Methodist, or Presbyterian denominations, although Episcopalian and Lutheran slaves were scattered throughout the South and Catholics abounded in

Louisiana and parts of Maryland and Florida. Seated in the back rows and balconies of their owners' churches, nineteenth-century slaves followed faiths familiar to their owners.

Yet if they shared church buildings, polity, and a variety of religious rituals with their owners, the slaves' religious beliefs and practices nevertheless stood apart. Slaves incorporated Christianity into the diverse African religious practices—some of them polytheistic, some of them Islamic, and some of them pretransfer Christian—that had evolved during the first two hundred years of American captivity into a religion that was itself an amalgam undergoing profound change. The genesis of African-American Christianity was as much the creation of a new faith as the expansion of the white man's religion.

Slaveowners meted out Christianity in carefully measured portions, but slaves were equally selective about what they accepted and how they incorporated it into their view of this world and the next. Patience in the face of earthly trial and obedience to earthly masters loomed large in the slaveholders' message, but slaves found other themes more to their liking. Theologically, they had little truck with the doctrines of Paul and, instead, maintained the egalitarianism of the eighteenth-century revivals, emphasizing the equality of mankind before God and the irrelevance of earthly status to one's chance for eternal life. They identified particularly with the people of the Old Testament and their heroic exodus from bondage. The message of the fundamental equality of all in the eyes of God and—when the master was out of range—in the eyes of man remained a central tenet of African-American Christianity long after it had ceased to echo in the slaveholder's church. But the theology of the black church did more than affirm the slaves' humanity and their worth before God: it envisioned a day of judgment, a "settling-up time" accompanied by a rebalancing of the moral scales.

So too with the theme of salvation, a flexible metaphor that joined earthly liberation and otherworldly redemption. Slave preachers presented the message of salvation skillfully so that, depending on the standpoint of the listener, it could be understood as either deeply conservative of the slave regime or utterly subversive of it. "Free At Last" could speak both to the release from earthy tribulations and the release from chattel bondage. The meaning of the message received by the congregants emerged from the antiphonal repartee of preacher and his flock. It was communicated by gesture and emphasis, long-winded biblical exegeses and significant silences. Because it depended as much on unstated assumptions as on stated doctrine, onlookers, particularly the masters, found it all but inaccessible.

African-American Christianity as it evolved in the nineteenth century thus had many parts, and slaves made use of all of them. Although Christian slaves drew strength from those elements that distinguished their religion from that of their white co-worshippers, they often found it useful to underline the similarities. Just as slaveholders cited the Bible to enjoin their slaves to obedience, slaves did the same, holding their owners accountable to the ethical standards embedded in the Ten Commandments, the Beatitudes, and the Sermon on the Mount.

The domestic and spiritual life of African-American slaves reflected the conflicting and contradictory evolution of the relationship between slaveholders and slaves in the antebellum years. Slaves found glimmerings of independence in the same domestic and religious institutions wherein slaveowners saw confirmation of the slaves' acquiescence to their rule. Indeed, what slaveholders often took as justification of their domination became a source of self-assertion for slaves and the basis of opposition to the masters' hegemony. What was true of family and church was equally true of art, cuisine, dance, language, and other cultural forms. African-American and European-American culture were connected in ways that belied the shifting balance of power between master and slave.

After 1861, when the long-simmering struggle between North and South bubbled over into civil war, the balance shifted sharply, if slowly, in the slaves' favor. Tossing aside the pronouncements of President Abraham Lincoln and other Union leaders that the conflict was a war for national unity, slaves put their own freedom and that of their posterity at the top of the national agenda. Steadily, as opportunities arose, slaves risked all for freedom. By fleeing from their owners, coming uninvited into Union lines, and offering their assistance as laborers, laundresses, cooks, and spies, slaves forced federal soldiers at the lowest level to recognize their importance to the Union's success. In time, that understanding ascended the chain of command. Eventually even the most obdurate federal commanders and policymakers came to appreciate that salvation of the Union depended on the destruction of slavery. In the summer of 1862, the U.S. Congress and President Lincoln sanctioned the exchange of freedom for military labor in the federal cause. By then, some Union generals were envisioning a more direct military role for slaves. They began to enlist slave men as soldiers, against the direct orders of their superiors. Those orders would soon change. On January 1, 1863, Lincoln's Emancipation Proclamation declared free all slaves within the Confederate states, announced the federal army's intention to recruit black men as soldiers, and officially transformed the war for Union into a war for liberty. By war's end, more than 200,000 black men, most of them former slaves, had served in the federal army and navy, whose steady advance brought freedom to an ever-larger portion of the slave population. Following the end of the war, the Thirteenth Amendment to the Constitution ended slavery forever.

From the start, the former slaves' recollections of slavery focused on the last years of the institution. The great events that had propelled them to freedom amid the tumult of Civil War loomed large. The last generation of slaves knew only dimly and indirectly—if they knew at all—of their ancestors' lives in Africa, of enslavement and the imposition of plantation discipline in the seventeenth and eighteenth centuries, and of the possibilities for freedom opened by the American Revolution. Rather than recalling the experience of their parents, grandparents, and great-grandparents, former slaves preferred to dwell on the immediate past: their direct experience of the Great Migration from the seaboard to the southwest, the Cotton Revolution, and the advent of African-American Christianity. In conveying the history of slavery to their own children and grandchildren, they also emphasized their own part in the drama of emancipation—partly because those stories were the ones their descendants wanted most to hear and partly because they were the ones the ex-slaves themselves wanted most to tell. Slavery's memory thus became increasingly short-term, with the direct, personal confrontations with slaveholders in the foreground.

The emphasis on relations between master and slave grew over time, as the memory of slavery itself came to play a critical role in postwar politics. With the final overthrow of Reconstruction, white Southerners celebrated the death of the short-lived experiment in biracial democracy by committing themselves to the maintenance of white supremacy. Determined to take back in peacetime what they had lost in wartime, they employed every means—from social ostracism and political skull-duggery to assassination and ritual murder—to maintain their rule. Undeterred by the new racial order, a rising generation of black men and women demanded full freedom and the right to make their lives unencumbered by the weight of the slave past. In response, white Southerners unleashed a reign of terror unseen in the South since the initial imposition of slavery. Exclusion, disfranchisement, and segregation followed.

As race relations deteriorated in the decades after Reconstruction, white and black Southerners justified their positions in terms of their own understandings of slavery. Former slaves and their free-born children described the endless indignities of chattel bondage; its numerous perils to family life; the trauma that accompanied beatings, mutilations, and murders; the prohibitions against education and religious worship; the denial of the basic civil rights they would claim as their own during Reconstruction. They lauded the slaves' heroic, if often futile, resistance to the old regime and their participation in the war for union and freedom. Viewing bondage as a prelude to freedom and all its possibilities—both fulfilled and unfulfilled—former slaves remembered slavery as a trial they had persevered through, as a condition they had (in Booker T. Washington's metaphor) come up from.

White Southerners remembered slavery very differently. Focusing on the paternalistic veneer that overlay antebellum plantation life, they emphasized the close personal relationships between slaves and owners while downplaying the violence and exploitation on which slavery ultimately rested. They glorified the docile "darkies" who had served so faithfully, the loyal mammies who had nursed both white and black children, and the trusted servants who protected the plantation against the hated Yankees. Whereas black Southerners boasted of how the last generation of slaves had resisted slavery and welcomed the coming of freedom, white Southerners denounced the changes that had accompanied emancipation. Although few would go so far as to defend slavery in the abstract, they nevertheless contrasted the antebellum South's ostensibly benign and humane social order with the misrule of Reconstruction. Sounding themes of racial declension, white Southerners compared unfavorably the "new Negro," with his unattainable demands for political equality, to the stereotypical "old-time Negro," who knew his place and quietly remained there. Former slaveholders and their descendants bemoaned the deaths of aged former slaves as the passing of a by-gone era, even as they terrorized the new generation of black men and women whose aspirations threatened the white supremacy of the new era.

Almost a century later, as a result of monumental struggle for racial equality, legal segregation has been outlawed and constitutional equality enshrined in law. But the work of creating an egalitarian multiracial society continues, as the American people labor to fulfill the ideals of the founders and, in the wake of the Second Reconstruction, grapple with issues left unresolved since the time of the first. As that struggle has intensified in the last decade of the twentieth century, the issue of slavery has once again rushed to the fore. The debate over the proposed official apology for slavery, the creation of a presidential commission to advance a "national conversation" on race, the furor over affirmative action programs, the popularity of the cinematic rendition of the Amistad revolt, and the appearance of a cover story on slavery in the nation's best-selling news magazine all suggest how fully the creation of an egalitarian society rests on the nation coming to terms with its slave past. There are no longer any Americans who have direct, personal memories of slavery, but the historical memory of slavery remains central to Americans' sense of themselves and the society in which they live.

In this context, the Library of Congress, The New Press, and Smithsonian Productions (the broadcasting and audio reproduction arm of the Smithsonian Institution) have joined together to make available the recollections of American ex-slaves as recorded more than a half century ago. These are presented in this book and a two-part radio documentary, both entitled *Remembering Slavery: African Americans Talk About Their Personal Experiences of Slavery and Freedom*. *Remembering Slavery* is a unique enterprise that draws together—in both printed word and recorded voices—first-hand accounts of former slaves confronting owners, laboring in the field, maintaining families without the legitimating force of law, and sustaining their dignity in the most degrading of circumstances. It seeks to put a human face on an inhumane social system that ended in the United States not that many generations ago, a system whose oldest survivors were the grandparents and great-grandparents of Americans still living. In so doing, *Remembering Slavery* allows readers and listeners to imagine the unimaginable, to reconsider the enslavement that so shaped the American past and whose legacy continues to cast a shadow over the American future.

EDITORIAL METHOD

With the notable exception of a handful of sound recordings, the recollections of former slaves in the twentieth century survive mainly in written form. The largest legacy is the "ex-slave stories" compiled by workers of the Federal Writers' Project (FWP) in the late 1930s, selections from which compose the bulk of this volume. These written documents, although based on interviews with former slaves, are several removes away from the spoken recollections. Few interviewers employed shorthand or other means of notating the narrators' words verbatim. Instead, they took written notes from conversations with the informants that often extended over several visits, later reconstructing them with the aid of the notes and their own memories. Interviewers and their editors "silently" intervened in numerous ways: they deleted material they deemed irrelevant, superfluous, or objectionable; they reordered text to suit their sense of the flow of the story; and they made untold other stylistic and substantive changes. Interviewers and editors followed no single protocol for transforming vernacular speech into print. A few painstakingly changed the ex-slaves' spoken recollections into standard English, "cleaning up" nonstandard pronunciation, grammar, and syntax. Others equally painstakingly transformed the ex-slaves' speech into stereotypical "Negro dialect," dropping terminal "g"s in *-ing* word endings and reducing "the," "them," and "these" to "de," "dem," and "dese." The worst bowdlerizers deployed patronizing "eye dialect," in which words such as "was," "of," and "from" were transformed into the phonetically indistinguishable "wuz," "uv," and "frum." So common were such contrived renderings that officials of the FWP eventually saw fit to prescribe "Approved Dialect Expressions" while banning others. ("De," "dem," "dese," "befo'," and "gwine," for example, made the approved list, while "wuz," "uv," "ovah," and "Ah" for "I" were taboo.) The best transcriptions manage to preserve a sense of the idiosyncracies of speech while remaining readable; the worst are cumbersome, artificial, and verge on minstrel-speak.

Loath to interpose yet another layer of editorial intervention between the ex-slaves' speech and the printed page, the editors of this volume have chosen to present the narratives exactly as they appear in the published transcriptions—irregularities, inconsistencies, and all. There are a few exceptions to this general principle. Narratives drawn from the *American Slave* series—where they appear as photoduplications of typewritten texts, sometimes with handwritten editorial markings—require special handling; several types of minor changes have been made without acknowledgment. First, where an irregularity seems to be a misspelling or typographical error rather than a purposeful attempt to render the spoken word, the editors of this volume have silently corrected it. Second, where an editorial marking on the typescript calls for revisions that do not affect the substance of the text—for example, correcting a misspelling or supplying a missing word—the editors of this volume have silently made the change. Third, in the many typescript narratives where every successive paragraph of the ex-slave's words is enclosed in quotation marks, the quotation marks have been silently omitted.

Other editorial interventions are marked in conventional ways. Text that is underlined in the typescript is rendered here in italics. Words or phrases added by the editors of this volume appear in brackets and italics, [*like this*]. Conjectural readings of illegible words appear in brackets and roman type, [like this]. Limitations of space and the topical chapter organization of this volume have dictated that most of the narratives be presented not in their entirety but as excerpts. Ellipses are employed only to indicate material omitted by the editors within an excerpt, not to indicate omissions of the text that preceded or followed the excerpt. (A citation to the full narrative is provided in the source note of each excerpt.)

The audio recordings of interviews with former slaves, nine excerpts of which appear in the body of this volume, present a different set of problems. Transcribed verbatim, they are encumbered by the sort of verbiage that is typical of spoken language but distracting in print: false starts; conversational "filler" such as "uh," "you know" and "mmm"; and other text that most readers will find superfluous, if not downright annoying. In presenting these interviews, the editors have therefore opted to sacrifice a measure of verisimilitude for the sake of readability. Most false starts and conversational filler have been silently omitted. Also silently omitted, in most cases, are reiterations of a word or phrase. Other editorial omissions are marked with ellipses. Conjectural renderings of semi-intelligible words appear in brackets in roman type, [like this], with a question mark if there is doubt about the conjecture; a 3-dot ellipsis in brackets, [. . .], denotes an indecipherable word.

Painstakingly detailed transcriptions of the audio recordings appear in Guy Bailey, Natalie Maynor, and Patricia Cukor-Avila, eds., *The Roots of Black English: Text and Commentary* (Amsterdam, 1991). The editors of the present volume wish to thank Guy Bailey and Jeutonne P. Brewer, linguists who have spent much of their professional lives studying the recordings, for helpful suggestions about presenting the transcriptions to an audience of nonspecialists.

CHAPTER

I.

THE FACES OF POWER: SLAVES AND OWNERS

SLAVERY, A SOCIAL SYSTEM THAT DEFINED MEN AND women as things, vested owners with enormous power over those they owned. Southern slaveholders—"masters" and "mistresses," as they liked to be known—enjoyed full command over the slaves' labor and nearly unchecked power over their persons. Owners could buy and sell slaves as they saw fit, for any reason or no reason at all. They could beat, whip, and physically abuse their slaves with virtual impunity. Laws against assault and rape—even murder—did not apply to violence perpetrated against a slave by an owner exercising his or her authority. Owners dictated where and how the slaves lived, how they worked and played, and with whom they associated. Slaves learned this fact early in their lives, and their owners never allowed them to forget it.

Violence and coercion were endemic to slavery, but there was far more to the institution than naked force. In the world of slaves and slaveholders, power wore a human face: relations between master and slave bore the complexity of all relations between men and women residing in close contact but with unequal power and conflicting interests and aspirations. Though convinced of their own superiority, slaveholders could never fully deny that the slaves, like themselves, were human beings with minds and souls, hopes and fears, physical desires and moral scruples. Slaves would not let them deny it.

Some owners exercised their dominion with such subtlety as to be nearly invisible; others were omnipresent, intrusive, and heavyhanded. Rather than wield the lash and the paddle themselves, many large slaveholders delegated that chore to white overseers or black "drivers." Standing above the fray, such planters liked to assume the role of patriarch and rule by precept and incentive rather than force. Others seemed to enjoy the dirty work of domination. However they ruled, though, slaveholders great and small often found it to their advantage to permit slaves modest creature comforts, to relax strict discipline on occasion, to allow slaves a small amount of time to do what they wished, and to reward a task well done. Like other dominant classes throughout history, slaveholders understood that a rule sustained solely by brute force produced discontented and thus dangerous subjects. But few masters doubted the necessity of brute force, at least as a last resort.

While acknowledging the power of masters and mistresses, slaves contested it with the weapons at their disposal. If they recognized the reality of their subordination, they did not accept it as inevitable, and they emphatically denied that it was right. Instead, they resisted the degradation of bondage and struggled to forge the best possible life for themselves within it. If owners monopolized the emblems of superiority with their great mansions and fine clothes, slaves ridiculed their pretensions. If slaveholders developed an ideology that affirmed the rights of masters and the innate inferiority of black people, slaves countered those beliefs with folk wisdom that celebrated the weak outwitting the strong. If owners resorted to force, slaves occasionally met violence with violence. The long struggle between masters and slaves, more than two hundred years old at the time of the Civil War, proceeded on many fronts at once. The home and church were sites of conflict no less than the field and the auction block. The weapons included words, symbols, and rituals as well as whips and guns.

An aged woman looking back on her girlhood in slavery, Harriet Smith had much to tell. She was interviewed by John Henry Faulk in 1941.

JHF: Well Aunt Harriet about how old are you?

HS: Well I don't know Mr. Faulk. I really don' know my age, only by the children telling me, of course. My ma died, an' she didn' know nothing about our age. But the children traced back from the ex-slave up to now.

JHF: Well how old were you when you were—

HS: Well, I was about thirteen years ol' at the break up.

JHF: Uh huh. Can you remember slavery days very well?

HS: Of course. I can 'member all our white folks. An' all the names of them, all the children. Call every one the children's names.

JHF: Who did you belong to?

HS: Jim Bunton, the baby boy.

JHF: Where was that? Where did he live?

HS: Back, out here in Hays County.

JHF: Sure enough? How many slaves did he have?

HS: Well, he had my grandma, an' my ma. My ma was the cook, an' grandma and them they worked in the field, an' everything. I remember when she use' to plow oxen. I plowed, I plowed oxen myself.

JHF: Is that right?

HS: I can plow an' lay off a corn row as good as any man.

JHF: Is that right?

HS: Course I can.

JHF: Well good for you.

HS: Chop, an' chop, pick cotton. I use' to pick my five hundred pounds of cotton.

JHF: Knock out five hundred pounds.

HS: Knock out around five hundred pounds of cotton. Then walk across the fiel' an' hunt watermelons, pomegranates an—

. . .

JHF: Well Aunt Harriet, do you remember church times?

HS: Yes, I remember church time. . . . I remember how our folks, they had prayer meeting from one house to another.

JHF: [T]he colored folks.

HS: Yes, I think it was [. . .]. An' over at the houses tha'd be in the section, a house, an' at different places they'd go an' we'd have prayer meeting. Ma an' pa an' them would go to prayer meeting. An' dances too.

JHF: And dances too?

HS: Yes. I've seen pa an' ma dance a many a time.

JHF: Is that right? During slavery times?

HS: Right. My grandma too. My grandma was name Rachel Proctor.

JHF: Rachel Proctor.

HS: Yes. But she belong to the Buntons. That's what she went by, her husband's name. Sure is, that's way back. Now in slavery time, there was my sister, my brother was a slave back. An' all of them stayed but me an' one of the girls an' she lives in San Antonio. Adelaide Taylor.

JHF: Adelaide Taylor. She was your sister?

HS: Yes. She's in the young bunch. Sister Ida, an' she was the next, brother George an' sister Ida an' myself were slaves. An' the others was born free. An' all of them, we the only two in slavery times.

JHF: Well I declare. Did you go to meetings? Did you ever go to church?

HS: We would go to the big house, prayer meetings you know. We children would put us in the corner. We was dared to cut up too.

JHF: Is that right?

HS: Yes, they'd carry us to prayer meetings.

JHF: Well did you go to the white folks' church any?

HS: Yes. I went to Mountain City to the white folks' church many a time. You see the white folks would have church in the morning, then they'd let the colored people have church at their church in the evening.

JHF: That was during slavery time.

HS: During slavery time, yes. During slavery time. I can remember that jus' as well as—

JHF: Well what would the preacher preach about in them days?

HS: I don' know. I didn' go. He'd preach about you know, maybe something or 'nother.

JHF: They didn't preach like they do today?

HS: No. They wasn't educated, you know, an' they would tell you how to do, an' how to get along, an' how to treat the white people an' so on. An' they'd read the Bible then. Yeah, I remember all about in slavery time. Ma an' them used to go to dances with the white folks.

JHF: Well did they treat, did the white folks treat you good? . . .

HS: They was good to us. Good. They never whipped none of their colored people, our colored people. They'd take big saddle horse, Mrs. Bunton's saddle horse, big gray animal, an' she'd have them riding. Grandma would ride to Mountain City to church. They had white preachers there. Mr. Porter, he was one of the preachers that lived across from us.

JHF: Well would the white preacher tell you to behave yourselves and be—

HS: Oh yes, they—

JHF: Be good to your master and mistress?

HS: Oh yes. That's what they preach. We sure didn' know there was any such thing as God. We thought that was a different man, but he was our master. Our white folks, preachers would refer to the white folks, master, an' so on that way. Preach that way. Didn' know no better. All of them would go up there to church. Then after we come to be free, they begin to, preach us. We begin to know there was a God an' so on.[1]

Enslaved for three decades and in three states, Delia Garlic knew the worst of slavery, including violent punishment and forced separation from family members. Decades later she offered an unsparing assessment: "Dem Days was Hell."

I was growed up when de war come . . . an' I was a mother befo' it closed. Babies was snatched from dere mother's breas' an' sold to speculators. Chilluns was separated from sisters an' brothers an' never saw each other ag'in.

Course dey cry; you think dey not cry when dey was sold lak cattle? I could tell you 'bout it all day, but even den you couldn't guess de awfulness of it.

It's bad to belong to folks dat own you soul an' body; dat can tie you

"It's bad to belong to folks dat own you soul an' body." Delia Garlic, formerly a slave in Virginia, Georgia, and Louisiana; pictured at Montgomery, Alabama. (See pages 8–11.)

up to a tree, wid yo' face to de tree an' yo' arms fastened tight aroun' it; who take a long curlin' whip an' cut de blood ever' lick.

Folks a mile away could hear dem awful whippings. Dey was a turrible part of livin'. . . .

I never seed none of my brothers an' sisters 'cept brother William. . . . Him an' my mother an' me was brought in a speculator's drove to Richmon' an' put in a warehouse wid a drove of other niggers. Den we was all put on a block an' sol' to de highes' bidder. I never seed brother William ag'in. Mammy an' me was sold to a man by de name of Carter, who was de sheriff of de county. No'm dey warn't no good times at his house. He was a widower an' his daughter kept house for him. I nursed for her, an' one day I was playin' wid de baby. It hurt its li'l han' an' commenced to cry, an' she whirl on me, pick up a hot iron an' run it all down my arm an' han'. It took off de flesh when she done it.

Atter awhile, marster married ag'in; but things warn't no better. I seed his wife blackin' her eyebrows wid smut one day, so I thought I'd black mine jes' for fun. I rubbed some smut on my eyebrows an' forgot to rub it off, an' she kotched me. She was powerful mad an' yelled: "You black devil, I'll show you how to mock your betters."

Den she pick up a stick of stovewood an' flails it ag'in' my head. I didn't know nothin' more 'till I come to, lyin' on de floor. I heard de mistus say to one of de girls: "I thought her thick skull and cap of wool could take it better than that."

I kept on stayin' dere, an' one night de marster come in drunk an' set at de table wid his head lollin' aroun'. I was waitin' on de table, an' he look up an' see me. I was skeered, an' dat made him awful mad. He called an overseer an' tol' him: "Take her out an' beat some sense in her."

I begin to cry an' run an' run in de night; but finally I run back by de quarters an' heard mammy callin' me. I went in, an' raght away dey come for me. A horse was standin' in front of de house, an' I was took dat very night to Richmon' an' sold to a speculator ag'in. I never seed my mammy any more.

I has thought many times through all dese years how mammy looked dat night. She pressed my han' in bofe of hers an' said: "Be good an' trus' in de Lawd."

Trustin' was de only hope of de pore black critters in dem days. Us jest prayed for strength to endure it to de end. We didn't 'spect nothin' but to stay in bondage 'till we died.

I was sol' by de speculator to a man in McDonough, Ga. I don't ricolleck his name, but he was openin' a big hotel at McDonough an' bought me to wait on tables. But when de time come aroun' to pay for me, his hotel done fail. Den de Atlanta man dat bought de hotel bought me, too. 'Fo' long, dough, I was sol' to a man by de name of Garlic, down in Louisiana, an' I stayed wid him 'till I was freed. I was a regular fiel' han', plowin' an' hoein' an' choppin' cotton.[2]

> While from the slaves' standpoint the best owner was none at all, owners differed greatly in their treatment of and relations with their slaves. Slaves had strong opinions about what distinguished a "good" master from a "bad" one. A good master punished his slaves lightly if at all; did not overwork them; did not break up families by sale; furnished adequate food, clothing, quarters, and medical care; and allowed slaves to visit relatives and friends, attend church, and work for their own benefit in their "free" time. A bad master did none of these things. Rare indeed was the owner who provided for the eventual freedom of his slaves, as did the owner of August Messersmith's parents. The presence of a harsh taskmaster on a neighboring plantation made Messersmith appreciate his owner all the more.

I was born in 1845, the fourth of July, near Rich Fountain, Osage County, Mo. not far from Jefferson City. My Father's name was Jim Messersmith, and my mother's maiden name was Martha Williams. I was called August Messersmith until I was old enough to vote, then I changed it to plain "Gus Smith." My friends nick-named me "Chinie" and I am called that today.

My marsters name was Bill Messersmith and he called himself a

Pennsylvania Dutchman. My marster's father settled in Missouri, near Jefferson City many years before the war. My marster owned 1500 acres of land. The old man, my marster's father had a good many slaves but the "chillun" didn't have so many after the old man died. Rufas, the old man's son and my marster's brother, took one of the negro boys; his sister Manisee, took a negro girl. These too, Rufas and Manisee never married and lived with my marster. Zennie, another sister took a girl and a boy. She married a man by the name of Goodman. My marster took my father and my mother.

My marster's father, before he died, told his chillun, that at his death he wanted each child to put their slaves out to work until they earned $800 a piece, to earn their own freedom, in that way each slave paid it themselves. He did not believe it was right to keep them in slavery all their lives. But the war came and they were free without having to work it out.

We all worn home-spun clothes, made of wool mostly. Mother carded, spun and wove all our clothes. My master let us come and go pretty much as we pleased. In fact we had much more freedom than the most of the slaves had in those days. He let us go to other places to work when we had nothing to do at home and we kept our money we earned, and spent it to suit ourselves. We had it so much better than other slaves that our neighbors would not let their slaves associate with us, for fear we would put "devilment" in their heads, for we had too much freedom.

My father and mother had their own cabin to live in, with their family, but the rest of the slaves stayed with our mistress.

We used to sing all the old plantation songs, but my father and mother were not such good singers. We all had good times along with the work. During Christmas times, and the whole month of January, it was the rulin' to give the slaves a holiday in our part of the country. A whole month, to go and come as much as we pleased and go for miles as far as we wanted to, but we had better be back by the first of February. If we wanted to go through a territory where it was hard to travel, or get by, we got a pass from our marster.

We had quiltin's, dancin', makin' rails, for days at a time. My goodness! We don't have nothin' to eat now like we did then. All kinds of game, wild ducks, geese, squirrels, rabbits, 'possum, pigeons and fried chicken, my, women in those days could cook. Great big "pound cakes" a foot and a half high. You don't see such things now-a-days.

I remember my father shooting so many pigeons at once that my mother just fed them to the hogs. Just shoot the game from our back yard. I have seen the wild pigeons so thick they looked like storm clouds coming. I'v seen them so thick they broke tree limbs down. Ducks and geese the same way. We could kill them by tow sacks full, with clubs. White folks and colored folks came to these "gatherings," from miles around, sat up all night, dancin', eatin', and drinkin'. People kept whiskey by the barrel in those days. You see, Miss, in those days they just loaded up ten or twelve bushel of corn, took it to the "still-house" and traded it for a barrel of whiskey. Not much selling in those days, everything was traded, even to labor. Our folks would tell us to go and help so-and-so and we did it.

Mother was the cook in those days at our place. The hewed log house we lived in was very big, about five or six rooms. In times of our holidays, we always had our own musicians. Sometimes we sent ten or twelve miles for a fiddler. He'd stay a week or so in one place and then he would go on the next farm, maybe four or five miles away, and they had a good time for a week. When we didn't have much work, we would get up about five o'clock every morning, but in busy season we had to be up and ready to work at daybreak.

There was plenty of work for every one then, even to the little darkeys, if only to pull weeds. We raised wheat, corn, cotton, tobacco, cabbage, potatoes, sheep, hogs and cattle. Had plenty of everything to eat.

Our closest neighbors were the Thorntons. Ol' man Thornton did not allow his slaves to go anyplace. He was a rough man, a low heavy set fellow, weighed about one hundred and sixty pounds. He was mean to his slaves. He whupped them all the time. I've seen their clothes sticking to their backs, from blood and scabs, being cut up with the cowhide. He just whupped them because he could. He use to say he "Allus give his niggers a 'breakfast spell' ever' mornin! Whupped them every morning. I remember he had a nigger woman about seventy years old on his place. The Thorntons did not feed their slaves good, they were nearly starved. One night that ol' woman was so hungry she stole a chicken from her marster—ol' Thornton, and was cooking it in her cabin. He found it out some way and started to her cabin, and caught her, while she had it on boiling. He was so mad, he told her to get a spoon and eat every bite before she stopped. It was scalding hot but he made her do it. She died right away, her insides burned.[3]

> While few owners were as relentlessly cruel as Old Man Thornton, most had little compunction about inflicting severe punishments on their slaves. Vinnie Busby, an ex-slave who grew up on a Mississippi plantation where "everything wuz kept jes' so," recalled the brutality that underlay the good order her owner so prized. Particularly fresh in her mind was an episode in which a slave had been punished by serving, literally, as a beast of burden.

I wuz raised up 'till I wuz right smart sized gal on Marse's plantation. Yes, I recollect way back in slave days an' how us lived, wuked an' wuz treated. I want [*wasn't*] as lucky as some ex-slaves as I happened to belong to a purty tough Master who alwas' wanted mo' wuk done an' wanted to be makin' more wealth. He owned a big plantation wid a big bunch ob slaves dat lived in small one-roomed cabins built in rows back o' his big fine two story house. His purty place wuz kept spic' an' span by slave servants. Deir wuz cooks, house maids, an' nurses a keepin' things a gwine, den der men wuked in de yards an' gardens. Now everything wuz kept jus' so 'round deir. De big kitchen alwas' had a good smell o' good things to eat sich as cakes ob all kinds, meat lak hams, chicken an' poke, taters an' good egg an' pone bread. De dairies wuz built out in de back yard under de big trees. Dese dairies wuz alwas' filled wid good milk an' butter. Now wid all de wuk an' hardships deir wuz alwas' plenty some 'em to eat.

De cabins we lived in wuz build ob logs split open an' pegged together. De fire places wuz big dat helt long logs. We could build big roarin' fires dat would light up de whole cabin bright as sunshine. Dese chimneys wuz made ob sticks, dirt and straw. De cabins didn't hab but 'bout one window an' two doors. One doo' at de front an' one a de back. Deir wuz never nothin' in 'em but beds which wuz home made, wid de matress made o' hay. De chairs wuz home made wid cow hide bottoms. Des chairs an' de cabin floors wuz kept scrubbed to a creamy whiteness.

De slaves went to wuk fo' day and wuked 'till night. Acres an' acres ob land wuz to be plowed and hoed—an in de fall ob de year de fiel's wuz white wid cotton.

Marse Easterlin wuz sho' a stern master. He believed in whippin' his slaves. I'se seed him put my ma 'cross a barrel an' whip her. She wuz a fiel' hand an' wuked powerfully hard. One ob de cruelest things I ever seen done to a slave wuz done by my Master. He wanted to punish one ob de slaves what had done some 'em dat he didn't lak, a kinda subborn one. He took dat darkie an' hitched him to a plow an' plowed him jes' lak a hors. He beat him an' jerked him 'bout 'till he got all bloody an' sore, but ole Marse he kept right on day after day. Finally de buzzards went to flyin' over 'em . . . dem buzzards kept a flyin' an' old Marse kept on a plowin him 'till one day he died. After dat Ole Marse got to being haunted by dat slave an' buzzards. He could alwas' see 'em an' hear de groans ob dat darkie an' he was hainted dat way de res' ob his life.

My pa an' ma wasn't owned by de same masters. My pa wuz owned by Marse Bill Brown who owned a plantation near Marse Easterlin. An' Marse being curious lak he wouldn't let pa come to see ma an' us. At night he would slip over to see us an' ole Marse wuz mos' alwa's on de look out fer everything. When he would ketch him he would beat him so hard 'till we could tell which way he went back by de blood. But pa, he would keep a comin' to see us an' a takin' de beatins.

We went to Church at de white folks Church. We waited on de white folks a totin' water an' seein' bout de horses and buggies an' a tendin' to de chillun. We had to go to whut ever Church our Marse went to. But de real times when we sho' nuf praised de Lord wuz in de fiel's. Dey tole tales an' praised de Lord an' sang de ole songs lak "Ole Time Religion." Dey shouted too but if ole Marse heard 'em he'd go make 'em quiet off. I don't know why he didn't want de singin' an' shoutin' a gwine on. Yo' know a nigger can alwa's wuk harder de mo' noise he's a makin'.[4]

Laura Smalley had not yet reached her teens when the Civil War broke out, but she had seen enough whippings to last a lifetime. In a conversation with John Henry Faulk, she discussed slave punishment.

LS: Mrs. Adeline, our mistress, jus' catched her [*a slave woman*] by her wrist, this way you know, both of them, an' pushed her down in the rocking chair. And when Mr. Bethany come home, she was crying. An' Mr. Bethany ask her what was the matter. She told Mrs. Adeline, Mrs., Aunt Martha Albert hurt her wrist. An' he ask her then, "What you doing in this house here, hurting her ol' mistress?" Say "She wasn't hurting no ol' mistress, she was jus', when mistress started whoop her, she sat her down." But they taken that ol' woman, poor ol' woman, carried her in the peach orchard, an' whipped her. An' jus' tied her han' this-a-way, 'roun' the peach orchard tree. . . . an' whipped her. You know she couldn' do nothing but jus' kick her feet. But they jus' had her clothes off down to her wais'. They didn' have her plum naked, but they had her clothes down to her waist. An' every now an' then they'd whip her, an' then snuff the pipe out on her. You know, the embers in the pipe, I don' know whether you ever see a pipe smoking.

JHF: Blow them out on her?

LS: Uh huh.

JHF: Good Lord have mercy.

LS: Blow them out on her.

JHF: Would she scream?

LS: Yeah, I reckon she would. I reckon she did. But we was dared to go out there, where it was. Because our old master would whip us an' then Uncle Saul would whip us. You see that was the overseer, Uncle Saul. Her papa was the overseer. Well he had to whip her. He whipped her too. Man he sure did whip her. Well he whipped her so that at night they had to grease her back. . . . An' after they whipped her so long that way, they quit. They quit an' give her her dinner. Late that evening they give her her dinner. . . . she was whipped so bad, she didn'

want to eat. If they whip you half a day, you ain't want to eat.
Not at all. No.

JHF: That's right.

LS: 'Cause a little chil', you can whip a little chil' now, he'll get mad,
an' don' want to eat nothing. So Uncle Saul, he was gonna whip
my mama. We had a brother, oldes' brother named Cal, an' he
was gonna whip my mother's boy [who] pack water. An' she
was gonna fight him.

JHF: Is that right?

LS: Yes sir. She was gonna fight him. You see one portion of the
people belong to Mr. Bethany, an' one portion belong to his
wife. Wife, you know, you'd have a lot of niggers, an' they give
you portion of them. Her people give you, people heap of them,
an' then your people give you some. Well that makes two parts.
You got part an' your wife got a part of colored folks that-a-way.
An' so Miss Adeline wouldn' let my Uncle Saul whip her. That
was her side. That was one of her niggers. She wouldn' let Uncle
Saul whip her, that-a-way. Well then they call her a sassy nigger,
sassy 'cause wouldn' let Uncle Saul whip her, about the boy
packing water. . . . Now, Uncle Jesse, he wasn' one of Mr.
Bethany's niggers. He was a Payne, my ol' stepdaddy, yes sir, he
was a Payne. An, he'd do anything, he would, they couldn' whip
them. Uh uh, couldn' whip them. . . .

JHF: Well where did he come from?

LS: Well, I think he come from at Louisiana, somewhere. Anyhow,
he come from somewhere. I couldn' 'xactly tell where he come
from, but my mama come from Mississippi. An' he'd back up,
you know. I don' know where you all ever see a [. . .] fence.

JHF: Yes, one of these rail fences.

LS: Yes sir. Well he'd back up in that, an' they wouldn' whip him.

He'd get him a stick an' keep them off. An' he was a great big ol'
man, an' he wouldn' let them whip him, you see, an' the master
wouldn' let them hurt him. An' the ol' master would tell him rather
than to kill him or something like that, don' hurt him. But don't,
don't kill him, but whip him. He wouldn' whip him, I tell you.

JHF: Well how would they punish him then?

LS: Give him an ear of corn. Jus' like you'd give me a ear of corn an'
that would be for my dinner or my breakfas'. When I come
home to dinner, he say to give me a ear of corn, say he shell it
off, an' plow along an' eat it. Night come, they'd give him a ear
of corn, an' tha's the way they fed him, you know, punish him
wouldn' give him nothing to eat. An' say look like he was
moving along too fast with that, too good with that, jus' giving
him corn, and he's eating it, an' drinking water an' going jus' the
same. Got so they wouldn' give him none. Wouldn' give him
nothing, but let him drink water. An' he live jus' the same. An'
he live with mama, thirty, thirty-two years, an' before he died.
An' he never did have a scar on him that the ol' boss put on him.

JHF: Did he talk like you all do or did he talk—

LS: No'm. He had a broken language.[5]

The violence of slavery left physical and psychological scars.
Henrietta King's mistress, angered by a child's petty offense,
disfigured her for life.

Well, here's how it happened. She put a piece of candy on her
washstan' one day. I was 'bout eight or nine years ole, an' it was my
task to empty de slop ev'y mornin'. I seed dat candy layin' dere, an' I
was hungry. Ain't had a father workin' in de fiel' like some of de

chillun to bring me eats—had jes' little pieces of scrapback each mornin' throwed at me from de kitchen. I seed dat peppermint stick layin' dere, an' I ain't dared go near it 'cause I knew ole Missus jus' waitin' for me to take it. Den one mornin' I so hungry dat I cain't resist. I went straight in dere an' grab dat stick of candy an' stuffed it in my mouf an' chew it down quick so ole Missus never fin' me wid it.

Nex' mornin' ole Missus say:

"Henrietta, you take dat piece o' candy out my room?" "No mam, ain't seed no candy." "Chile, you lyin' to me. You took dat candy." "Deed, Missus, I tel de truf. Ain't seed no candy." "You lyin' an' I'm gonna whup you. Come here." "Please, Missus, please don't whup me. I ain't seed no candy. I ain't took it." Well, she got her rawhide down from de nail by de fire place, an' she grabbed me by de arm an' she try to turn me 'cross her knees whilst she set in de rocker so's she could hol' me. I twisted an' turned till finally she called her daughter. De gal come an' took dat strap like her mother tole her and commence to lay it on real hard whilst Missus holt me. I twisted 'way so dere warn't no chance o' her gittin' in no solid lick. Den ole Missus lif' me up by de legs, an' she stuck my haid under de bottom of her rocker, an' she rock forward so's to hol' my haid an' whup me some mo'. I guess dey must of whupped me near a hour wid dat rocker leg a-pressin' down on my haid.

Nex' thing I knew de ole Doctor was dere, an' I was lyin' on my pallet in de hall, an' he was a-pushin' an' diggin' at my face, but he couldn't do nothin' at all wid it. Seem like dat rocker pressin' on my young bones had crushed 'em all into soft pulp. De nex' day I couldn' open my mouf and' I feel it an dey warn't no bone in de lef' side at all. An' my mouf kep' a-slippin' over to de right side an' I couldn't chaw nothin'—only drink milk. Well, ole Missus musta got kinda sorry 'cause she gits de doctor to come regular an' pry at my mouf. He git it arterwhile so's it open an' I could move my lips, but it kep' movin' over to de right, an' he couldn't stop dat. Arter a while it was over jes' whar it is now. An' I ain't never growed no mo' teef on dat side. Ain't never been able to chaw nothin' good since. Don't even 'member what it is to chaw. Been eatin' liquid, stews, an' soup ever since dat day, an' dat was eighty-six years ago.

Here, put yo' han' on my face—right here on dis lef' cheek—dat's what slave days was like. It made me so I been goin' roun' lookin' like a false face all my life. What chilluns laugh at an' babies gits to cryin' when dey see me. Course, I don't min' it no mo'. I been like dis so long now dat I don' never think on it, 'ceptin' when I see someone starin' hard an' wonderin' what debbil got in an' made me born dis way. An' it was a debbil dat done it—a she-debbil what's burnin' and twistin' in hell. She never would bother me much arter dat. Maybe it was 'cause Marsa raised such a rumpus 'cause of what she done. Never did beat me again. Used to see her sometime lookin' at me whilst I was dustin' or sweepin'. Never did say nothin', jus' set there lookin' widdout knowin' I knew it. Guess she got tired of havin' me round. When I got 'bout thirteen years ole she an Marsa give me to Marsa's cousin. Dey was good: all I had to do was mind de chillun. Was wid dem when freedom come an' dey let me stay on dere same as befo', 'ceptin' dey give me money each month. Stayed wid dem 'till I got married. Soon arter I got married, I heard dat ole Missus had died. Didn't make me drap no tears.[6]

> Even those slaves who themselves never felt the lash and the paddle witnessed the physical punishment of relatives, friends, and acquaintances. Leah Garrett recalled in vivid detail the punishments favored by her former owners and the extraordinary measures that one slave couple took to escape such treatment.

I know so many things 'bout slavery time 'til I never will be able to tell 'em all. . . . In dem days, preachers wuz just as bad and mean as

anybody else. Dere wuz a man who folks called a good preacher, but
he wuz one of de meanest mens I ever seed. When I wuz in slavery
under him he done so many bad things 'til God soon kilt him. His wife
or chillun could get mad wid you, and if dey told him anything he
always beat you. Most times he beat his slaves when dey hadn't done
nothin' a t'all. One Sunday mornin' his wife told him deir cook wouldn't
never fix nothin' she told her to fix. Time she said it he jumped up
from de table, went in de kitchen, and made de cook go under de
porch whar he always whupped his slaves. She begged and prayed but
he didn't pay no 'tention to dat. He put her up in what us called de
swing, and beat her 'til she couldn't holler. De pore thing already had
heart trouble; dat's why he put her in de kitchen, but he left her
swingin' dar and went to church, preached, and called hisself servin'
God. When he got back home she wuz dead. Whenever your marster
had you swingin' up, nobody wouldn't take you down. Sometimes a
man would help his wife, but most times he wuz beat afterwards.

Another marster I had kept a hogshead to whup you on. Dis
hogshead had two or three hoops 'round it. He buckled you face down
on de hogshead and whupped you 'til you bled. Everybody always
stripped you in dem days to whup you, 'cause dey didn't keer who seed
you naked. Some folks' chillun took sticks and jobbed (jabbed) you all
while you wuz bein' beat. Sometimes dese chillun would beat you all
'cross your head, and dey Mas and Pas didn't know what stop wuz.

Another way marster had to whup us wuz in a stock dat he had in
de stables. Dis wuz whar he whupped you when he wuz real mad. He
had logs fixed together wid holes for your feet, hands, and head. He
had a way to open dese logs and fasten you in. Den he had his
coachman give you so many lashes, and he would let you stay in de
stock for so many days and nights. Dat's why he had it in de stable so

it wouldn't rain on you. Everyday you got dat same number of lashes. You never come out able to sit down.

I had a cousin wid two chillun. De oldest one had to nuss one of marster's grandchildren. De front steps wuz real high, and one day dis pore chile fall down dese steps wid de baby. His wife and daughter hollered and went on turrible, and when our marster come home dey wuz still hollerin' just lak de baby wuz dead or dyin'. When dey told him 'bout it, he picked up a board and hit dis pore little chile 'cross de head and kilt her right dar. Den he told his slaves to take her and throw her in de river. Her ma begged and prayed, but he didn't pay her no 'tention; he made 'em throw de chile in.

One of de slaves married a young gal, and dey put her in de "Big House" to wuk. One day Mistess jumped on her 'bout something and de gal hit her back. Mistess said she wuz goin' to have Marster put her in de stock and beat her when he come home. When de gal went to de field and told her husband 'bout it, he told her whar to go and stay 'til he got dar. Dat night he took his supper to her. He carried her to a cave and hauled pine straw and put in dar for her to sleep on. He fixed dat cave up just lak a house for her, put a stove in dar and run de pipe out through de ground into a swamp. Everybody always wondered how he fixed dat pipe, course dey didn't cook on it 'til night when nobody could see de smoke. He ceiled de house wid pine logs, made beds and tables out of pine poles, and dey lived in dis cave seven years. Durin' dis time, dey had three chillun. Nobody wuz wid her when dese chillun wuz born but her husband. He waited on her wid each chile. De chillun didn't wear no clothes 'cept a piece tied 'round deir waists. Dey wuz just as hairy as wild people, and dey wuz wild. When dey come out of dat cave dey would run everytime dey seed a pusson.

"De seven years she lived in de cave, diffunt folks helped keep 'em in food. Her husband would take it to a certain place and she would go and git it. People had passed over dis cave ever so many times, but nobody knowed dese folks wuz livin' dar. Our Marster didn't know whar she wuz, and it wuz freedom 'fore she come out of dat cave for good.[7]

> Whippings on some Southern plantations and farms were public spectacles, intended to awe the witnesses as well as the recipient of the punishment. For impressionable young slaves, the flogging of a fellow slave—especially a close relative—was a never-to-be-forgotten event. William Colbert, who had been a slave in Georgia, recalled a whipping his older brother, January, had received and the stoic manner in which he had endured it.

My name am William Colbert and I'se fum Jawja. I was bawn in 1844 on my massa's plantation in Fort Valley. My massa's name was Jim Hodison. At one time he had 165 of us niggers. . . .

Nawsuh, he warn't good to none of us niggers. All de niggers 'roun' hated to be bought by him kaze he wuz so mean. When he wuz too tired to whup us he had de overseer do it; and de overseer wuz meaner dan de massa. But, Mister, de peoples wuz de same as dey is now. Dere wuz good uns and bad uns. I jus' happened to belong to a bad un. One day I remembers my brother, January wuz cotched ober seein' a gal on de next plantation. He had a pass but de time on it done gib out. Well suh, when de massa found out dat he wuz a hour late, he got as mad as a hive of bees. So when brother January he come home, de massa took down his long mule skinner and tied him wid a rope to a pine tree. He strip' his shirt off and said:

"Now, nigger. I'm goin' to teach you some sense."

Wid dat he started layin' on de lashes. January was a big, fine lookin' nigger, de finest I ever seed. He wuz jus' four years older dan

"Dere wuz good uns and bad uns. I jus' happened to belong to a bad un."
William Colbert, formerly a slave in Georgia; pictured in Alabama.
(See pages 24–26.)

me, an' when de massa begin a beatin' him, January neber said a word.
De massa got madder and madder kaze he couldn't make January
holla.

"What's de matter wid you, nigger?" he say. "Don't it hurt?"

January, he neber said nothin', and de massa keep a beatin' till little
streams of blood started flowin' down January's chest, but he neber

holler. His lips wuz a quiverin' and his body wuz a shakin', but his
mouf it neber open; and all de while I sat on my mammy's and pappy's
steps a cryin'. De niggers wuz all gathered about and some uv 'em
couldn't stand it; dey hadda go inside dere cabins. Atter while,
January, he couldn't stand it no longer hisself, and he say in a hoarse,
loud whisper:

"Massa! Massa! have mercy on dis poor nigger."[8]

> The hand wielding the lash was not always white. On many
> large plantations, planters employed slave foremen, usually
> known as "drivers," to enforce discipline among the field hands.
> "Uncle Big Jake," the driver on the Texas sugar plantation that
> Sarah Ford once called home, had a reputation for brutality ri-
> valing any white overseer. Ford's father once ran away rather
> than submit to the driver's wrath, then remained at large for
> more than a year before returning home to be with his wife and
> children, even though he knew what punishment awaited him.

Now, I tells you 'bout de plantation what I's born on. You all knows
where West Columbia is at? Well, dat's right where I's born, on Massa
Kit Patton's Plantation, dey calls it de Hogg place now. (Owned by
children of Gov. Will Hogg.)

Mama and papa belongs to Massa Kit and mama born there, too.
Folks called her "Little Jane," 'cause she no bigger'n nothing.

Papa's name was Mike and he's a tanner and he come from
Tennessee and sold to Massa Kit by a nigger trader. He wasn't all
black, he was part Indian. I heared him say what tribe, but I can't 'lect
now. When I's growed mama tells me lots of things. She say de white
folks don't let de slaves what works in de field marry none, dey jus'
puts a man and breedin' woman together like mules. Iffen the woman

"[E]ven does your stomach be full, and does you have plenty clothes,
dat bullwhip on your bare hide make you forgit de good part. . . ."
Sarah Ford, formerly a slave in Texas; pictured at Houston, Texas.
(See pages 26–30.)

don't like the man it don't make no diff'rence, she better go or dey
gives her a hidin'.

Massa Kit has two brothers, Massa Charles and Massa Matt, what
lives at West Columbia. Massa Kit on one side Varney's Creek and
Massa Charles on de other side. Massa Kit have a Arfican woman from

Kentucky for he wife, and dat's de truth. I ain't sayin' iffen she a real
wife or not, but all de slaves has to call her "Miss Rachel." But iffen a
bird fly up in de sky it mus' come down sometime, and Rachel jus' like
dat bird, 'cause Massa Kit go crazy and die and Massa Charles take
over de plantation and he takes Rachel and puts her to work in de
field. But she don't stay in de field long, 'cause Massa Charles puts her
in a house by herself and she don't work no more. . . .

I guess Massa Charles what taken us when Massa Kit die, was 'bout
de same as all white folks what owned slaves, some good and some
bad. We has plenty to eat—more'n I has now—and plenty clothes and
shoes. But de overseer was Uncle Big Jake, what's black like de rest of
us, but he so mean I 'spect de devil done make him overseer down
below long time ago. Dat de bad part of Massa Charles, 'cause he lets
Uncle Jake whip de slaves so much dat some like my papa what had
spirit was all de time runnin' 'way. And even does your stomach be
full, and does you have plenty clothes, dat bullwhip on your bare hide
make you forgit de good part, and dat's de truth.

Uncle Big Jake sho' work de slaves from early mornin' till night.
When you is in de field you better not lag none. When its fallin'
weather de hands is put to work fixin' dis and dat. De women what
has li'l chillen don't have to work so hard. Dey works 'round de sugar
house and come 11 o'clock dey quits and cares for de babies till 1
o'clock, and den works till 3 o'clock and quits.

Massa Charles have a arbor and dat's where we has preachin'. One
day old Uncle Lew preachin' and he say, "De Lawd make everyone to
come in unity and on de level, both white and black." When Massa
Charles hears 'bout it, he don't like it none and de next mornin' old
Uncle Jake git Uncle Lew and put him out in de field with de rest.

Massa Charles run dat plantation jus' like a factory. Uncle Cip was
sugar man, my papa tanner and Uncle John Austin, what have a

wooden leg, am shoemaker and make de shoes with de brass toes. Law me, dey heaps of things go on in slave time what won't go on no more, 'cause de bright light come and it ain't dark no more for us black folks. Iffen a nigger run away and dey cotch him, or does he come back 'cause he hongry, I seed Uncle Jake stretch him out on de ground and tie he hands and feet to posts so he can't move none. Den he git de piece of iron what he call de "slut" and what is like a block of wood with little holes in it, and fill de holes up with tallow and put dat iron in de fire till de grease sizzlin' hot and hold it over de pore nigger's back and let dat hot grease drap on he hide. Den he take de bullwhip and whip up and down, and after all dat throw de pore nigger in de stockhouse and chain him up a couple days with nothin' to eat. My papa carry de grease scars on he back till he die.

Massa Charles and Uncle Jake don't like papa, 'cause he ain't so black, and he had spirit, 'cause he part Indian. Do somethin' go wrong and Uncle Big Jake say he gwine to give papa de whippin', he runs off. One time he gone a whole year and he sho' look like a monkey when he gits back, with de hair standin' straight on he head and he face. Papa was mighty good to mama and me and dat de only reason he ever come back from runnin' 'way, to see us. He knowed he'd git a whippin' but he come anyway. Dey never could cotch papa when he run 'way, 'cause he part Indian. Massa Charles even gits old Nigger Kelly what lives over to Sandy Point to track papa with he dogs, but papa wade in water and dey can't track him.

Dey knows papa is de best tanner 'round dat part de country, so dey doesn't sell him off de place. I 'lect papa sayin' dere one place special where he hide, some German folks, de name Ebbling, I think. While he hides dere, he tans hides on de sly like and dey feeds him, and lots of mornin's when us open de cabin door on a shelf jus' 'bove is food for mama and me, and sometime store clothes. No one ain't see

papa, but dere it is. One time he brung us dresses, and Uncle Big Jake
heered 'bout it and he sho' mad 'cause he can't cotch papa, and he say
to mama he gwine to whip her 'less she tell him where papa is. Mama
say, "Fore God, Uncle Jake, I don't know, 'cause I ain't seed him since
he run 'way," and jus' den papa come 'round de corner of de house. He
save mama from de whippin' but papa got de hot grease drapped on
him like I told you Uncle Big Jake did, and got put in de stockhouse
with shackles on him, and kep' dere three days, and while he in dere
mama has de goin' down pains and my sister, Rachel, is born.[9]

> If some slaveholders used the whip with abandon, others were
> more discriminating, weighing the disciplinary effect against
> the possibility of incapacitating a valuable worker. After Jenny
> Proctor received a severe flogging at the hands of the plantation
> driver, her owner disapproved on the grounds that her wounds
> would keep her from several days of field labor.

I's hear tell of dem good slave days but I ain't nev'r seen no good times
den. My mother's name was Liza and when I was a very small chile I
hear dat driver goin' from cabin to cabin as early as 3 o'clock in de
mornin' and when he comes to our cabin he say, "Liza, Liza, git up
from dere and git dat breakfast." My mother, she was cook and I don't
recollect nothin' 'bout my father. If I had any brothers and sisters I
didn' know it. We had old ragged huts made out of poles and some of
de cracks chinked up wid mud and moss and some of dem wasn't. We
didn' have no good beds, jes' scaffolds nailed up to de wall out of
poles and de ole ragged beddin' throwed on dem. Dat sho' was hard
sleepin' but even dat feel good to our weary bones after dem long hard
days work in de field. I 'tended to de chillun when I was a little gal and
tried to clean de house jes' like ole miss tells me to. Den soon as I was

10 years ole, ole marster, he say, "Git dis yere nigger to dat cotton patch." I recollects once when I was tryin' to clean de house like ole miss tell me, I finds a biscuit and I's so hungry I et it, 'cause we nev'r see sich a thing as a biscuit only some times on Sunday mornin'. We jes' have co'n braid and syrup and some times fat bacon, but when I et dat biscuit and she comes in and say, "Whar dat biscuit?" I say, "Miss, I et it 'cause I's so hungry." Den she grab dat broom and start to beatin' me over de head wid it and callin' me low down nigger and I guess I jes' clean lost my head 'cause I know'd better dan to fight her if I knowed anything 'tall, but I start to fight her and de driver, he comes in and he grabs me and starts beatin' me wid dat cat-o'-nine-tails, and he beats me 'til I fall to de floor nearly dead. He cut my back all to pieces, den dey rubs salt in de cuts for mo' punishment. Lawd, Lawd, honey! Dem was awful days. When ole marster come to de house he say, "What you beat dat nigger like dat for?" And de driver tells him why, and he say, "She can't work now for a week, she pay for several biscuits in dat time." He sho' was mad and he tell ole miss she start de whole mess. I still got dem scars on my ole back right now, jes' like my grandmother have when she die and I's a-carryin' mine right on to de grave jes' like she did.[10]

> Although the whip was a fearsome disciplinary tool, perhaps the ultimate weapon in the slaveholders' arsenal was the power to sell a slave away from family and friends. As Sam Kilgore remembered, his owner's threats to sell rebellious slaves to an itinerant slave trader were so effective as to render whipping unnecessary.

Dat plant'tion am run on system lak a big factory an' it am kep up to date, everythin' am clean an' in ordah. 'Twas not lak lot of de plant'tions wid tools scattered 'round an' dirt piled up heah an' thar.

"Weuns all skeert 'bout gettin' sold to de nigger driver." Sam Kilgore, formerly
a slave in Texas; pictured at Fort Worth, Texas. (See pages 31–33.)

Thar am de chief overseer an' de seconds. De undah overseers am
cullud fo'ks, de ones dat am de head of de diffe'ent departments.
'Twas lak dis, Stein was cullud overseer in de shoe makin'
department, he am boss of de helpers makin' de harness an' tan de
hides too. Aunt Darkins am de cullud overseer dat bosses de spinnin',
weavin' an' de makin' of de clothes. Aunt Lou am de one dat tuks de

measure an' see what clothes am needed. She gives de measure an' orders to Aunt Darkins.

De place am so well managed by de Marster dat whuppin's am not necessary. Ise don't ever 'membahs of one whuppin's even. Marster had a method of keepin' de cullud fo'ks in line. If one of dem do somethin' not right to dem he say: "Don't go to wo'k tomorrow Ise 'spect de nigger drive am a-comin' pass an' Ise gwine to sell youse." Weuns all skeert 'bout gettin' sold to de nigger driver. Youse see de nigger driver am a nigger trader. Deys go through de country buyin an' sellin' slaves. W'en a slave gets in de hands of a driver 'twas a big chance of him gettin' sold to a cruel Marster an' de cullud fo'ks am powerful skeert 'bout sich. Den 'twas a plant'tion next to weuns, Ledbetter am de name, who use de whup an' hard. Weuns could hear de cullud fo'ks pleadin', "Marster, oh Marster please have de mercy" and sich. W'ens weuns heah de pleadin' de Marster say to weuns, "Boys youse heah dat misery, weuns don't want any sich on dis place an' tis up to youse." Weuns know how it may be wid some tudder Marster. W'en de Marster call a slave an' say, "Don't go to wo'k 'cause Ise have to sell youse to de nigger driver." Youse den heah de nigger pleadin', "Forgive me Marster, dis time Ise sho wont does it 'gain."[11]

> Sam Kilgore's owner was one of many slaveholders who preferred to discipline slaves by means other than the lash. Another was Alexander H. Stephens, a planter and lawyer who rose to be a U.S. Congressman and eventually vice president of the Confederate States of America. A paternalistic sort who enjoyed displays of benevolence toward his slaves, Stephens played a minor part in their day-to-day supervision. That chore he left to a kinsman who provided well for the slaves but ran a tight ship. Georgia Baker, who grew up surrounded by relatives on Stephens's estate, had generally fond memories of her youth in slavery.

Whar was I born? Why I was born on de plantation of a great man. It was Marse Alec Stephens' plantation 'bout a mile and a half from Crawfordville, in Taliaferro county. Mary and Grandison Tilly was my Ma and Pa. Ma was cook up at the big house and she died when I was jus' a little gal. Pa was a field hand, and he belonged to Marse Britt Tilly.

Dere was four of us chillun: me, and Mary, and Frances, and Mack. . . . Marse Alec let Marse Jim Johnson have Mack for his bodyguard. Frances, she wuked in de field, and Mary was de baby—she was too little to wuk. Me, I was 14 years old when de war was over. I swept yards, toted water to de field and played 'round de house and yard wid de rest of de chillun.

De long, log houses what us lived in was called "shotgun" houses 'cause dey had three rooms, one behind de other in a row lak de barrel of a shotgun. All de chillun slept in one end room and de grown folkses slept in de other end room. De kitchen whar us cooked and et was de middle room. Beds was made out of pine poles put together wid cords. Dem wheat-straw mattresses was for grown folkses mostly 'cause nigh all de chillun slept on pallets. How-some-ever, dere was some few slave chillun what had beds to sleep on. Pillows! Dem days us never knowed what pillows was. Gals slept on one side of de room and boys on de other in de chilluns room. Uncle Jim, he was de bed-maker, and he made up a heap of little beds lak what dey calls cots now.

Becky and Stafford Stephens was my Grandma and Grandpa. Marse Alec bought 'em in Old Virginny. I don't know what my Grandma done 'cause she died 'fore I was borned, but I 'members Grandpa Stafford well enough. I can see him now. He was a old man what slept on a trundle bed in the kitchen, and all he done was to set by de fire all day wid a switch in his hand and tend de chillun whilst dere mammies was at wuk. Chillun minded better dem days dan dey does now. Grandpa Stafford never had to holler at 'em but one time. Dey knowed dey would git de switch next if dey didn't behave. . . .

. . . Marse Alec, had plenty for his slaves to eat. Dere was meat, bread, collard greens, snap beans, 'taters, peas, all sorts of dried fruit, and just lots of milk and butter. Marse Alec had 12 cows and dat's whar I learned to love milk so good. De same Uncle Jim what made our beds made our wooden bowls what dey kept filled wid bread and milk for de chillun all day. You might want to call dat place whar Marse Alec had our veg'tables raised a gyarden, but it looked more lak a big field to me, it was so big. You jus' ought to have seed dat dere fireplace whar dey cooked all us had to eat. It was one sho 'nough big somepin, all full of pots, skillets, and ovens. Dey warn't never 'lowed to get full of smut neither. Dey had to be cleant and shined up atter evvy meal, and dey sho was pretty hangin' dar in dat big old fireplace.

George and Mack was de hunters. When dey went huntin' dey brought back jus' evvything: possums, rabbits, coon, squirrels, birds, and wild turkeys. Yessum, wild turkeys is some sort of birds I reckon, but when us talked about birds to eat us meant part'idges. Some folkses calls 'em quails. De fishes us had in summertime was a sight to see. Us sho et good dem days. Now us jus' eats what-some-ever us can git. . . .

Marse Lordnorth Stephens was de boss on Marse Alec's plantation. Course Marse Alec owned us and he was our sho 'nough Marster. Neither one of 'em ever married. Marse Lordnorth was a good man, but he didn' have no use for 'omans—he was a sissy. Dere warn't no Marster no whar no better dan our Marse Alec Stephens, but he never stayed home enough to tend to things hisself much 'cause he was all de time too busy on de outside. He was de President or somepin of our side durin' de war. . . .

Ma, she was Marse Alec's cook and looked atter de house. Atter she died Marse Lordnorth got Mrs. Mary Berry from Habersham County to keep house at de big house, but Aunt 'Liza, she done de cookin' atter Miss Mary got dar. Us little Niggers sho' did love Miss Mary. Us called her "Mammy Mary" sometimes. Miss Mary had three sons and one of 'em was named Jeff Davis. I 'members when dey came and got him and tuk him off to war. Marse Lordnorth built a four-room house on de plantation for Miss Mary and her boys. Evvybody loved our Miss Mary, 'cause she was so good and sweet, and dere warn't nothin' us wouldn't have done for her.

No Lord! Marse Lordnorth never needed no overseer or no carriage driver neither. Uncle Jim was de head man what got de Niggers up evvy mornin' and started 'em off to wuk right. De big house sho was a pretty place, a-settin' up on a high hill. De squirrels was so tame dar dey jus' played all 'round de yard. Marse Alec's dog is buried in dat yard.

No Mam, I never knowed how many acres dere was in de plantation us lived on, and Marse Alec had other places too. He had land scattered evvywhar. Lord, dere was a heap of Niggers on dat place, and all of us was kin to one another. Grandma Becky and Grandpa Stafford was de fust slaves Marse Alec ever had, and dey sho had a passel of chillun. One thing sho Marse Lordnorth wouldn't keep no bright colored Nigger on dat plantation if he could help it. Aunt Mary was a bright colored Nigger and dey said dat Marse John, Marse Lordnorth's brother, was her Pa, but anyhow Marse Lordnorth never had no use for her 'cause she was a bright colored nigger.

Marse Lordnorth never had no certain early time for his slaves to git up nor no special late time for 'em to quit wuk. De hours dey wuked was 'cordin' to how much wuk was ahead to be done. Folks in Crawfordville called us "Stephens' Free Niggers."

Us minded Marse Lordnorth—us had to do dat—but he let us do pretty much as us pleased. Us never had no sorry piece of a Marster. He was a good man and he made a sho 'nough good Marster. I never seed no Nigger git a beatin', and what's more I never heard of nothin' lak dat on our place. Dere was a jail in Crawfordville, but none of us Niggers on Marse Alec's place warn't never put in it.

No Lord: None of us Niggers never knowed nothin' 'bout readin' and writin'. Dere warn't no school for Niggers den, and I ain't never been to school a day in my life. Niggers was more skeered of newspapers dan dey is of snakes now, and us never knowed what a Bible was dem days.

Niggers never had no churches of deir own den. Dey went to de white folkses' churches and sot in de gallery. One Sunday when me and my sister Frances went to church I found 50¢ in Confederate money and showed it to her. She tuk it away from me. Dat's de onliest money I seed durin' slavery time. Course you knows dey throwed Confederate money away for thrash atter de war was over. Den us young chaps used to play wid it.

I never went to no baptizin's nor funerals neither den. Funerals warn't de style. When a Nigger died dem days, dey jus' put his body in a box and buried it. I 'members very well when Aunt Sallie and Aunt Catherine died, but I was little den, and I didn't take it in what dey done 'bout buryin' 'em.

None of Marse Alec's slaves never run away to no North, 'cause he so good to 'em dey never wanted to leave him. De onliest Nigger what left Marse Alec's place was Uncle Dave, and he wouldn't have left 'cept he got in trouble wid a white 'oman. You needn't ax me her name 'cause I ain't gwine to tell it, but I knows it well as I does my own name. Anyhow Marse Alec give Uncle Dave some money and told him to leave, and nobody never seed him no more atter dat.

Oh, yessum! Us heared 'bout 'em, but none of us never seed no
patterollers on Marse Alec's plantation. He never 'lowed 'em on his
land, and he let 'em know dat he kept his slaves supplied wid passes
whenever dey wanted to go places so as dey could come and go when
dey got good and ready. Thursday and Sadday nights was de main
nights dey went off. Uncle Stafford's wife was Miss Mary Stephen's
cook, Uncle Jim's wife lived on de Finley place, and Uncle Isom's
belonged to de Hollises, so dey had regular passes all de time and no
patterollers never bothered 'em none.

Whenever Marse Alec or Marse Lordnorth wanted to send a
message dey jus' put George or Mack on a horse and sont 'em on but
one thing sho, dere warn't no slave knowed what was in dem
letters. . . .

Most times when slaves went to deir quarters at night, mens rested,
but sometimes dey holped de 'omans cyard [card] de cotton and wool.
Young folkses frolicked, sung songs, and visited from cabin to cabin.
When dey got behind wid de field wuk, sometimes slaves wuked atter
dinner Saddays, but dat warn't often. But, Oh, dem Sadday nights! Dat
was when slaves got together and danced. George, he blowed de
quills, and he sho could blow grand dance music on 'em. Dem Niggers
would jus' dance down. Dere warn't no foolishment 'lowed atter 10:00
o'clock no night. Sundays dey went to church and visited 'round, but
folks didn't spend as much time gaddin' 'bout lak dey does now days.

Christmas Day! Oh, what a time us Niggers did have dat day! Marse
Lordnorth and Marse Alec give us evvything you could name to eat:
cake of all kinds, fresh meat, lightbread, turkey, chickens, ducks,
geese, and all kinds of wild game. Dere was allus plenty of pecans,
apples, and dried peaches too at Christmas. Marse Alec had some
trees what had fruit dat looked lak bananas on 'em, but I done forgot
what was de name of dem trees. Marse Alec would call de grown

folkses to de big house early in de mornin' and pass 'round a big pewter pitcher full of whiskey, den he would put a little whiskey in dat same pitcher and fill it wid sweetened water and give dat to us chillun. Us called dat "toddy" or "dram." Marse Alec allus had plenty of good whiskey, 'cause Uncle Willis made it up for him and it was made jus' right. De night atter Christmas Day us pulled syrup candy, drunk more liquor, and danced. Us had a big time for a whole week and den on New Year's Day us done a little wuk jus' to start de year right and us feasted dat day on fresh meat, plenty of cake, and whiskey. Dere was allus a big pile of ash-roasted 'taters on hand to go wid dat good old baked meat. Us allus tried to raise enough 'taters to last all through de winter 'cause Niggers sho does love dem sweet 'taters. No Mam, us never knowed nothin' 'bout Santa Claus 'til atter de war.

No Mam, dere warn't no special cornshuckin's and cotton pickin's on Marse Alec's place, but of course dey did quilt in de winter 'cause dere had to be lots of quiltin' done for all dem slaves to have plenty of warm kivver and you knows, lady, 'omans can quilt better if dey gits a passel of 'em together to do it. Marse Alec and Marse Lordnorth never 'lowed dere slaves to mix up wid other folkses business much. . . .

De fust time I ever seed Marse Alec to know who he was, I warn't more'n 6 years old. Uncle Stafford had went fishin' and catched de nicest mess of fish you ever seed. He cleant 'em and put 'em in a pan of water, and told me to take 'em up to de big house to Marse Alec. I was skeered when I went in de big house yard and axed, what looked lak a little boy, whar Marse Alec was, and I was wuss skeered when he said: "Dis is Marse Alec you is talkin' to. What you want?" I tole him Uncle Stafford sont him de fishes and he told me: "Take 'em to de kitchen and tell 'Liza to cook 'em for me." I sho ain't never gwine to forgit dat.

One day dey sont me wid a bucket of water to de field, and I had to go through de peach orchard. I et so many peaches, I was 'most daid when I got back to de house. Dey hed to drench me down wid sweet milk, and from dat day to dis I ain't never laked peaches. From den on Marse Alec called me de "peach gal."

Marse Alec warn't home much of de time, but when he was dar he used to walk down to de cabins and laugh and talk to his Niggers. He used to sing a song for de slave chillun dat run somepin' lak dis:

> Walk light ladies
> De cake's all dough
> You needn't mind de weather,
> If de wind don't blow."

. . . Us didn't know when he was a-singin' dat tune to us chillun dat when us growed up us would be cake walkin' to de same song.[12]

Manda Boggan's master, a Bible-quoting Mississippian, eschewed whipping and gave his slaves other privileges they valued. His death, however, brought the division of his estate among his heirs and, consequently, the separation of many slave families, including Boggan's.

I believes I had de bes' master in de worl'. I gits ter thinkin' ob de days back in slavery time an' wishes ole Mars could ev alwa's cared fo' us. He wuz a preacher an' sho' did live his religion, an' taught us slaves ter walk in de straight an' narrow way. He wouldn't 'low no overseers wukin' his slaves, 'cause he wont gwine ter hab 'em beat. He got wuk a plinty out en us, fer when yo' turn a bunch ob niggers a loose an' let 'em sing, pray, an' shout all dey wants ter he's sho' gwine ter turn de wuk off.

I don't know who mars bought my mudder from, but I knows my pa wuz bought from a man in Virginia. He married my mudder after he come to mar's plantation. Dey lived in one ob de little log cabins back ob mar's who lived in a big low, ramblin', log house, wid a big kitchen an' dinnin' room built away from de main house. Dey had a slave cook what wuz named Hannah, dat done de cookin' fer mar's family an' all de wukin' slaves. I jes' wish I could tell yo' all ob all de good grub deir wuz cooked an' served. All I can say is dat hit wuz good grub in 'bundence.

Afore I wuz big 'nuf to be sont to de fields, I jes' played 'round ever whar wid de chilluns. Us made play houses under de big oak trees. Us raked up big piles ob leaves fer beds, an' made rag-dolls, us made dresses an' hats out 'en leaves pined tergether wid pine straws. Den us played run and ketch games us made up.

My first wuk wuz 'round mar's house, totin' cule water a mile from a spring, an milkin' de cows. Hit took a heap ob us ter milk all dem cows. De milk den had to be strained in big stone crocks and put in de dairies dat wuz built out under de trees ter keep de milk cool. Deir wuz a heap o' churnin' ter be done. Hit 'peared lak us had ter churn fer hours 'afore dat butter would be deir.

When I wuz put in de fields, hit wuz wuk from early till late. De fields would be full o' slaves a wukin' hard. Us would look up an see Mars acomin' across de field wid his bible under his arm. He would walk along whar us wuz a wukin' an' read a text, den us would sing an' pray. De song us laked bes' wuz, "De Day ob Jubilee es come." . . .

Eber Sunday mornin' Mars went to de slave cabins an' read de bible an' prayed. He come in de cabins wid a smile. Us went to meetin' once a month wid de white folks an' set in de back. Us waited on 'em, toted in water an' tended ter de chilluns. When de meetin' wuz ober us kotched de horses an' led 'em to deir blocks an' brung de carriages 'round fer 'em.

I wants yo' all ter know, us had gran' times at de frolics. On Satuday nites us would dance all nite long. I can hear dem fiddles an' guitars yet, wid dat loud, "swing yo' pardners." Hit wuz all gran'.

One ob de saddest days of us' lives wuz when Ole Mars died. He wuz de bes' friend us all had or eber will hab. After he wuz burried in de ole church yard, de slaves wuz divided amoungst his chillun. My dear brudder wuz took slap off to Texas an' us ain't neber heard ob him since. A heap ob de families wuz tore apart lak dat.[13]

> As property, slaves could be bought and sold, traded for other goods, offered as security for a loan, inherited, or given as gifts. Slaves dreaded such transactions. Few events so dramatized the slaves' powerlessness as a sale on the auction block or the movement of a "coffle" of slaves by an itinerant slave trader (colloquially, a "speculator"). Transfers of slaves meant not only changes of owners and residence but, more important, separation from friends and family. Delicia Patterson of Missouri described the circumstances of her sale at the age of about fifteen.

I was born in Boonville, Missouri, January 2, 1845. My mother's name was Maria and my father's was Jack Wiley. Mother had five children but raised only two of us. I was owned by Charles Mitchell until I was 15 years old. They were fairly nice to all of their slaves and they had several of us. I only got whipped once in the whole 15 years there, and that was because I was working in the garden with one of my owner's daughters and I pulled up something that she did not want pulled up, so she up and slapped me for it.

I got so mad at her, I taken up a hoe and run her all the way in the big house, and of course I got whipped for that. I did not even have to sleep in the cabins. I slept on a pallet in the bedrooms with old marse's children. I was a pet anywhere I worked, because I was always very neat and clean, and a good worker.

When I was 15 years old, I was brought to the courthouse, put up on the auction block to be sold. Old Judge Miller from my county was there. I knew him well because he was one of the wealthiest slave owners in the county, and the meanest one. He was so cruel all the slaves and many owners hated him because of it. He saw me on the block for sale, and he knew I was a good worker so when he bid for me, I spoke right out on the auction block and told him: "Old Judge Miller don't you bid for me, 'cause if you do, I would not live on your plantation, I will take a knife and cut my own throat from ear to ear before I would be owned by you."

So he stepped back and let someone else bid for me. My own father knew I was to be for sale, so he brought his owner to the sale for him to buy me, so we could be together. But when father's owner heard what I said to Judge Miller, he told my father he would not buy me, because I was sassy, and he never owned a sassy niggah and did not want one that was sassy. That broke my father's heart, but I couldn't help that. Another nigger trader standing right beside my father's owner said, I wouldn't own a nigger that didn't have some spunk. So I was sold to a Southern Englishman named Thomas B. Steele for $1500. He had an old slave he had in his home for years as their housekeeper, and his wife did not like her and, he had to sell her to keep peace at home so he put me in his buggy and taken me home to his wife and told her, "I bought you another girl, Susianna, but I don't want you to lay the weight of your finger on her when she disobeys. Let me know and I will punish her myself."

I lived in that family until after the Civil War was over. Mr. Steele's wife's people had a big family and they visited the Steeles a great deal. Mr. Tom didn't like them because they were Yankees and the Steeles were Union.* So one time Mr. Tom was going away on a trip and he knew when he was gone, his wife would have all of her folks in the home visiting, and that was against his wishes. He told me to keep tab on every time her relatives come to the house and how long they stayed, and tell him when he come back home, and that he would leave orders in the home to let me work in the field, so I would not have to bother with that great big family. When he left all his wife's folks come right down on our plantation, so I had to work in the house for them so hard, I did not have time to even look at the field.

When old boss come home I told him, I had not worked in the field and why. Him and his wife had a big fight about that, and she hated me for a long time, and said, the idea of her husband taking a nigger's word to hers and mistreat her on account of it. But he did not let her bother me about nothing, so I stayed on with them until one day, while I had a fly brush in my hand fanning flies while they ate, she told him something I done she didn't like. Just to please her, he taken the fly brush out of my hand and just tapped me with it. It didn't hurt me a bit, but it made me so mad I just went straight to the kitchen left all the dishes, put on my sunbonnet and run away. I stayed two weeks. He sent everybody he thought knew where I was after me, and told them to tell me if I would only come on back home, no one would ever bother me anymore. I hid in the woods that whole two weeks and was not afraid. I would be afraid out in those woods now, but I wasn't then. At night I would come up to some of the slave cabins who were my friends and eat and stay all night. So I went back home after my 2 weeks off as a runaway nigger and no one ever bothered me any more either. I came to St. Louis with them, during the Civil War.[14]

---

*A handwritten [?] in the margin of the original marks the apparent misidentification of either the Steeles' politics or those of their relatives.

Delicia Patterson was sold to another owner in her home state, but for many slaves a change of masters meant traveling hundreds of miles to a new residence. Betty Simmons carried vivid memories of how the collapse of her owner's finances forced her sale away from her family in Alabama. Sold to a speculator, she embarked on a journey that ended at her purchaser's plantation in Texas.

Betty Simmons

"I's satisfy den I los' my people and ain't never goin' to see dem no more in dis world. . . ." Betty Simmons, formerly a slave in Alabama, Texas, and points between; pictured in Texas with an unidentified woman. (See pages 45–48.)

When Massa Engford was ruint and dey goin' to take de store 'way from him, dey was trouble, plenty of dat. One day massa send me down to he brudder's place. I was dere two days and den de missy tell me to go to de fence. Dere was two white men in a buggy and one of 'em say, "I thought she bigger den dat." Den he asks me, "Betty, kin you cook?" I tells him I been cook helper two, three month, and he say, "You git

dressed and come on down three mile to de other side de post office."
So I gits my little bundle and when I gits dere he say, "Gal, you want to
go 'bout 23 mile and help cook at de boardin' house?" He tries to make
me believe I won't be gone a long time, but when I gits in de buggy dey
tells me Massa Engford done los' everything and he have to hide out
he niggers for to keep he credickers from gittin' dem. Some of de
niggers he hides in de woods, but he stole me from my sweet missy
and sell me so dem credickers can't git me.

When we gits to de crossroads dere de massa and a nigger man. Dat
another slave he gwine to sell, and he hate to sell us so bad he can't
look us in de eye. Dey puts us niggers inside de buggy, so iffen de
credickers comes along dey can't see us.

Finally dose slave spec'lators puts de nigger man and me on de train
and takes us to Memphis, and when we gits dere dey takes us to de
nigger traders' yard. We gits dere at breakfast time and waits for de
boat dey calls de "Ohio" to git dere. De boat jus' ahead of dis Ohio, Old
Capt. Yabra's boat, was 'stroyed and dat delay our boat two hours. When
it come, dey was 200 niggers out of dem nigger yards in Memphis what
gits on dat boat. Dey puts de niggers upstairs and goes down de river
far as Vicksburg, dat was de place, and den us gits offen de boat and
gits on de train 'gain and dat time we goes to New Orleans.

I's satisfy den I los' my people and ain't never goin' to see dem no
more in dis world, and I never did. Dey has three big trader yard in
New Orleans and I hear de traders say dat town 23 mile square. I ain't
like it so well, 'cause I ain't like it 'bout dat big river. I hears some of
'em say dere's gwineter threw a long war and us all think what dey
buy us for if we's gwine to be sot free. Some was still buyin' niggers
every fall and us think it too funny dey keep on fillin' up when dey
gwineter be emptyin' out soon.

Dey have big sandbars and planks fix 'round de nigger yards and dey
have watchmans to keep dem from runnin 'way in de swamp. Some of

de niggers dey have jus' picked up on de road, dey steals dem. Dey
calls dem "wagon boy" and "wagon gal." Dey has one bit mulatto boy
dey stole 'long de road dat way and he massa find out 'bout him and
come and git him and take him 'way. And a woman what was a
seamster a man what knowed her seed her in de pen and he done told
her massa and he come right down and git her. She sho' was proud to
git out. She was stole from 'long de road, too. You sees, if dey could
steal de niggers and sell 'em for de good money, dem traders could
make plenty money dat way.

At las' Col. Fortescue, he buy me and kep' me. He a fighter in de
Mexican War and he come to New Orleans to buy he slaves. He takes
me up de Red River to Shreveport and den by de buggy to Liberty, in
Texas.[15]

> A slave's personal relationship with his or her owner could af-
> fect every area of life. Slaves who won the affection and trust of
> their owner typically enjoyed easier treatment and more privi-
> leges than their fellows. Such ties stemmed from various
> sources: perhaps the slave had skills or personality traits the
> owner appreciated; perhaps he or she had been a childhood
> playmate; perhaps he or she was a blood relative—a sibling,
> cousin, or even a child. Privileged slaves' close connection to
> their owners was a mixed blessing, however. Their special sta-
> tus often alienated them from their fellow slaves. And strains in
> the personal relationship that underlay their favored position
> could bring dire consequences. Salomon Oliver's mother, Mary,
> the daughter of her wealthy owner, enjoyed the benefits and
> suffered the liabilities of her status.

John A. Miller owned the finest plantation in Washington County,
Mississippi, about 12-mile east of Greenville. I was born on this
20,000-acre plantation November 17, 1859, being one of about four
hundred slave children on the place.

About three hundred negro families living in box-type cabins made it seem like a small town. Built in rows, the cabins were kept whitewashed, neat and orderly, for the Master was strict about such things. Several large barns and storage buildings were scattered around the plantation. Also, two cotton gins and two old fashioned presses, operated by horses and mules, made Miller's plantation one of the best equipped in Mississippi.

Master John was quite a character. The big plantation didn't occupy all his time. He owned a bank in Vicksburg and another in New Orleans, and only came to the plantation two or three times a year for a week or two visit.

Things happened around there mighty quick when the Master showed up. If the slaves were not being treated right—out go the white overseer. Fired! The Master was a good man and tried to hire good boss men. Master John was bad after the slave women. A yellow child show up every once in a while. Those kind always got special privileges because the Master said he didn't want his children whipped like the rest of them slaves.

My own Mammy, Mary, was the Master's own daughter! She married Salomon Oliver (who took the name of Oliver after the War), and the Master told all the slave drivers to leave her alone and not whip her. This made the overseers jealous of her and caused trouble. John Santhers was one of the white overseers who treated her bad, and after I was born and got strong enough (I was a weakling for three-four years after birth), to do light chores he would whip me just for the fun of it. It was fun for him but not for me. I hoped to whip him when I grew up. That is the one thing I won't ever forget. He died about the end of the War so that's one thing I won't ever get to do.

My mother was high-tempered and she knew about the Master's orders not to whip her. I guess sometimes she took advantage and tried to do things that maybe wasn't right. But it did her no good and one of the white men flogged her to death. She died with scars on her back![16]

As a favored house servant, young Anna Baker enjoyed her master's confidence. He tried to enlist her as an informant, notifying him of goings-on in the slave quarter, but she became something of a double agent.

I 'members a pow'ful lot 'bout slavery times an' 'bout 'fore surrender. I know I was a right smart size den, so's 'cording to dat I mus' be 'roun' 'bout eighty year old. I aint sho' 'bout dat an' I don't want to tell no untruth. I know I was right smart size 'fore de surrender, as I was a-sayin', 'cause I 'members Marster comin' down de road past de house. When I'd see 'im 'way off I'd run to de gate an' start singin' dis song to 'im:

> Here come de marster, root toot too!
> Here come Marster, comin' my way!
> Howdy, Marster, howdy do!
> What you gwine a-bring from town today?

Dat would mos' nigh tickle him to death an' he'd say, "Loosanna (dat was his pet name for me) what you want today?" I'd say, "Bring me some goobers, or a doll, or some stick candy, or anything. An' you can bet yo' bottom dollar he'd always bring me somp'n'.

One reason Marse Morgan thought so much o' me, dey say I was a right peart young'n' an' caught on to anything pretty quick. Marster would tell me, "Loosanna, if you keep yo' ears open an' tell me what de darkies talk 'bout, dey'll be somp'n' good in it for you." (He meant for me to listen when dey'd talk 'bout runnin' off an' such.) I'd stay 'roun' de old folks and' make lak I was a-playin'. All de time I'd be a-listenin'. Den I'd go an' tell Marster what I hear'd. But all de time I mus' a-had a right smart mind, 'cause I'd play 'roun' de white folks an' hear what dey'd say an' den go tell de Niggers. Don't guess de marster ever thought 'bout me doin' dat.[17]

As Anna Baker understood, privilege brought opportunity. Joe Sutherland, a slave coachman in Virginia, used his privileged status to learn the rudiments of literacy without his master's knowledge. By means of his expertly forged passes, several slaves managed to escape to freedom in the North. In his wide-ranging recollections of his youth, William Johnson, who lived on the same plantation as Sutherland, told the story of the coachman's deception and his ultimate betrayal by a fellow slave.

I was born in Albermarle County, February 14th, 1840 on the George's Estate. My childhood up to age ten was spent in playing around the house—minding chickens. Between age 10 and 12, to mind the sheep and cows, and pasturing.

Old man George died and in the division of the estate I was given to his daughter as was also my parents. She was married to a man by the name of Johnson.

With this family I was taken into the house and trained to be a butler. When I was 17 years old they hired me out to a man in Richmond, Virginia by the name of Brooks. I served in this house as butler during 1858–1859, and since our time always expired on Xmas Eve; on that day 1859 the Johnsons took me back to their home in Goochland County, where I remained as their butler until the Civil War. . . .

My master Johnson, always had more slaves than he could work but he preferred to hire them out to selling them. When a slave was hired out, the man would have to sign a contract to pay the owner $250.00 at the end of the year and to give the slave food, shelter, two suits of clothes and the necessary medicine during the year. Whether the slaves stayed with the person who hired him or not, the leasee would have to pay that contact at the end of the year.

I had two Uncles, Edmund and John Johnson who never worked

more than four months during the four or five years that they were hired out. They would go with the person who hired them, work about a month, then steal off into the woods and stay until their time was out. Then they would return to their original owners in Goochland. Of course, the master never punished them for doing this—he didn't care cause he collected his contract just the same. Edmund and John always worked all right when they were at home but they were always determined not to work for anyone else. . . .

We had one smart slave on our plantation, Joe Sutherland, who was master's coachman. Joe always hung around the courthouse with master. He went on business trips with him, and through this way, Joe learned to read and write unbeknown to master. In fact, Joe got so good that he leaned how to write passes for the slaves. Master's son Carter Johnson, was clerk of the county court, and by going around the court everyday Joe forged the county seal on these passes and several slaves used them to escape to free states. I remember three slaves who escaped that way; they were App Seldom, who carried his wife, Moses Bollock and Daniel Prosser. Joe was doing a big business—the slaves always paid him for the passes—but he was finally caught and sold way down south, somewhere. It was always said that a man on the adjourning farm by the name of Ned Lee, who was a close friend of Joe's betrayed him. Anyway, the thing was quieted down and Joe was put in shackles until he was sold to a man in Mississippi.[18]

The common practice of slave-hiring, in which an owner rented out a slave to a third party, complicated the master–slave relationship. The slave remained the owner's property, but fell temporarily to the supervision and control of the hirer. Slave hirers, who had no long-term interest in the slaves they employed, often abused them. Slaves were quick to appeal to their owner. Adelaide Vaughn's mother, dissatisfied at her treatment by the wife of her hirer, sought and obtained redress from her owners.

My mother, she was sold from her father when she was four years old. The rest of the children were grown then. Master Hickman was the one who bought her. I don't know the one that sold her. Hickman had a lot of children her age and he raised her up with them. They were nice to her all the time.

Once the pateroles came near capturing her. But she made it home and they didn't catch her.

Mr. Candle hired her from her master when she was about eighteen years old. He was nice to her but his wife was mean. Just because mother wouldn't do everything the other servants said Mis' Candle wanted to whip her. Mother said she knew that Mis' Candle couldn't whip her alone. But she was 'fraid that she would have Sallie, another old Negro woman slave, and Kitty, a young Negro woman slave, to help whip her.

One day when it was freezing cold, she wanted mother to stand out in the hall with Sallie and Clara and wash the glasses in boiling hot water. She was making her do that because she thought she was uppity and she wanted to punish her. When mother went out, she rattled the dishes 'round in the pan and broke them. They was all glasses. Mis' Candle heard them breaking and come out to see about it. She wanted to whip mother but she was 'fraid to do it while she was alone; so she waited till her husband come home. When he come she told him. He said she oughtn't to have sent them out in the cold to wash the glasses because nobody could wash dishes outside in that cold weather.

The first morning she was at Mis' Candle's, they called her to eat and they didn't have nothing but black molasses and corn bread for mother's meal. The other two ate it but mother didn't. She asked for something else. She said she wasn't used to eating that—that she ate what her master and mistress ate at home.

Mis' Candle didn't like that to begin with. She told my mother that she was a smart nigger. She told mother to do one thing and then before she could do it, she would tell her do something else. Mother would just go on doing the first thing till she finished that, and Mis' Candle would git mad. But it wasn't nobody's fault but her own.

She asked mother to go out and git water from the spring on a rainy day. Mother wouldn't go. Finally mother got tired and went back home. Her mistress heard what she had to tell her about the place she'd been working. Then she said mother did right to quit. She had worked there for three or four months. They meant to keep her but she wouldn't stay. Mis' Hickman went over and collected her money.

When mother worked out, the people that hired her paid her owners. Her owners furnished her everything she wanted to eat and clothes to wear, and all the money she earned went to them.

Mis' [Mr.] Candle begged Mr. Hickman to let him have mother back. He said he'd talk to his wife and she wouldn't mistreat her any more but mama said that she didn't want to go back and Mrs. Hickman said, "No, she doesn't want to go back and I wouldn't make her." And the girls said, "No, mama, don't let her go back." And Mis' Hickman said, "No, she was raised with my girls and I am not going to let her go back."[19]

Few figures loomed as large in the ex-slaves' memory as the patrollers, white men who policed the plantation countryside. These white men, often nonslaveholders, captured and punished slaves who ran away, took leave without a pass from their owner, violated curfews, or breached other laws or customs. Slaves despised them. Owners had an ambiguous relationship with them. On the one hand, patrollers were essential to the security of slavery and an important means of incorporating nonslaveholders into the plantation regime; on the other hand, in punishing slaves they often trespassed on the authority that masters preferred to retain for themselves. Nonslaveholders sometimes took out their hostility toward their wealthier neighbors by damaging the slaveholders' valued property, the slaves. Daniel Dowdy, who had been a slave in Georgia, related an incident in which an owner warned the patrollers away from "his people."

Oh, them patrollers! They had a chief and he git'em together and iffen they caught you without a pass and sometimes with a pass, they'd beat you. But iffen you had a pass, they had to answer to the law. One old master had two slaves, brothers, on his place. They was both preachers. Mitchell was a hardshell Baptist and Andrew was a Missionary Baptist. One day the patroller chief was rambling thoo' the place and found some letters writ to Mitchell and Andrew. He went to the master and said, "Did you know you had some niggers that could read and write?" Master said, "No, but I might have, who do you 'spect?" The patroller answered, "Mitchell and Andrew." The old master said, "I never knowed Andrew to tell me a lie 'bout nothing!"

Mitchell was called first and asked could he read and write. He was scared stiff. He said, "Naw-sir." Andrew was called and asked. He said, "Yes-sir." He was asked iffen Mitchell could. He said, "Sho', better'n me." The master told John Arnold, the patroller chief, not to bother 'em. He gloried in they spunk. [20]

W. B. Allen, who became a minister after emancipation, described how patrollers in his Alabama neighborhood disrupted slaves' prayer meetings. Yet while the slaves lacked horses, guns, and whips, they were not entirely without weapons to use against the night riders.

They had a hard time trying to serve God. The patrolers would break up their prayer meetings and whip all caught in attendance—unless, of course, a Nigger saved himself in flight.

My father was once attending a prayer meeting in a house which had only one door. The slaves had turned a large pot down in the center of the floor to hold the sounds of their voices within. (No sounds can escape from a closed room, if a big pot be turned down in the middle of it.) But, despite their precaution, the patrolers found them and broke in. Of course, every Nigger present was "in" for a severe whipping, but the Lord must have spoken to my father. Thinking fast and acting quickly (as if he were inspired), my father stuck a big shovel in the fireplace, drew out a peck or more of hot ashes and cinders and flung them broadcast into the faces of them patrolers. The room was soon filled with smoke and the smell of burning clothes and white flesh and, in the confusion and general hubbub that followed, every Negro escaped.

Teasing, and playing pranks on, the patrolers were favorite pastimes of some of the slaves. One of their choicest stunts was to tie a grapevine across some narrow, dark stretch of road where they knew the patrolers would pass. And, as the patrolers usually rode in a gallop, these vines would be sure to catch the foremost rider or riders somewhere between their saddle horns and necks and unhorse at least one or more of them." [21]

Despite the occasional episode of open resistance, slaves' sense of self-preservation ordinarily made them cautious about directly challenging the impositions of their owners and other defenders of the slave system. They knew that frontal attacks on the master's authority entailed grave risk and would likely bring swift, sure, and possibly lethal punishment. On occasion, however, a brave, foolhardy, or desperate slave openly defied the owner or tried to escape slavery altogether. Fannie Berry, an ex-slave from Virginia, related the story (possibly apocryphal) of Sukie, a domestic slave who forcibly rebuffed the sexual advances of her owner and was sold away as a result.

Sukie was her name. She was a big strappin' nigger gal dat never had nothin' to say much. She used to cook for Miss Sarah Ann, but ole Marsa was always tryin' to make Sukie his gal. One day Sukie was in the kitchen makin' soap. Had three gra' big pots o' lye jus' comin' to a bile in de fireplace when ole Marsa come in for to get arter her 'bout somep'n.

He lay into her, but she ain't answer him a word. Den he tell Sukie to take off her dress. She tole him no. Den he grabbed her an' pull it down off'n her shoulders. When he done dat, he fo'got 'bout whuppin' her, I guess, 'cause he grab hold of her an' try to pull her down on de flo'. Den dat black gal got mad. She took an' punch ole Marsa an' made him break loose an' den she gave him a shove an' push his hindparts down in de hot pot o' soap. Soap was near to bilin', an' it burnt him near to death. He got up holdin' his hindparts an' ran from de kitchen, not darin' to yell, 'cause he didn't want Miss Sarah Ann to know 'bout it.

Well, few days later he took Sukie off an' sol' her to de nigger trader. An' dey put Sukie on de block, an' de nigger traders 'zamined her an' pinched her an' den dey open her mouf, and stuck dey fingers in to see how her teeth was. Den Sukie got awful mad, and she pult up her dress an' tole ole nigger traders to look an' see if dey could fin' any teef down dere. Ole Jim, Marsa's coachman, tel' us all 'bout it, 'cause he done see it. Marsa never did bother slave gals no mo'.[22]

A few slaves did escape to freedom. W. P. Jacobs recounted the story of his Uncle Charlie, who with the aid of the Underground Railroad passed from slavery in the western Virginia hills to freedom in Canada.

My father often told me about his brother Charlie. I remember him faintly. I was about six years old when Uncle Charlie escaped, and I never saw him again. Father says he and Uncle Charlie used to work in the woods making rails. This was out in the mountain country beyond Roanoke, and they had to have fences or else the cattle would get out and get lost. These rails were from eight to ten feet long, and each slave had to cut and finish a hundred rails a day.

First you had to cut a tree down three feet wide. This would make two good rail cuts. After you cut down your tree, you'd top off the branches, wedge and split the tree and make rails. That was some job. Those who couldn't make the number had a whipping coming when the nigger-driver counted up each evening. Uncle Charlie was one of the slaves that couldn't get his number finished. Almost every night he would get 39 lashes and that made him sore as could be, and he wouldn't work well the next day.

The nigger-driver was Uncle Charlie's half-brother, and one day he was beating Uncle Charlie pretty hard. Uncle Charlie made up his mind he wouldn't stand it any longer, so he jumped on the nigger-driver. They fought and Uncle Charlie won. Uncle Charlie ran away. He swam the Ohio and was almost drowned. That's where they caught him. They brought him back and scouraged him mightily. Then they threatened to sell him.

The second time he ran away he fared better. He said that he was walking in the woods one day when a strange white man approached him. This white man was an abolitionist. He asked Uncle Charlie if he would like to be a free man just like his master and Charlie said, "Yes." The man said, "Come with me then." So Uncle Charlie ran away again. They traveled at night and slept in the day. Finally they escaped to Chicago and crossed the lake on a boat to Canada. When he got over there, he was put with some white friends to stay. They gave him a home, sent him to school, and told him he was a man able to do what he pleased. They asked him if [he] had anyone he wished particularly to have them bring up from the plantation. He told them he would love to have his girl friend.

Days went by and nothing happened. Then one night, when he came home from work to supper, he was shocked to see his Rachel at the table. Tears flooded his eyes, and he almost broke his neck by falling over a chair as he rushed to greet her. Uncle Charlie married that girl at once and later became a Methodist minister. He wrote his master. He told him he was a free man in a free land, told the master who his wife was and informed the master that he would be welcome to the hospitality of their home anytime he cared to call, since they had the same father. The year before Hayes was president, my uncle was discovered by his relatives again. He was preaching at a Methodist conference and mentioned his delivery from slavery. That was in Chicago. My Aunt Lucy happened to be in the audience and recognized him. After the service was completed, she went up to the altar and asked Uncle Charlie if he remembered her. He looked at her a moment and burst out crying, "My sister! My sister!" It was a very happy reunion. [23]

Despite the odds against successful flight, enough slaves succeeded in escaping bondage to inspire other would-be runaways. As a plantation foreman, Frank Bell's uncle, Moses Bell, enjoyed a privileged position within the slave community.

Nevertheless, he yearned for freedom and sought repeatedly to
obtain it by flight. His owner John Fallons valued Moses,
though, and for years declined to punish him for his truancy.
But one day Fallons's patience finally reached its breaking
point.

Uncle Moses was a caution. Everybody skeered of him, even ole
Marser. Never whip him, don't believe he ever had a whippin' in his
life. Had it easy, he did. All he had to do was see dat de other niggers
did de work. Was married to Aunt Martha, who was a slave on Parson
Lipskin's farm, down near Hamilton Station, 'bout 12 miles from
Vienna. Every Sunday Marser let Uncle Moses take a horse an' ride
down to see his wife an' their two chillun, an' Sunday night he come
riding back; sometimes early Monday morning just in time to start de
slaves working in de field.

But Uncle Moses never was satisfied. Wanted to be free, he did.
Soon as all de crops was harvested an' in de barn, den he would run
away. Every year, when Indian Summer come, Uncle Moses git hisself
some food together an' de next day he be gone. Yessir, run away far as
I can recollec' nine or ten times, but every time they caught him trying
to get up North, he was. Just had made up his mind he gotta be free.
Everytime Marser go and get him he come back mad as blazes, but he
never whip him. If it been any other slave he give him a good
whipping, but not Uncle Moses. Just wasn't going to whip him. Don't
know why, ah guess he was little bit skeered to whip dat big man.
Everybody else was skeered of him too. But ole Marser was some kind
of mad. Cost a lot of money, it did, when you go git a runaway slave.
"Hue and Cry" dey called it, you got to put notice in de papers, an' you
got to pay a reward to whoever catches de runaway. Finally ole
Marser got plumb tired of looking all over Alexandria and Washington

for Uncle Moses. Swore he was gonna sell him de very next time he
run away. Uncle Moses ain't said nothing, just went on working,
getting in de crops as usual.

Sure enough Marser sold him. It was the next year, an' Marser had
hired me out to Washington. It was long 'bout '60, it was, just before
the war, and Marser used to hire out a bunch of the young slaves to
merchants in Washington. You see, dey was running all the slaves out
of Washington, an' it was all right if you was hired to a storekeeper, so
long as he didn't own you.

Well on dis day, August I think it was, I was working in Bacon and
Brothers store, on Pennsylvania Avenue, 'tween sixth and seventh
Streets when ole Marser stepped to the door an' called me, "Come on,
boy, an' tell your Uncle goodbye."

Well, I come on out an' got in the wagon an' ole Marser drove me
down to the 7th Street Wharf, to ole Joe Bruin's omnibus where they
had them. Uncle Moses was standing there chained up with 40 or 50
other slaves what had been sold along with him. They all was
runaways, there was a gang of them what had tried to get to Canada.
All but ten had been caught, including Uncle Moses. He was de only
one what belonged to Marser John, though. And all these runaways
what had been sold was chained round they legs in rows of 12 each,
an' each one had handcuffs round they wrist. [24]

> Sometimes slaves fled not in expectation of permanent escape
> but, rather, as a protest or a means of wresting some concession
> from their owner. Lorenzo Ivy related how his grandmother es-
> caped a threatened punishment.

Sometimes slaves jus' run' 'way to de woods fo' a week or two to git a
res' fum de fiel', an' den dey come on back. Never come back till dey

git de word, dough. Arter dey been gone 'long 'nough old Marse would come down to de quarters an' let out, "Guess Jim gittin' purty hongry out in de woods. Rained de other night, an' he must of got good an' wet." Den someone say, "Guess dat nigger scared to come back, marse, scared you gonna whup him." "Who said I was gonna whup him?" answered Marse. "But I will whup him ef he don' hurry back here." Dat de word, you see. Marse mean by dat dat ef Jim come back fo' work de nex' Monday mornin' he wasn't gonna beat him, an' dat was all Jim was waitin' for.

My grandmother, named Sallie Douchard, stayed in de woods for three or four weeks. I warn't born 'cause it was long fo' my time, but dey say dat her ole Marsa, named Allen, treated her jus' like a dog. She was de cook, an' he would beat her ef he didn't like what she cooked. So she run 'way to de woods an' stayed in hidin' in de day time an' come out onlies' at night. My mama say she used to always put out food fo' her an' she would slip up nights an' git it. After gramma been out in de woods fo' couple of weeks, ole Marsa come down to my mama an' tell her to tell ole Sallie to come on back—he wasn't gonna hide her. Mama swore she ain't seed her—didn't know where she was. "Sho, I know, Mamie, but if you do see her you tell her if she gits back Monday I ain't gonna hide her, but if she don't I gonna give her 500 lashes." Mama told gramma dat night, an' dey talked 'bout it tryin' to decide what to do. Finally gramma decided to come on back, so on Monday mornin' dar she was in de kitchen', an Marsa kept his word—didn't give her nary a lick. [25]

Many runaways had no intention of returning—at least not as slaves. Ishrael Massie, a former Virginia slave, remembered some of the tricks used by fugitive slaves to avoid recapture and described how his half-brother Bob managed to remain at liberty for an extended period.

Aw chile, woods stayed full of niggers an' sometimes dey would ketch 'em by dogs (sometimes) called bloodhounds. Lord, Lord, dem ole dogs scent ya up to de crick. Ef ya ar' runnin' 'way, jump in de crick. Dogs loose de scent of ya an' too, ef ya take a raw onion [and] rub feet bottom ya make de dogs loose ya.

Dese slaves stay in woods 'til dey git tired. Come back to marster, git a beatin'—"nine and thirty," dey use to call hit.

We had one slave dat runned away an' he had a vault in th' woods fixed jes' like dis room an' he had a wife an' two boys dat he raised under dar. Waal, ya say, "'Scribe"—ya mean tell how 'twas built? Dar wuz a hole cut in de groun'. I don' cut a many a one an' stole lumber at night to kiver hit over wid. Den dirt wuz piled on top of dis plank so dat hit won't rain in dar. Den he has him some piping—trough-like—made of wood dat runned so many feet in de groun'. Dis carried smoke way away from dis cave. Fer fir used oak bark 'cause hit didn't give much smoke. He had him a hole to come up on lan'. Dar wuz sticks, pine beard, and trash on top to kiver de hole. Ha, ha, ha. Ya could stan' right over dis hole an' wouldn't kno' hit.

Dis cave wuz not far from de crick. Reasons fer dat is ya could git water—an' de dirt we throwd in crick to be washed down. Bob 'longst to de Masses an' so dar he an' his family lived 'til Lee surrendered. He wuz a half-brother of mine an' all us slaves knew whar he wuz but, in dem days ya kno', nigger didn't tell on each other. Yas, yas, I don' et many er good meal of vituals in Bob's den.

T'other part of dis is de room wuz 10 feet square. In dis room dar wuz a bed made out of rails. De mattress wuz made out of his wife's old dresses an' somebody else's dat he could steal. De fiah place wuz made of rocks an' bricks. Dar wuz no stoves. Sawed off blocks wuz used fer his chairs. Cooking things wuz old pieces of pots an' pans broken at de great house. [26]

As Morris Hillyer explained, one ungovernable slave near
Rome, Georgia, fled and was recaptured many times before suc-
cessfully escaping. Thereafter, he lived a precarious—but
free—existence in the woods until the end of the Civil War.

They used to scare us kids by telling us dat a runaway nigger would git
us. De timber was awful heavy in de river bottoms, and dey was one
nigger dat run off from his master and lived for years in these bottoms.
He was there all during de War and come out after de surrender. Every
man in dat country owned him at some time or other. His owner sold
him to a man who was sure he could catch him—he never did, so he
sold him to another slave owner and so on till nearly everybody had
him. He changed hands about six or seven times. They would come in
droves with blood hounds and hunt for him but dey couldn't catch him
for he knowed them woods too well. He'd feed de dogs and make
friends with 'em and they wouldn't bother him. He lived on nuts, fruit,
and wild game, and niggers would slip food to him. He'd slip into town
and get whiskey and trade it to de niggers for food. [27]

A successful escape could be oh so sweet. Arnold Gragston, a
Kentucky slave, ferried scores of slaves across the river to freedom in Ohio before gaining his own liberty.

Most of the slaves didn't know when they was born, but I did. You see,
I was born on a Christmas mornin'—it was in 1840; I was a full grown
man when I finally got my freedom.

Before I got it, though, I helped a lot of others get theirs. Lawd only
knows how many; might have been as much as two-three hundred. It
was 'way more than a hundred, I know.

But that all come after I was a young man—"grown" enough to

know a pretty girl when I saw one, and to go chasing after her, too. I was born on a plantation that b'longed to Mr. Jack Tabb in Mason County, just across the river in Kentucky.

Mr. Tabb was a pretty good man. He used to beat us, sure; but not nearly so much as others did, some of his own kin people, even. But he was kinda funny sometimes; he used to have a special slave who didn't have nothin' to do but teach the rest of us—we had about ten on the plantation, and a lot on the other plantations near us—how to read and write and figger. Mr. Tabb liked us to know how to figger. But sometimes when he would send for us and we would be a long time comin', he would ask us where we had been. If we told him we had been learnin' to read, he would near beat the daylights out of us—after gettin' somebody to teach us; I think he did some of that so that the other owners wouldn't say he was spoilin' his slaves.

He was funny about us marryin', too. He would let us go a-courtin' on the other plantations near anytime we liked, if we were good, and if we found somebody we wanted to marry, and she was on a plantation that b'longed to one of his kin folks or a friend, he would swap a slave so that the husband and wife could be together. Sometimes, when he couldn't do this, he would let a slave work all day on his plantation, and live with his wife at night on her plantation. Some of the other owners was always talking about his spoilin' us.

He wasn't a Dimmacrat like the rest of 'em in the county; he belonged to the "know-nothin' party" and he was a real leader in it. He used to always be makin' speeches, and sometimes his best friends wouldn't be speaking to him for days at a time.

Mr. Tabb was always specially good to me. He used to let me go all about—I guess he had to; couldn't get too much work out of me even when he kept me right under his eyes. I learned fast, too, and I think he kinda liked that. He used to call Sandy Davis, the slave who taught me, "the smartest Nigger in Kentucky."

It was 'cause he used to let me go around in the day and night so much that I came to be the one who carried the runnin' away slaves over the river. It was funny the way I started it, too.

I didn't have no idea of ever gettin' mixed up in any sort of business like that until one special night. I hadn't even thought of rowing across the river myself.

But one night I had gone to another plantation, 'courtin', and the old woman whose house I went to told me she had a real pretty girl there who wanted to go across the river and would I take her. I was scared and backed out in a hurry. But then I saw the girl, and she was such a pretty little thing, brown-skinned and kinda rosy, and looking as scared as I was feelin', so it wasn't long before I was listenin' to the old woman tell me when to take her and where to leave her on the other side.

I didn't have nerve enough to do it that night, though, and I told them to wait for me until tomorrow night. All the next day I kept seeing Mister Tabb laying a rawhide across my back, or shootin' me, and kept seeing that scared little brown girl back at the house, lookin' at me with her big eyes and asking me if I wouldn't just row her across to Ripley. Me and Mr. Tabb lost, and soon as dust settled that night, I was at the old lady's house.

I don't know how I ever rowed the boat across the river the current was strong and I was trembling. I couldn't see a thing there in the dark, but I felt that girl's eyes. We didn't dare to whisper, so I couldn't tell her how sure I was that Mr. Tabb or some of the other owners would "tear me up" when they found out what I had done. I just knew they would find out.

I was worried, too, about where to put her out of the boat. I couldn't ride her across the river all night, and I didn't know a thing about the other side. I had heard a lot about it from other slaves but I thought it was just about like Mason County, with slaves and masters, overseers and rawhides; and so, I just knew that if I pulled the boat up and went to asking people where to take her I would get a beating or get killed.

I don't know whether it seemed like a long time or a short time, now—it's so long ago; I know it was a long time rowing there in the cold and worryin'. But it was short, too, 'cause as soon as I did get on the other side the big-eyed, brown-skin girl would be gone. Well, pretty soon I saw a tall light and I remembered what the old lady had told me about looking for that light and rowing to it. I did; and when I got up to it, two men reached down and grabbed her; I started tremblin' all over again, and prayin'. Then, one of the men took my arm and I just felt down inside of me that the Lord had got ready for me. "You hungry, Boy?" is what he asked me, and if he hadn't been holdin' me I think I would have fell backward into the river.

That was my first trip; it took me a long time to get over my scared feelin', but I finally did, and I soon found myself goin' back across the river, with two and three people, and sometimes a whole boatload. I got so I used to make three and four trips a month.

What did my passengers look like? I can't tell you any more about it than you can, and you wasn't there. After that first girl—no, I never did see her again—I never saw my passengers. It would have to be the "black nights" of the moon when I would carry them, and I would meet 'em out in the open or in a house without a single light. The only way I knew who they were was to ask them; "What you say?" And they would answer, "Menare." I don't know what that word meant—it came from the Bible. I only know that that was the password I used, and all of them that I took over told it to me before I took them.

I guess you wonder what I did with them after I got them over the

river. Well, there in Ripley was a man named Mr. Rankins; I think the
rest of his name was John. He had a regular station in there on his
place for escaping slaves. You see, Ohio was a free state and once they
got over the river from Kentucky or Virginia, Mr. Rankins could strut
them all around town, and nobody would bother 'em. The only reason
we used to land 'em quietly at night was so that whoever brought 'em
could go back for more, and because we had to be careful that none of
the owners had followed us. Every once in a while they would follow a
boat and catch their slaves back. Sometimes they would shoot at
whoever was trying to save the poor devils.

Mr. Rankins had a regular "station" for the slaves. He had a big
lighthouse in his yard, about thirty feet high and he kept it burnin' all
night. It always meant freedom for a slave if he could get to this light.

Sometimes Mr. Rankins would have twenty or thirty slaves that had
run away on his place at the time. It must have cost him a whole lots
to keep them and feed 'em, but I think some of his friends helped him.

Those who wanted to stay around that part of Ohio could stay, but
didn't many of 'em do it, because there was too much danger that you
would be walkin' along free one night, feel a hand over your mouth,
and be back across the river and in slavery again in the morning. And
nobody in the world ever got a chance to know as much misery as a
slave that had escaped and been caught.

So a whole lot of 'em went on North to other parts of Ohio, or to
New York, Chicago or Canada; Canada was popular then because all
of the slaves thought it was the last gate before you got all the way
inside of heaven. I don't think there was much chance for a slave to
make a living in Canada, but didn't many of 'em come back. They
seem like they rather starve up there in the cold than to be back in
slavery.

The Army soon started taking a lot of 'em, too. They could enlist in the Union Army and get good wages, more food than they ever had, and have all the little gals wavin' at 'em when they passed. Them blue uniforms was a nice change, too.

No, I never got anything from a single one of the people I carried over the river to freedom. I didn't want anything; after I had made a few trips I got to like it, and even though I could have been free any night myself, I figgered I wasn't gettin' along so bad so I would stay on Mr. Tabb's place and help the others get free. I did it for four years.

I don't know to this day how he never knew what I was doing; I used to take some awful chances, and he knew I must have been up to something; I wouldn't do much work in the day, would never be in my house at night, and when he would happen to visit the plantation where I had said I was goin' I wouldn't be there. Sometimes I think he did know and wanted me to get the slaves away that way so he wouldn't have to cause hard feelin's by freein' 'em.

I think Mr. Tabb used to talk a lot to Mr. John Fee; Mr. Fee was a man who lived in Kentucky, but Lord! how that man hated slavery! He used to always tell us (we never let our owners see us listenin' to him, though) that God didn't intend for some men to be free and some men be in slavery. He used to talk to the owners, too, when they would listen to him, but mostly they hated the sight of John Fee.

In the night, though, he was a different man, for every slave who came though his place going across the river he had a good word, something to eat and some kind of rags, too, if it was cold. He always knew just what to tell you to do if anything went wrong, and sometimes I think he kept slaves there on his place 'till they could be rowed across the river. Helped us a lot.

I almost ran the business in the ground after I had been carrying the slaves across for nearly four years. It was in 1863, and one night I carried across about twelve on the same night. Somebody must have seen us, because they set out after me as soon as I stepped out of the boat back on the Kentucky side; from that time on they were after me. Sometimes they would almost catch me; I had to run away from Mr. Tabb's plantation and live in the fields and in the woods. I didn't know what a bed was from one week to another. I would sleep in a cornfield tonight, up in the branches of a tree tomorrow night, and buried in a haypile the next night; the River, where I had carried so many across myself, was no good to me; it was watched too close.

Finally, I saw that I could never do any more good in Mason County, so I decided to take my freedom, too. I had a wife by this time, and one night we quietly slipped across and headed for Mr. Rankins' bell and light. It looked like we had to go almost to China to get across that river; I could hear the bell and see the light on Mr. Rankins' place, but the harder I rowed, the farther away it got, and I knew if I didn't make it I'd get killed. But finally, I pulled up by the lighthouse, and went on to my freedom—just a few months before all of the slaves got theirs. I didn't stay in Ripley, though; I wasn't taking no chances. I went on to Detroit and still live there with most of 10 children and 31 grandchildren.

The bigger ones don't care so much about hearin' it now, but the little ones never get tired of hearin' how their grandpa brought Emancipation to loads of slaves he could touch and feel, but never could see.[28]

CHAPTER

II.

WORK AND SLAVE LIFE: "FROM CAN TO CAN'T"

SLAVES SPENT MOST OF THEIR WAKING HOURS, MOST OF their days, and most of their lives working for their owners without compensation. Compulsory labor shaped their existence from cradle to grave. Slave children grew up watching their parents and other fellow slaves work. By the age of eight or so most children were working at least part-time; by their early teens, they were toiling as hard and as long as full-grown adults. Thereafter, only illness, disability, and (for women) childbirth exempted them from year-round labor until they reached old age.

The dictates of their owners in large measure determined the slaves' labor routines. The tasks slaves performed, the hours and days they worked, the composition of their work groups, and the extent of supervision were all decisions made by their owners. Slaveholders sometimes gave their slaves a degree of latitude to work for themselves on their "own" time—nights, Sundays, and perhaps Saturday afternoons. Depending on circumstances, slaves might use that privilege to cultivate gardens, hunt and fish, make and sell handcrafted goods, or even hire themselves to neighboring owners for wages. But owners insisted that outside work remain subordinate to the main business at hand.

For the great majority of slaves, the main business was agricultural labor. Slave field hands produced the bulk of the South's export staple crops—cotton, tobacco, sugar cane, rice, and wheat. They also raised the lion's share of the food that sustained themselves and their owners, plus fodder for farm animals. About half of the field hands worked on plantations with hundreds of acres under cultivation and twenty or more slaves; the remainder worked on farms with smaller land- and slave-holdings. Plantation hands typically labored in large gangs, supervised by a white overseer and sometimes by a slave driver. Slaves on smaller farms worked in smaller groups, in many cases alongside their owner or members of his family.

Not all slaves performed field labor. On large plantations and in towns and cities, a handful of slaves worked as domestics—personal servants, cooks, butlers, nurse maids—in their owner's home. A few men practiced skilled trades. Blacksmithing, carpentry, shoemaking, and cooperage were the most common occupations, but slave artisans could be found among the most highly skilled metalworkers, ironmongers, machinists, and cabinetmakers. Skilled occupations for slave women were less varied, and confined largely to weaving, sewing, and midwifery. The work experience of domestics and skilled slaves differed in important ways from that of field hands.

Although driven to labor for the benefit of others, slaves nonetheless found ways to draw satisfaction and pride from their work. Knowledge of agricultural practices or the secrets of a trade—whether it be the ability to plow a straight furrow, select the best seed, shoe a mule, weave a coverlet, or fashion a tight barrel—not only affirmed the slaves' humanity but also allowed them (at least in some matters) to surpass those who lorded over them. Their competence at their work gave slave men and women a basis to counter the owners' assertion of the slaves' natural and irredeemable inferiority. Work, in short, was both a source of oppression and a seed of liberation.

Sarah Gudger, who claimed to have been born in 1816, had put in many a long, grueling workday by the time freedom came. Labor on a large grain-growing farm in North Carolina, she recalled, was hard and unremitting, with punishment awaiting any slave who failed to meet its rigors.

I wah bo'n 'bout two mile fum Ole Fo't on de Ole Mo'ganton Road. I sho' has had a ha'd life. Jes wok, an' wok, an' wok. I nebbah know nothin' but wok. Mah boss he wah Ole Man Andy Hemphill. He had a la'ge plantation in de valley. Plenty ob ebbathin'. All kine ob stock: hawgs, cows, mules, an' hosses. When Marse Andy die I go lib wif he son, William Hemphill. . . .

No'm, I nebbah knowed whut it wah t' rest. I jes wok all de time f'om mawnin' till late at night. I had t' do ebbathin' dey wah t' do on de outside. Wok in de field, chop wood, hoe cawn, till sometime I feels lak mah back sholy break. I done ebbathin' 'cept split rails. Yo' know, dey split rails back in dem days. Well, I nevah did split no rails.

Ole Marse strop us good effen we did anythin' he didn' lak. Sometime he get hes dandah up an' den we dassent look roun' at him. Else he tie yo' hands afoah yo' body an' whup yo', jes lak yo' a mule. Lawdy, honey, I's tuk a thousand lashins in mah day. Sometimes mah poah ole body be soah foah a week.

Ole Hoss he send us niggahs out in any kine ob weathah, rain o' snow, it nebbah mattah. We had t' go t' de mountings, cut wood an'

"Jes wok, an' wok, an wok. I nebbah know nothin' but wok." Sarah Gudger,
formerly a slave in North Carolina; pictured in North Carolina.
(See pages 73–75.)

drag it down t' de house. Many de time we come in wif ouh cloes stuck
t' ouh poah ole cold bodies, but 'twarn't no use t' try t' git 'em dry. Ef
de Ole Boss o' de Ole Missie see us dey yell: "Git on out ob heah yo'
black thin', an' git yo' wok outen de way!" An' Lawdy, honey, we
knowed t' git, else we git de lash. Dey did'n cah how ole o' how young
yo' wah, yo' nebbah too big t' git de lash.

De rich white folks nebbah did no wok; dey had da'kies t' do it foah dem. In de summah we had t' wok outdoo's, in de wintah in de house. I had t' ceard an' spin till ten o'clock. Nebbah git much rest, had t' git up at foah de nex' mawnin' an' sta't agin. Didn' get much t' eat, nuthah, jes a lil' cawn bread an' 'lasses. Lawdy, honey, yo' caint know whut a time I had. All cold n'hungry. No'm, I aint tellin' no lies. It de gospel truf. It sho is. [1]

> Field slaves on plantations generally worked under overseers, who supervised the proceedings with a watchful eye—and often with a ready lash. Wes Brady described the regimen imposed by the overseer of the Texas cotton estate on which he grew up.

Some white folks might want to put me back in slavery if I tells how we was used in slavery time, but you asks me for the truth. The overseer was 'straddle his big horse at three o'clock in the mornin', roustin' the hands off to the field. He got them all lined up and then come back to the house for breakfas'. The rows was a mile long and no matter how much grass was in them, if you leaves one sprig on your row they beats you nearly to death. Lots of times they weighed cotton by candlelight. All the hands took dinner to the field in buckets and the overseer give them fifteen minutes to git dinner. He'd start cuffin' some of them over the head when it was time to stop eatin' and go back to work. He'd go to the house and eat his dinner and then he'd come back and look in all the buckets and if a piece of anything that was there when he left was et, he'd say you was losin' time and had to be whipped. He'd drive four stakes in the ground and tie a nigger down and beat him till he's raw. Then he'd take a brick and grind it up in a powder and mix it with lard and put it all over him and roll him in

"The overseer was 'straddle his big horse at three o'clock in the mornin',
roustin' the hands off to the field." Wes Brady, formerly a slave in Texas;
pictured in Harrison County, Texas. (See pages 75–77.)

a sheet. It'd be two days or more 'fore that nigger could work 'gain. I
seed one nigger done that way for stealin' a meat bone from the
meathouse. That nigger got fifteen hundred lashes. The li'l chaps
would pick up egg shells and play with them and if the overseer seed
them he'd say you was stealin' eggs and give you a beatin'. I seed long

lines of slaves chained together driv by a white man on a hoss down
the Jefferson road.[2]

> Slaves did what they could to shield their co-workers from the
> lash. A Virginia ex-slave related how his grandmother, faced
> with punishment for failure to meet her quota during cotton-
> picking, received assistance from her fellow slaves.

Grandma said slaves had to pick so many pounds of cotton a day, and
they were given an awful whipping if they didn't get this amount. My
grandma said she was small and just couldn't get her proper amount,
but was jolly and always ran to get water for the other slaves when
they wanted it. At the end of the day one of the men would tell
another, "Give that little black gal five pounds of cotton. She's all
right." When they evened her up, she wouldn't get a beatin', but lots of
time she would come up short and would have to take the whippin'.
All the slaves who had fallen short had to stand in line with their
backs bare for their whippin'. Grandma said that often she was
whipped until she could barely grunt.[3]

> Born in 1854, George Fleming grew up on an estate in up-
> country South Carolina he described as "de biggest planta-
> tion . . . I is ever seed or heard tell of." Decades later, Fleming
> depicted a regimen in which every slave who could work did so,
> either at raising cotton and other crops, maintaining the own-
> er's house, or performing one of the innumerable other tasks
> necessary for the operation of a great plantation.

Some of de women dat didn't have a passel of lil' brats was 'signed to
de job of cooking fer de field hands. Some of 'em come home to eat,

but mostly dey stayed in de fields. De dinner horn blow'd 'zactly at 12 o'clock and dey know'd it was time fer grub. Everybody drapped what dey was doing and compiled demselves in groups. Dey could see de buckets coming over de hill. Dar was more dan one group, fer de fields was so big dat dey couldn't all come to one place. Cose all dat was planned out by de overseers. Had lots of overseers and dey had certain groups to look out fer.

Most of de food was brung to de fields in buckets, but sometimes de beans and de like of dat come in de same pots dey was cooked in. It took two big niggers to tote de big pots. Dar was no want of food fer de hands. Marse know'd if dey worked dey had to eat. Dey had collards, turnips and other good vegetables wid cornbread. Chunks of meat was wid de greens, too, and us had lots of buttermilk.

Women worked in de field same as de men. Some of dem plowed jes' like de men and boys. Couldn't tell 'em apart in de field, as dey wore pantelets or breeches. Dey tied strings 'round de bottom of de legs so de loose dirt wouldn't git in deir shoes. De horn blow'd to start work and to quit. In de morning when de signal blow'd, dey all tried to see who could git to de field first. Dey had a good time and dey liked to do deir work. Us didn't pay much mind to de clock. We worked frum sun to sun. All de slaves had to keep on de job, but dey didn't have to work so hard. Marse allus said dey could do better and last longer by keeping 'em steady and not overworking 'em.

Dar was all kinds of work 'sides de field work dat went on all de time. Everybody had de work dat he could do de best. My daddy worked wid leather. He was de best harness maker on de place, and he could make shoes. Dey had a place whar dey tanned cow-hides. Dat was called de tannos. Dey didn't do much spinning and weaving in de home quarters; most of it was done in one special place Marse had made fer dat purpose. Some of de slaves didn't do nothing but spin and weave, and dey sho was good at it, too. Dey was trained up jes' fer dat particular work.

I don't know how many spinning wheels and looms and dem things Marse had, but he sho had lots of 'em. Dat business making cloth had lots to it and I don't know much 'bout it, but it was sort of dis way. Dey picked de seeds out of de cotton; den put de cotton in piles and carded it. Dey kept brushing it over and over on de cards till it was in lil' rolls. It was den ready fer de spinning wheels whar it was spun in thread. Dis was called de filling. I don't know much 'bout de warp, dat is de part dat run long ways.

Dem spinning wheels sho did go on de fly. Dey connected up wid de spindle and it go lots faster dan de wheel. Dey hold one end of de cotton roll wid de hand and 'tach de other to de spindle. It keep drawing and twisting de roll till it make a small thread. Sometimes dey would run de thread frum de spindle to a cornshuck or anything dat would serve de purpose. Dat was called de broach. Some of dem didn't go any further dan dat, dey had to make sech and sech broaches a day. Dis was deir task. Dat's de reason some of dem had to work atter dark, dat is, if dey didn't git de task done befo' dat.

Dey run de thread off de broach on to reels, and some of it was dyed on de reels. Dey made deir own dyes, too. Some of it was made frum copperas, and some frum barks and berries. Atter while, de thread was put back on de spinning wheel and wound on lil' old cane quills. It was den ready fer de looms. Don't know nothing, de looms—boom! boom! sho could travel. Dey put de quills, atter de thread was wound on dem, in de shettle and knocked it back and forth twixt de long threads what was on de beams. Can't see de thread fly out of dat shettle it come so fast. Dey sho could sheckle it through dar. Day peddled dem looms, zip! zap! making de thread rise and drap while de shettle zoom twixt it. Hear dem looms booming all day long 'round de weaving shop. De weaving and spinning was done in de same place.

Overseers lived on de plantation. No, dey wasn't poor whites. All Marse Sam's overseers was good men. Dey lived wid deir families, and Marse's folks 'sociated wid dem, too. Dey had good houses to live in. Dey built better dan ours was. Marse didn't 'low dem to whip de slaves, but dey made us keep straight. If any whipping had to be done, Marse done it, but he didn't have to do much. He didn't hurt 'em bad, den, jes' git a big hickry and lay on a few. He would say if dat nigger didn't walk de chalk, he would put him on de block and settle him. Dat was usually enough, 'cause Marse mean't dat thing and all de niggers know'd it. . . .

Slaves started to work by de time dey was old enough to tote water and pick up chips to start fires wid. Some of dem started to work in de fields when dey about ten, but most of 'em was older. Lawd, Marse Sam must have had more dan a dozen house niggers. It took a lot of work to keep things in and 'round de house in good shape. Cose most of de slaves was jes' field hands, but some of dem was picked out fer special duties. Slaves didn't get any pay in money fer work, but Marse give 'em a lil' change sometimes.

Everybody have plenty to eat. Lots of times we had fish, rabbits, possums and stuff like dat; lots of fishing and hunting in dem days. Some slaves have lil' gardens of deir own, but most de vegetables come frum de big garden. Missus was in charge de big garden, but cose she didn't have to do no work. She sho seed atter us too. Even de poor white trash had plenty to eat back in dem times. Marse have a hundred head of hogs in de smokehouse at one time. Never seen so much pork in my life. We sho lived in fine fashion in hog killing time, cose de meats was cured and us had some all de year. Yes sir, Marse ration out everybody some every week. Watermelons grow awful big, some of 'em weigh a hundred pounds. Dey big stripes ones, called "rattlesnakes," so big you can't tote it no piece. All de baking and biling was done over de big fireplaces.

Didn't wear much clothes in summer 'cause we didn't need much, but all de grown niggers had shoes. Lawd, I wore many pair of Marse Lyntt's boots, I means sho 'nuff good boots. Marse had his own shoemakers, so twan't no use us gwine widout. Had better clothes fer Sunday. Most de washing was done on Saturday afternoons, and we be all setting purty fer Sunday. Cold weather we was dressed warm, and we had plenty bed kivvers, too. Cose all slaves didn't have it as good as Marse Sam's did. Lawd, I is seed lil' naked niggers setting on de rail fences like pa'cel of buzzards; but Marse Sam's niggers never had to go dat way. . . .

When de slaves come from de field, deir day's work was done. Fact is, everybody's work was done 'cept maybe some of de spinners or weavers dat didn't quite finish deir task. Dey was de onliest ones dat had to ever work atter dark, and dat not often. Sometimes on Saturdays we didn't have to work a-tall, dat is in de fields, and sometimes we had to work till 12 o'clock. Lots of de men went fishing and hunting, and mostly de women washed. Saturday nights some groups would git together and sing. I can still hear dem old songs in my mind, but I doesn't recalls de words.[4]

> Hundreds of miles separated upcountry South Carolina from eastern Arkansas, where Cora Carroll moved just before the Civil War; but the organization of work and the daily routine on her owner's cotton plantation did not differ greatly from that of the plantation where George Fleming lived and worked.

Most of the slaves on our place worked in the field—cotton and corn and so on. Had a man for each thing. One would be over the horses, and so on. They raised everything we ate on the farm. Did n't have to buy anything. They would buy their meat, of course. But they did n't have to buy that often because they raised hogs, and killed and cured their own meat. But in the summer, they would buy fresh meat if they wanted it.

As I said, there was a man to take care of the horses; a man for the cattle stock—to see that they were in of evenings; one for the hogs. They fed the stock twice—morning and evening. They had hog pens and stables for the cows and horses. Nothing had to stand out in the open, especially in the winter time. We had field hands. All the stock men worked in the field also—so many hours. They had a bell for them to go to work in the morning, a bell for them to get up by, and another one for noon, and another in the evening when they would knock off for dark.

They had a woman to nurse the children while the mothers were in the field. If the mothers were nursing the baby, they allowed them to come back to the nursery every hour to nurse them. The women who took care of them was an old woman who was too old to go into the field. She was "Aunt Kizzie." I don't know what her real name was. She was a tall brownskin woman. She had children, too,—grand children. But she would treat them all alike. You could n't say she made any difference.

In the field the slaves wore jeans. They would make the cloth and dye it red, brown or blue. For summer they had cotton pants made out of cotton cloth. They made the cloth and the clothes. They called the pants jeans.

The youngest age they worked in the field was twelve. Then they would just give them tasks—mostly carrying water.

The grown people were in the field early in the morning. It was about six, I reckon. It was early. The master would give them time to eat their breakfast. They had an hour for dinner, and they would stop about dark unless there was something the matter urgent. If it was late in the season and they were afraid the rain or something would catch them, then they would have to work later sometimes. If it were hot in the hot part of summer, they would allow the slaves to stop during the hot part of the day and rest. They worked in the early and late part of the day then. . . .

My work was to answer the door bell and wait on my mistress and go round with her wherever she went. I had to sleep in the house with her. Sometimes at night I would have to go down to the quarters for her, and I would run every step of the way. The old master had been buried in the garden (He died at Vicksburg), and folks said he was a "hant." I never did see nothing, but I was scared I would. When I would get back, Mistress would say, "You did n't take so long to go." And I would say to her "I was scared I would see 'Master.'" She and I were the only two persons in the house.

A colored man called the yard man lived right near the house. Whenever there was a noise at night, he would have to get up and see what it was that made it. He would get up any time she called. Round about then there was a lot of soldiers—Rebs and Yanks both—who would steal meat and stock, and you would have to watch out for them. She was a mighty brave woman though. She was n't scared. She would just talk up to any of them. Henry the yard man had nothing to do but keep the yard round the house clean and see after the fowls and so on.

Some of the men on the farm were mechanics. They had a man that could fix the horses' shoes when they needed it. They had a carpenter to fix the houses, and build things. They did n't have nobody to teach them. They just picked up the knowledge, I guess. You know some people can. They had women to sew and spin. Old Miss would cut out men's clothes, and on rainy days, the women would sew them. And these clothes were issued out as they were needed. There were old ladies who could knit stockings, sock, wristbands, sweaters, and anything. There were men who could mend shoes.

There used to be trade boats going down the river, and the slaves that were smart enough used to raise vegetables and chickens. Everyone of the slave houses in the quarters had a plot of ground attached to it. My mother used to raise vegetables and chickens and sell them to the trading boats. Then there were peddlars that would come round with different things, and they would take eggs and chickens and things in trade. My mother raised hogs in her lot, too. Some of them raised their own milk cows as well as their hogs. It was about an acre, I guess. I'm not sure. They would knock off early on Saturdays and give them time to work for themselves. All farmers did n't do that, just them that had hearts and thought you was human.[5]

> Charley Williams, "a great big hulking buck of a boy" on the eve of the Civil War, worked in the field in the larger of his owner's two plantations near Monroe, Louisiana. He vividly remembered the regimentation of work, beginning at daybreak.

When de day began to crack de whole plantation break out wid all kinds of noises, and you could tell what going on by de kind of noise you hear.

Come de daybreak you hear de guinea fowls start potracking down at de edge of de woods lot, and den de roosters all start up 'round de barn and de ducks finally wake up and jine in. You can smell de sow belly frying down at the cabins in de "row," to go wid de hoecake and de buttermilk.

Den purty soon de wind rise a little, and you can hear a old bell

"Bells and horns! Bells for dis and horns for dat! All we knowed was go and come by de bells and horns!" Charley Williams, formerly a slave in Louisiana; pictured at Tulsa, Oklahoma, with unidentified girl. (See pages 84–86.)

donging way on some plantation a mile or two off, and den more bells at other places and maybe a horn, and purty soon younder go old Master's old ram horn wid a long toot and den some short toots, and here come de overseer down de row of cabins, hollering right and left, and picking de ham out'n his teeth wid a long shiny goose quill pick.

Bells and horns! Bells for dis and horns for dat! All we knowed was go and come by de bells and horns!

Old ram horn blow to send us all to de field. We all line up, about seventy-five field niggers, and go by de tool shed and git our hoes, or maybe go hitch up de mules to de plows and lay de plows out on de side so de overseer can see iffen de points is sharp. Any plow gits broke or de point gits bungled up on de rocks it goes to de blacksmith nigger, den we all git on down in de field.

Den de anvil start dangling in de blacksmith shop: Tank! Deling-ding! Tank! Deling-ding!", and dat ole bull tongue gitting straightened out!

Course you can't hear de shoemaker awling and pegging, and de card spinners, and de old mammy sewing by hand, but maybe you can hear de ole loom going "frump, frump," and you know it all right iffen your clothes do be wearing out, 'cause you gwine git new britches purty soon!

We had about a hundred niggers on dat place, young and old, and about twenty on de little place down below. We could make about every kind of thing but coffee and gunpowder dat our whitefolks and us needed.

When we needs a hat we gits inside cornshucks and weave one out, and makes horse collars de same way. Jest tie two little soft shucks together and begin plaiting.

All de cloth 'cepting a de Mistress' Sunday dresses come from de sheep to de carders and de spinners and de weaver, den we dye it wid "butternut" and hickory bark and indigo and other things and set it wid copperas. Leather tanned on de place made de shoes, and I never see a store boughten wagon wheel 'cepting among de stages and de freighters along de big road.

We made purty, long back-combs out'n cow horn, and knitting neddles out'n second hickory. Split a young hickory and put in a big wedge to prize it open, then cut it down and let it season, and you got good bent grain for wagon hames and chair rockers and such.[6]

Agricultural work for slaves, as for free farmers, followed the sun and the seasons and was shaped by the demands of particular crops. Gabe Hunt, a Virginia ex-slave, recalled tobacco-picking time.

You see, de fust pickin' come roun' de fust of August. You git de wheat in, den come de tobacco. Ole Marse go roun' pluckin' at de leaves, den one mornin' he say, "Come on, boys, git de smoke house in order." Den one go down an' clean out de barn. Got to rake out all de leavin's and dirt an' clean de mud an' dirt out whar de fire box is. Barns was built on hills, you see. Build dem on hills so's you kin lay de sticks way fum top to bottom. Pack de top fum de upper winder right level wid de groun' an' pack de bottom fum de do'. Spend one day gittin' de barn ready, den de nex' day you go to pickin'. Got to pick dem leaves what's jus' startin to brown. Pick 'em too soon dey don't cure, an' you pick 'em too late dey bitters. Got to break 'em off clean at de stem an' not twist 'em cause if dey bruised dey spile. Hands git so stuck up in dat old tobaccy gum it git so yo' fingers stick together. Dat ole gum was de worse mess you ever see. Couldn't brush it off, couldn't wash it off, got to wait tell it wear off. Spread de leaves on a cyart an' drag it to de barn. Den de women would take each leaf up an' fix de stem 'tween two pieces of board, den tie de ends together. Den hand 'em all up in dat barn an' let it smoke two days an' two nights. Got to keep dat fire burnin' rain or shine, 'cause if it go out, it spile de tobaccy. Ev'ybody happy when de tobaccy curin' is done, 'cause den ole Marse gonna take it to market an' maybe bring back new clothes fo' de slaves.[7]

> The work of Katie Darling, whose owner was a middling Texas farmer with three families of slaves, included tending the master's children in the house and milking cows in the barn. Darling's fellow slaves, among them her brothers and father, labored in the field and performed other tasks that sometimes required them to work into the night and on Sundays.

You is talkin now to a Nigger what nu'sed seven white chil'ren in them "bull-whip" days. Miss Stella, my young mistress, got all our ages down

"Master had six children when the war come on. . . . I nu'sed all of them."
Katie Darling, formerly a slave in Texas; pictured at Marshall, Texas.
(See pages 87–90.)

in a Bible, dat is how I knows I was bo'n in '49. I was a slave of Master
William (Bill) McCarty what lived southeast of Marshall close to
Louisiana line. I was the only girl, but had three brother, Peter, Adam,
and Willis. We all lived to be grown and married. Mammy died in
slavery, and Pappy run away while he and Master William was on the
way to the Battle of Mansfield. Master say when he come back from

the War. "That trifling Nigger ran away and jined up with them dam Yankees."

Master had six children when the war come on, Herbert, Walter, Jennie, Stella, Bell, and Harvey. I nu'sed all of them. I stayed there in the house with them and slep on a pallet on the floor. By the time I was big enough to tote a cow pail they put me to milking. Master had over a hundred head of cows and most of the time me and Violet, another house girl, did all the milking. We was up before five and by five we better be in that cow pen. We better milk all of them cows too or they'd bull-whip us. But we didn't allus do it. Them calves got lots of that milk. One mon'nin Master cotched me letting one of the calves do the "milking." It was cold and snow was on the ground and I was barefooted. Master says, "I'll let you off this time." But that don't mean he was allus good to us, cause them cows had more feeling for us than they did. Several times Master would say to Mistress that it was cold and bad and hadn't she better try to find some old shoes for us. Mistress say, "Them Niggers don't need no shoes, they better get out of here to that cow pen."

Master McCarty only had three families of slaves on the place. They lived in one-room log houses that had two bunks to the house. They slep' on straw matresses. They et peas, greens, collards and middlings. Niggers had better let that ham alone. The McCarty place jined the Henry Ware Place. His niggers would wo'k for Master Ware some, and Master Ware's niggers worked for him. The slaves on our place drank meal coffee. They'd parch meal in the oven, bile (boil) it and drink the liquor. When Master Ware's fo'k would have company they bring Mammy's fo'ks the biscuits and "Lincoln" coffee that was left. Dat "Lincoln" coffee was sumpin' to us Niggers. Master Williams fo'ks had it too, but Mistress saw to it that they didn't get anything extra.

Master William done all the bossing his-self. When the Niggers done anything he would bull-whip them, but didn't skin them up very often. He tie the men up with ropes when he whipped them. He'd whip them for half doing the plowing or the hoeing, but if they done it right he find something else to whip them for. At night the men had to shuck co'n and the wimmen would card and spin. The Niggers got two garments apiece for winter and two for summer, but no shoes. Sometimes they'd give us the shoes the white fo'ks wore out. We warn't 'lowed to go no where hardly. We worked Saturday jist like Monday, and if that grass was in the field we didn't git no Sunday.[8]

> Among field hands, women worked alongside men at most tasks, even the most physically demanding ones. Enslaved for nearly forty years, Anne Clark saw much of the brutality of slavery. But at age 112, she still boasted of her ability to perform a slave's work as well as any man.

I'll be 112 years old, come first day of June (1937). Bo'n in Mississippi. I had two marsters, but I've been free nearly 80 years. I was freed in Memphis. . . .

You know, the white folks hated to give us up worse thing in the world. I ploughed, hoed, split rails. I done the hardest work ever a man ever did. I was so strong, iffen he needed me I'd pull the men down so the marster could handcuff 'em. They'd whop us with a bullwhip. We got up at 3 o'clock, at 4 we done et and hitched up the mules and went to the fiel's. We worked all day pullin' fodder and choppin' cotton. Marster'd say, "I wan' you to lead dat fiel' today, and if you don' do it I'll put you in de stocks." Then he'd whop me iffen I didn' know he was talkin' to me.

My poppa was strong. He never had a lick in his life. He helped the marster, but one day the marster says, "Si, you got to have a whoppin'," and my poppa says, "I never had a whoppin' and you cain't whop me." An' the marster says, "But I kin kill you," an' he shot my poppa down. My mama tuk him in the cabin and put him on a pallet. He died.

My mama did the washin' for the big house. She tuk a big tub on her head and a bucket of water in her hand. My mama had two white chillen by marster and they were sold as slaves. I had two chillen, too. I never married. They allus said we'd steal, but I didn' take a thing. Why, they'd put me on a hoss with money to take into town and I'd take it to the store in town, and when I'd git back, marster'd say, "Anne, you didn' take a thing."

When women was with child they'd dig a hole in the groun' and put their stomach in the hole, and then beat 'em. They'd allus whop us."[9]

> Slave children worked. Emma Knight, one of a family of five people enslaved by a Missouri farmer, remembered that she and her sisters performed a variety of chores so that her master's children would not have to work.

We lived on a Creek near Florida. We belonged to Will Ely. He had only five slaves, my father and mother and three of us girls. I was only eight or nine years old. The Ely's had eight children. There was Paula, Ann, Sarah, Becky, Emily, Lizzie, Will, Ike, and Frank. Lizzie was the oldest girl and I was to belong to her when she was married.

The master of the house was better to us than the mistress. We didn't have to work very hard, because we was so young, I guess. We cut weeds along the fences, pulled weeds in the garden and helped the mistress with the hoeing. We had to feed the stock, sheep, hogs, and calves, because the young masters wouldn't do the work. In the

evening we were made to knit a finger width and if we missed a stitch
we would have to pull all the yarn out and do it over. The master's
girls taught us to read and write. We didn't have hardly any clothes
and most of the time they was just rags. We went barefoot until it got
real cold. Our feet would crack open from the cold and bleed. We
would sit down bawl and cry because it hurt so. Mother made
moccasins for our feet from old pants. Late in the fall master would go
to Hannibal or Palmyra and bring us shoes and clothes. We got those
things only once a year. I had to wear the young master's overalls for
underwear and linseys for a dress.[10]

> Slaveholders began training their slaves at an early age, prepar-
> ing them for a lifetime of labor. An elderly free man looking
> back on his childhood in bondage, Ebenezer Brown described
> how he and other children gradually assumed their places in the
> workforce of a Mississippi plantation.

I is now eighty five years old; I wus born 'bout twelve miles south uf
Liberty, on de road dat goes frum Liberty to Jackson, Louisiana, on Mr.
Bill McDowell's place, an' dat wus er big farm. Marse Bill wus mi'ty
tough on his slaves. I wus jes' a boy, but I will niver fergit how he
whup'ed his slaves. I ken name ebry one uf his slaves: dar was
Viney—she done de cookin'; Zias wus er fiel' han' an' he driv de
carriage; my uncle Irwin, he fed de hosses, an' he wus a bad nigger an'
got whup'd fur stealin' all de time; Jim was de rice beater, an' he beat
de rice ebery Friday; Sara wus er fiel' han'—Relia wurk in de fiel' an'
milked, an' had ter go to de cow pen bar' footed an' her feet got frost
bit, an' dat made her cripple; Hager wus er fiel' han' an' Peggy wus er
fiel' han' an' afte' Relia got crippled Peggy he'p milk; Monday wus er
fiel' hand' but he wus bad 'bout runnin' way from home an' de patroller

wud git him; Patience, dat was my mammy, she milked an' wurk in de fiel' an' den dar wus sum big chulluns dat he'ped in de fiel' an' we all hed ter wurk round de house. Dar wus Tom, a nigger boy 'bout my age, an' we played tergedder an' done wurk tergedder. . . .

Marse Bill's wife wus named Miss Hester an' deir chulluns was named, young Marse Russ; he wud grown an' toted a big whip all de time; he he'ped Marse Bill look afte' de darkies in de fiel'; an' den dar wus young Marse Tom, an' Miss Lizzie, an' Miss Mary, an' Miss Ella, an' Miss Ethel, and Miss Dulcie, an' dat wus all.

Marse Bill hed two brudders: one wus named Tom, an' one wus named John' an' Mr. Tom wus a mi'ty rich man; he uster loan money. One time Marse Bill put me on his big fine black pony, named "Snap," an' give me er note, an' sont me to Mr. Tom's; when I got dar, Mr. Tom sed "whut's de matter wid Bill now?"; den I giv him de note—he sed "Lord, Jesus Christ; peas an' rice: dat is whut Bill is allus wantin'— Money! money! money!"—and he give me de money an' put me back on de black hoss an' sont me home.

As a child, I played in de yard wid another black boy named Tom Hardin; but dey didn't 'low fur us to play much. We shot china berries frum er pop-gun, an' we made de shots hit de udder chaps, an' wud git whup'ed fur it. We done dat all de time. We toted in wood fur Viney, so she culd cook, an' she cooked in a big fire place with racks in de chimbly; den we had ter pick up de eggs ebery day; we brung de eggs ter de house in er baskit; ebery time de wind wud blow we hed to pick up de plums frum under de trees and tote 'em in baskits to de hogs; an' den we picked up de peaches an' apples dat fell offen de trees an' toted dem to de hogs an' dat made de hogs fat. Den Marse Bill made cider outern de apples an' dat wus good. Den I hed to churn ebery udder day; dat churn was 'bout three feet high an it hed er long handle dasher, an' I hed ter stand der an wurk dat handle up an' down till de

buter wud cum; when I seed de lil'l lumps uf butter stickin on de
handle I wud take my finger an' wipe it off an' den suck my
finger—but I dar'sent let old Mistis see me do dat, an' iffen she
kotched me doin' it I wud git a whup'in—

Tom an' me had ter sweep de yard an' stamp ebery Sa'day we had
whut yer call "brush-brooms" an' we brushed dem leaves up in er pile
an' put dem in er baskit an' toted 'em to er pen behin' de barn an' dar
let 'em rot. . . .

My pappy wus a carpenter, an' wurk in de fiel' an' dun de buildin' dat
wus dun on de place, an' he driv de ox team to Osyka to git sugar an'
flour, an' he allus hed ter grease de wagon wid tar. Dat wud make it
run easy.

Marse Bill had no overseer dat I remember: he an' young Marse
Russ toted de whup, an' wud ride ober de fiel' an' make de slaves wurk
an' day wud shore whup iffen dat wurk wusnt dun. Den Marse Bill had
er old poll parrot dat he put on a limb in de fiel' sum times, an' dat
parrot wud tell who it wus dat didnt wurk. Marse Bill wud tie dem
slaves an' whup hard, and all de slaves wud say "O, pray, marster; O,
pray, Marster!"—

When de slaves was wurkin good dey wud sing like dis—

> Watch de sun; see how she run;
> Niver let her ketch yo' wid yer wurk undun.
>
> Howdy, my brethern, Howdy yo' do,
> Since I bin in de lan'
> I do mi'ty well, an' I thank de Lord, too,
> Since I bin in de lan'
> O yes, O yes, since I bin in de lan'
> O, yes, O yes, since I bin in de lan'

I do mi'ty well an' I thank de Lord too,
Since I bin in de lan'—

Dar wus 'nudder song dat went sorta like dis—

See my brudder down de hill; fall down on he knees;
Send up your prayers' I'll send up mine; de good Lord ter please.
Raise de heabens, high as de skies; fall down on yer knees;
Send up your prayers; I'll send up mine; de good Lord ter please.

When cum quitin' time dem slaves wud sing all de way ter de house.[11]

> Mary Island's initiation into slaves' work began at the unusually
> early age of four, supervised by the "aunty" who raised her after
> her mother's death.

I was born in Union Parish, Louisiana in the year of 1857, so the white
folks told me, and I am eighty years old. My mama died when I was
two years old and my aunty raised me. She started me out washing
dishes when I was four years old and when I was six she was learning
me how to cook. While the other hands was working in the field I
carried water. We had to cook out in the yard on an old skillet and lid,
so you see I had to tote brush and bark and roll up little logs such as I
could to keep the fire from one time of cooking to the other. I was not
but six years old either. When I got to be seven years old I was cutting
sprouts almost like a man and when I was eight I could pick one
hundred pounds of cotton. When it rained and we could not go to the
field my aunty had me spinning thread to make socks and cloth, then I
had to card the bats and make the rolls to spin.

My auntie was a slave and she lived in the edge of the field. Of
course I was born a slave but didn't know much about it because my

aunty did the bossing of me but I had a pretty hard time. Our wash tubs, water buckets, bread trays and such were made out of tupelo gum logs dug out with some kind of an axe and when aunty would wash I had to use the battling stick. I would carry the wet clothes to a stump and beat them with that battling stick and we hung the clothes out on bushes and on the fence. We used water from a spring.

In my young days all we wore was homespun and lowel. We lived in a log house with a dirt floor and the cracks was chinked with mud and our bed was some poles nailed against the wall with two legs out on the dirt floor, and we pulled grass and put in a lowel bed tick. My aunty would get old dresses, old coats, and old pants and make quilts.[12]

> Domestic labor was mainly women's and children's work, performed under the supervision of the owner's wife or another female household member. As a house slave of a "very aristocratic" family with twelve children, Marie Askin had much to do, especially making, cleaning, and maintaining clothing.

I was born June the eighth, but I do not remember the year. I know I was about seven or eight years old during the Civil War. My mother and father were both slaves, but belonged to different owners. My mother was Lucy Askin and my father's name was Washington Halbert. That was the sir names of their owners. I did not carry my father's name because I belonged to the Askin white folks. At that time it was the law or rule for slaves to bear the owner's name regardless of marriage between slaves.

I can well remember the soldiers of the Civil War, passing our home, with their bayonets and guns. I was about eight years old as near as I can remember.

Our home was in Crawford County, near Steelville, Missouri. There was no real fighting in that part of the country. Most of the soldiers were from General Price's Regiment. My father's marster had about one hundred slaves. They all lived in little cabins, near him, almost like a little village. He hired out most of his slaves to white folks that had no slaves and needed work done.

Our white folks, the Askins, had my mother, two sisters and myself and two brothers as slaves. They were very aristocratic, they had a large family, of six sons and six daughters. I was just a little girl but I can remember how they kept me busy waiting on them. Carrying water from the spring, hunting eggs and a lot of other little things.

Mother did most of the cooking and washing and ironing. In those days they did the washing with battlin' sticks and boards. They layed the clothes on this board and battled them with battlin sticks. We had little "piggins" to carry the water, a little thing, made of cedar, with little handles. Much smaller than the regular water buckets. It could be carried anywhere, easily. They were pretty little things, with bright brass bindings, and they kept them brightly polished, too.

We boiled our clothes in big iron kettles, over a fire in the yard. We made our own lye and soap. The ash-hopper was made of boards, a sort of trough that was set slant-wise over a big iron kettle. The wood ashes from the fire place were dumped in this hopper. Hot water was poured over the ashes and they drained down into the kettle. It dripped slowly. When we thought the lye was strong enough, we got a turkey feather, (a chicken feather won't do, 'cause it would eat up too quick) and if the lye from the hopper was strong enough it would eat up the turkey feather. Then a fire was started under the kettle.

Into this big kettle of boiling ash-lye, we stirred in "cracklin'." This was the fried out fats left over from hog killin'. Old meat rinds, old meats that had turned strong, any kind of fat meat that was not used to eat, was thrown into this hot boiling lye. When the meat did not melt anymore we know that there was enough fat in the lye to make soap.

This was boiled down until it got "ropey." We tested it by dripping some of it in cold water. If it floated on top, it wasn't done. If it sunk to the bottom, we pulled the fire from under it and let it get cold. That was called hard soap. Next day, it was cut into chunks, placed on boards and put in the smoke house or attic to dry. If a body wanted soft soap, they just didn't let it "cook" so long. Soft soap was jelly like and looked like molasses. Nobody had any other soap but home made soap, to wash, scrub or use on their bodies. Soft soap was a little handier to use to boil the clothes with. Some folks made as much as a barrel and a half, owing to the old grease they had.

The ironing was done with hand wrought flat irons. They were kept hot by setting them up before the fireplace and heaping nice clean hot coals to them.

Dresses in those days were tight fitting waists and full skirts. The dresses and petticoats had yards of lace and tucks. There were no sewing machines. All the women learned to sew by hand. I never learned to sew very young because I had to nurse the children, so the older ones could be free to sew. I would take them off to themselves, wash and dress them and rock them to sleep, or play with them.

We had our own wool. Raised our own sheep, carded and spun, wove and knit. The yarn was dyed all sorts of pretty colors, red, black, yellow, blue, brown, and purple.

Indigo made blues and purples. Just according to how long or how strong the dye was used. The indigo was bought at the drugstore. Ol' Doc Gibson had the drugstore. I remember he had a "withered hand." He had the prettiest colored bottles, red and blue with black and gold letters to keep his medicines in.

For brown dye, we used walnut hulls. If we wanted black dye, we used the ripe black hulls and for all shades of brown we used young green hulls. We boiled them good, then strained it. The yarn was laid in the cold juice of the walnut, until it "took" on the shade we wanted. Then it was hung to dry without squeezing.

Elder and Poke berries made red dyes. We would gather them ripe and squeeze the juice. Yellow dye was made of some kind of "Yellow Root"—I don't remember the real name of the plant.

Our floors were kept scrubbed white as could be with sand. No carpets or other floor coverin's in those days.

I remember that we had big wooden trays, hewed out of cedar, about one and a half feet across, to knead light bread or mix salads or other foods. Our wash tubs were handmade, hewed out of cedar and other woods. They looked like half barrels.

We had a big skillet with a deep lid on it. We sat this before the fire place and heaped a few hot coals under it and more on top of it. This was used to bake bread or meat. I remember how nice and brown and good the bread was.

We had plenty to eat, but we did not have good times. We could not go off the place, without asking, we better not or we would get "whupped" to pieces. My mother was often whupped before she was grown. I was whupped good and plenty myself.[13]

Interviewed in 1941 by Robert Sonkin, Isom Moseley of Alabama described how molasses and soap were made and leather was tanned.

IM: My name is Isom Moseley. Raised up in ol' time without a mother. My ol' master an' mistress raised me. My master was named Lewis Moseley. My mistress was name Blanche Moseley . . . My mother was a house woman, an' after she died, my father was a fiel' han', an' white folks kep' me aroun' the house to tote cool water. Houseboy like. . . . they made 'lasses way back then, an' they had no iron mills like they got. They made wood, the carpenters made wooden mills. An' they'd grin' that 'lasses an' they had a vat, big kettle to make it in, you know, had [. . .] put the kettles on. An' when that 'lasses was made, they had poplar trough to pour that 'lasses in. No barrels at all. I never seed a barrel 'long then, nothing but troughs. An' when you get your 'lasses made, they had plank to cover them troughs.

RS: You told me something about the way they made soap in the old days. . . .

IM: Now, when I was a boy they use' to make soap. Well I was large enough to tote water to the soap makers to put on ash hopper. Now they didn' have no barrels, they had boards, you know. An' them boards come in that-a-way. . . . Well, all these here an' you'd lay some crossway to hol' the ashes. An' then I'd tote water an' put on that ash hopper for the soap maker. Now he'd make soap for the whole plantation, an' make about two or three barrels. An' 'long then captain, I ain't seed no bar soap. They might have had some but I never seed none. An' they had something dug in the groun', deep hole an' board up one each side, it was plank. Well it was about three foot deep I reckon, as nigh as I can come at it, an' about eight or ten foot long. Well, they'd tan leather. They'd lay a bark down in that hole, an' then they'd lay a hide over that bark. An' then they would lay another layer of bark an' another layer of hide, till they got it like they want. An' then they'd full that thing up with water. But now, 'fore they'd tan that leather, they had a place to put it in to lay a while an' get the hair off. An' when they got done with that leather i's jus' like any tan leather, an' they had a man there to make shoes for all us. Now we was children, good-size children, going about, that shoemaker make shoes for we children. An' the ol' folks too. We had mighty good white folks, my memory, far as I can remember, mighty good, mighty good.[14]

> Work in the master's house differed considerably from work in the field; slaves often found it difficult to switch between the two settings. Accustomed to domestic work as a youth, Ella Wilson remembered an episode in which she was ordered to serve a stint in the field. Her performance did not satisfy her owner.

I was born in Atlanta, Georgia. I don't remember the month. But when the Civil War ceased I was here then and sixteen years old. I'm a hundred years old. Some folks tries to make out like it ain't so. But I reckon I oughter know.

The white folks moved out from Georgia and went to Louisiana. I was raised in Louisiana, but I was born in Georgia. I have had several people countin' up my age and they all say I is a hundred years old. I had eight childen. All of them are free born. Four of them died when they were babies. I lost one just a few days ago.

I had such a hard time in slavery. Them white folks was slashing me and whipping me and putting me in the buck, till I don't want to hear nothin' about it. . . .

The first work I ever did was nursing the white children. My old mis' called me in the house and told me that she wanted me to take care of her children and from then till freedom came, I stayed in the house nursing. I had to get up every morning at five when the cook got up and make the coffee and then I had to go in the dining-room and set the table. Then I served breakfast. Then I went into the house and cleaned it up. Then I 'tended to the white children and served the other meals during the day. I never did work in the fields much. My old mars said I was too damned slow.

They carried me out to the field one evening. He never did show me nor tell me how to handle it and when I found myself, he had knocked me down. When I got up, he didn't tell me what to do, but when I picked up my things and started droppin' the seeds ag'in, he picked up a pine root and killed me off with it. When I come to, he took me up to the house and told his wife he didn't want me into the fields because I was too damned slow.

My mars used to throw me in a buck and whip me. He would put my hands together and tie them. Then he would make me squat down. Then he would run a stick through behind my knees and in front of my elbows. My knees was up against my chest. My hands was tied together just in front of my shins. The stick between my arms and my knees held me in a squat. That's what they called a buck. You could stand up an' you couldn't git your feet out. You couldn't do nothin' but just squat there and take what he put on you. You couldn't move no way at all. Just try to. You just fall over on one side and have to stay there till you turned over by him.

He would whip me on one side till that was sore and full of blood and then he would whip me on the other side till that was all tore up. I got a scar big as the place my old mis' hit me. She took a bull whip once—the bull whip had a piece of iron in the handle of it—and she got mad. She was so mad she took the whip and hit me over the head with the butt end of it, and the blood flew. It run all down my back and dripped off my heels. But I wasn't dassent to stop to do nothin' about it. Old ugly thing! The devil's got her right now! They never rubbed no salt nor nothin' in your back. They didn't need to.[15]

Work around the house often extended to midwifery and other
tasks relating to childbirth and medical care. Some slaves became skilled medical practitioners in their own right. Mildred
Graves, who had been a slave in Virginia, found her skills as a
healer much in demand.

I was born in Hanover County, Virginia about a hundred years ago. My
owner was name Tinsley.

The Tinsleys was good to me. Cose at times things was pretty bad,
but on a whole dey was decent people.

What kind of work I did? Most everything chile. I cooked, den I was
house maid, an' I raised I don't know how many chillun. You know in
dem days dey didn' have many doctors. Well I was always good when
it come to de sick, so dat was mostly my job. I was also what you call
a midwife too. Whenever any o' de white folks 'roun' Hanover was
goin' to have babies dey always got word to Mr. Tinsley dat dey want
to hire me fer dat time. Sho he let me go—twas money fer him, you
know. He would give me only a few cents, but dat was kinda good o'
him to do dat. Plenty niggers was hired out an' didn't get nothin'.
Sometimes I had three an' four sick at de same time. Marser use to tell
me I was a valuable slave. Dey use to come fer me both day an'
night—you know it's a funny thing how babies has a way of comin'
heah when it's dark.

One night Mrs. Leake sent fer me. 'Twas 'roun' twelve o'clock an'
ev'ybody was sleep when her husban' Judge Leake, come all out o'
breaf a-askin' fer me. He said to Mr. Tinsley dat his wife was mighty
sick an' dey was 'fraid she was goin' to die an' please let me come to
see her. I went an' when I got dare she had two doctors f'om Richmond, but dey won't doin' nothin' fer her. Something was very wrong
wid Mrs. Leake dey say, an' dey want to call another doctor—

min' you, dere was two dere already. I tol' dem I could bring her 'roun',
but dey laugh at me an' say, "Get back darkie, we mean business an'
don' won't any witch doctors or hoodoo stuff." Mrs. Leake heard dem
an' she said 'tween pains she want me; so dey said if you want her fer
your doctor we would go. I stayed an' wuked f'om 'bout one o'clock to
eight o'clock. I tell you dat was de toughes' case I ever had. I did
ev'ything I knowed an' somethings I didn' know. I don' know how I
done it, but anyway a son was born dat mornin' an' dat boy lived. He
didn' weigh five pounds I know, but I fix him up. Mrs. Leake got well
too. Even de doctors dat had call me bad names said many praise fer
me. De baby was named Andrew an' he was my chile. After he got
older he use to steal over to Mr. Tinsley's to see me. He would bring
me things—eats, money, candy, an' purty earrings. One I wore in my
ear 'till de Yankees come an' stole 'em. He use to teach me to write my
name an' I learn lots o' things f'om dat boy. He tol' me his father tried
to buy me, but Mr. Tinsley wouldn't sell me. Den he went to war an'
dat blessed chile was kilt; I knowed he died fightin'.[16]

> Sarah Wilson, who was owned by a Cherokee Indian in the
> western frontier of Arkansas, labored at whatever work she
> was told to do, whether outdoors or indoors. Her proficiency at
> sewing gave her special standing in the neighborhood.

Besides hoeing in the field, chopping sprouts, shearing sheep, carrying
water, cutting firewood, picking cotton and sewing I was the one they
picked to work Mistress' little garden where she raised things from
seed they got in Fort Smith. Green peas and beans and radishes and
things like that. If we raised a good garden she give me a little of it,
and if we had a poor one I got a little anyhow even when she didn't
give it.

Ben Horry, formerly a slave in South Carolina.

For clothes we had homespun cotton all the year round, but in winter we had a sheep skin jacket with the wool left on the inside. Sometimes sheep skin shoes with the wool on the inside and sometimes real cow leather shoes with wood peggings for winter, but always barefooted in summer, all the men and women too.

Lord, I never earned a dime of money in slave days for myself but

Amy Chapman, formerly a slave in Alabama.

plenty for the old Master. He would send me out to work the
neighbors field and he got paid for it, but we never did see any money.

I remember the first money I ever did see. It was a little while after
we was free, and I found a greenback in the road at Fort Gibson and I
didn't know what it was. Mammy said it was money and grabbed for it,
but I was still a hell cat and I run with it. I went to the little sutler store
and laid it down and pointed to a pitcher I been wanting. The man

Emma Howard, formerly a slave in Alabama.

took the money and give me the pitcher, but I don't know to this day how much money it was and how much was the pitcher, but I still got that pitcher put away. It's all blue and white stripedy.

Most of the work I done off the plantation was sewing. I learned from my Granny and I loved to sew. That was about the only thing I was industrious in. When I was just a little bitsy girl I found a steel needle in the yard that belong to old Mistress. My Mammy took it and I

George Young, formerly a slave in Alabama.

cried. She put it in her dress and started for the field. I cried so old
Mistress found out why and made Mammy give me the needle for my
own.

We had some neighbor Indians named Starr, and Mrs. Starr used me
sometimes to sew. She had nine boys and one girl, and she would sew
up all they clothes at once to do for a year. She would cut out the cloth
for about a week, and then send the word around to all the neighbors,

Lucindy Jurdon, formerly a slave in Georgia.

and old Mistress would send me because she couldn't see good to sew. They would have stacks of drawers, shirts, pants and some dresses all cut out to sew up.

I was the only Negro that would set there and sew in that bunch of women, and they always talked to me nice and when they eat I get part of it too, out in the kitchen.

One Negro girl, Eula Davis, had a mistress sent her too, one time,

Laura Clark, formerly a slave in North Carolina and Alabama.

but she wouldn't sew. She didn't like me because she said I was too white and she played off to spite the white people. She got sent home, too.

When old Mistress die I done all the sewing for the family almost. I could sew good enough to go out before I was eight years old, and when I got to be about ten I was better than any other girl on the place for sewing.

I can still quilt without my glasses, and I have sewed all night long
many a time while I was watching Young Master's baby after old
Mistress died.[17]

Emanuel Elmore was a slave ironworker of great strength and
skill. His extraordinary ability at the forge impressed the entire
neighborhood at the Cherokee Iron Works in upcountry South
Carolina. His son and namesake took pride in his father's mas-
tery of a difficult and dangerous craft.

I was born on June 20th and I remember when the war broke out, for I
was about five years old. We lived in Spartanburg County not far from
old Cherokee Ford. My father was Emanuel Elmore, and he lived to be
about 90 years old. . . .

I used to go and watch my father work. He was a moulder in the
Cherokee Iron Works, way back thare when everything was done by
hand. He moulded everything from knives and forks to skillets and
wash pots. If you could have seen pa's hammer, you would have seen
something worth looking at. It was so big that it jarred the whole earth
when it struck a lick. Of course it was a forge hammer, driven by
water power. They called the hammer "Big Henry." The butt end was
as big as an ordinary telephone pole.

The water wheel had fifteen or twenty spokes in it, but when it was
running it looked like it was solid. I used to like to sit and watch that
old wheel. The water ran over it and the more water came over, the
more power the wheel gave out.

At the Iron Works they made everything by hand that was used in a
hardware store, like nails, horse shoes and rims for all kinds of
wheels, like wagon and buggy wheels. There were moulds for
everything no matter how large or small the thing to be made was. Pa

Oliver Bell, formerly a slave in Alabama.

could almost pick up the right mould in the dark, he was so used to doing it. The patterns for the pots and kettles of different sizes were all in rows, each row being a different size. In my mind I can still see them.

Hot molten iron from the vats was dipped with spoons which were handled by two men. Both spoons had long handles, with a man at each handle. The spoons would hold from four to five gallons of hot

Nicey Pugh, formerly a slave in Alabama.

iron that poured just like water does. As quick as the man poured the
hot iron in the mould, another man came along behind them and
closed the mould. The large moulds had doors and the small moulds
had lids. They had small pans and small spoons for little things, like
nails, knives and forks. When the mould had set until cold, the piece
was prized out.

Pa had a turn for making covered skillets and fire dogs. He made them so pretty that white ladies would come and give an order for a "pair of dogs," and tell him how they wanted them to look. He would take his hammer and beat them to look just that way.[18]

> Although slaves worked first and foremost for their owners, they often had to work for themselves, particularly if they wanted a little extra beyond the monotonous ration of corn meal, pork, and standard-issue clothing. Octavia George, who had been a slave in Louisiana, recalled how she and some of her fellow slaves enjoyed the privilege of working "our little crops" on Sundays and the difference their labors made.

I was born in Mansieur, Louisiana, 1852, Avoir Parish. I am the daughter of Alfred and Clementine Joseph. I don't know much about my grandparents other than my mother told me my grandfather's name was Fransuai, and was one time a king in Africa.

Most of the slaves lived in log cabins, and the beds were home-made. The mattresses were made out of moss gathered from trees, and we used to have lots of fun gathering that moss to make those mattresses.

My job was taking care of the white children up at the Big House (that is what they called the house where our master lived), and I also had to feed the little Negro children. I remember quite well how those poor little children used to have to eat. They were fed in boxes and troughs, under the house. They were fed corn meal mush and beans. When this was poured into their box they would gather around it the same as we see pigs, horses and cattle gather around troughs today.

We were never given any money, but were able to get a little money this way: our Master would let us have two or three acres of land each year to plant for ourselves, and we could have what we raised on it.

We could not allow our work on these two or three acres to interfere with Master's work, but we had to work our little crops on Sundays. Now remind you, all the Negroes didn't get these two or three acres, only good masters allowed their slaves to have a little crop of their own. We would take the money from our little crops and buy a few clothes and something for Christmas. The men would save enough money out of the crops to buy their Christmas whiskey. It was all right for the slaves to get drunk on Christmas and New Years Day; no one was whipped for getting drunk on those days. We were allowed to have a garden and from this we gathered vegetables to eat; on Sundays we could have duck, fish and pork.

We didn't know anything about any clothes other than cotton; everything we wore was made of cotton, except our shoes, they were made from pieces of leather cut out of a raw cowhide.[19]

> The man who owned Henry Pettus, a "very liberal" Georgia planter-physician, allowed his slaves to keep pigs in addition to raising crops in their garden patches.

I was born in Wilkes County, near Washington, Georgia. My mother's owners was Dr. Palmer and Sarah Palmer. They had three boys; Steve, George, and Johnie. They lived in Washington and the farm I lived on was five miles southeast of town. It was fifty miles from Augusta, Georgia. He had another farm on the Augusta Road. He had a white man overseer. His name was Tom Newsom and his nephew, Jimmie Newsom, helped. He was pretty smooth most of the time. He got rough sometimes. Tom's wife was named Susie Newsom.

Dick Gilbert had a place over back of ours. They sent things to the still at Dick Gilbert's. Sent peaches and apples and surplus corn. The

still was across the hill from Dr. Palmer's farm. He didn't seem to
drink much but the boys did. All three did. Dr. Palmer died in 1861.
People kept brandy and whiskey in a closet and some had fancy
bottles they kept, one brandy, one whiskey, on their mantel. Some
owners passed drinks around like on Sunday morning. Dr. Palmer
didn't do that but it was done on some places before the Civil War. It
wasn't against the law to make spirits for their own use. That is the
way it was made. Meal and flour was made the same way then.

Mother lived in Dr. Palmer's office in Warren County. It was a very
nice log house and had a fence to make the front on the road and the
back enclosed like. Inside the fence was a tanyard and house at some
distance and a very nice log house where Mr. Hudson lived. Dr. Palmer
and Mr. Hudson had that place together. The shoemaker lived in
Washington in Dr. Palmer's back yard. He had his office and home all
in the same. Mr. Anthony made all the shoes for Dr. Palmer's slaves
and for white folks in town. He made fine nice shoes. He was
considered a high class shoemaker.

Mother was a field hand. She wasn't real black. My father never did
do much. He was a sort of a foreman. He rode around. He was lighter
than I am. He was old man Pettus' son. Old man Pettus had a great big
farm—land! land! land! Wiley and Milton Roberts had farms between
Dr. Palmer and old man Pettus' farm. Mother originally belong to old
man Pettus. He give Miss Sarah Palmer her place on the Augusta Road
and his son the place on which his own home was. They was his white
children. He had two. Mother was hired by her young mistress, Dr.
Palmer's wife, Miss Sarah. Father rode around, upheld by the old man
Pettus. He never worked hard. I don't know if old man Pettus raised
grandma or not; he never grandpa. He was a Terral. He died when I
was small. Grandpa was a field hand. He was the only colored man on
the place allowed to have a dog. He was Dr. Palmer's stock man. They

raised their own stock; sheep, goats, cows, hogs, mules, and horses. . . .

We raised a pet pig. Nearly every year we raised a pet pig. When mother would be out that pig would get my supper in spite of all I could do. The pig was nearly as large as I was. I couldn't do anything. We had a watermelon patch and sometimes sold Dr. Palmer melons. He let us have a melon patch and a cotton patch our own to work. Mother worked in moonlight and at odd times. They give that to her extra. We helped her work it. They give old people potato patches and let the children have goober rows. Land was plentiful. Dr. Palmer wasn't stingy with his slaves—very liberal. He was a man willing to live and let live so far as I can know of him.[20]

In her youth in Alabama, the centenarian ex-slave Laura Thornton was owned by Tom Eford, whom she remembered as a humane master. Eford made relatively light demands on his slaves' labor compared to neighboring slaveholders and permitted them time and land to work for their own benefit. Taking advantages of these privileges, Thornton's father managed to acquire valuable property of his own.

My native home is Alabama. I was born not far from Midway, Alabama, about twelve miles from Clayton. Midway, Clayton, and Barber are all near-by towns. We used to go to all of them.

"My master was Tom Eford. . . . We got up after daylight. Tom Eford didn't make his folks git up early. But after he was dead and gone, things changed up. The res' made 'em git up before daylight. He was a good man. The Lord knows. Yes Lord, way before day. You'd be in the field to work way before day and then work way into the night. The white folks called Eford's colored people poor white folks because he was so good to them. Old Tom Eford was the sheriff of Clayton.

His folks came back to the house at noon and et their dinner at the house. He had a cook and dinner was prepared for them just like it was for the white folks. The colored woman that cooked for them had it ready when they came there for it. They had a great big kitchen and the hands ate there. They came back to the same place for supper. And they didn't have to work late either. Old Tom Eford never worked his hands extra. That is the reason they called his niggers poor white folks. Folks lived at home them days and et in the same place. When my old man was living, I had plenty. Smokehouse was full of good meat. Now everything you git, you have to buy.

Next morning, they all et their breakfast in the same kitchen. They et three meals a day every day. My mother never cooked except on Sunday. She didn't need to. . . .

Slaves had money in slave time. My daddy bought a horse. He made a crop every year. He made his bale of cotton. He made corn to feed his horse with. He belonged to his white folks but he had his house and lot right next to theirs. They would give him time you know. He didn't have to work in the heat of the day. He made his crop and bought his whiskey. The white folks fed 'im. He had no expenses, 'cept tending to his crop. He didn't have to give Tom Eford anything he made. He just worked his crop in his extra time. Many folks too lazy to git theirselves somethin' when they have the chance to do it. But my daddy wasn't that kind. His old master gave him the ground and he made it give him the money.

My daddy left me plenty but I ain't got it now. I didn't care what happened when he died. People made out like they was goin' to put my money in the bank for me and took it and destroyed it. Used it for theirselves I reckon. How I need it and ain't got it—ain't got a penny.

For five or six years at my home, I made good crops. We raised everything we needed at home. Didn't know what it was to come to town to buy anything. If anybody had told me twenty years ago I would be in this shape, I wouldn't have believed it because I had plenty.[21]

CHAPTER

III.

FAMILY LIFE IN SLAVERY: "OUR FOLKS"

FOR SLAVEHOLDERS AND SLAVES, THE FAMILY REPRE-
sented the center of society and the wellspring of culture. Slaveholders often likened the plantation to an extended household in which
the master presided over his "family, white and black." Their interest as
owners, masters believed, entitled them to intervene in the slaves' domestic lives as they saw fit.

Slaves had very different notions of family. They understood kinship
in terms of their obligations to one another, not to their owners. Their
connection to fellow slaves—as husband and wife, parent and child,
and uncles, aunts, and cousins—affirmed the humanity that slavery
sought to deny and provided a basis for opposition to the master's rule.
Such diametrically different views of domestic life made the family contested terrain, where slaves and masters struggled to realize their own
vision.

In law, the masters' power to transgress the boundaries of the slave family was nearly limitless. Slave marriages had no legal standing. The unions were mere couplings that could be sundered by their owners, and any children produced, like the slaves' labor, could be employed at the owners' pleasure. In the eyes of the law, slaves could not exercise the authority of husbands, wives, fathers, or mothers. Since the slaveholders' rights were preeminent, slave parents lacked authority to discipline their children or sustain their own aged parents. Slaveholders had no legal obligation to respect the sanctity of the slave's marriage bed, and slave women—married or single—had no formal protection against their owners' sexual advances.

Some owners, motivated by moral convictions and deference to their slaves' wishes, sanctioned slave marriages and respected the slave household. But such scruples frequently came into conflict with an owner's material interests. A few slaveholders were willing to incur serious financial loss or other inconveniences for the sake of preserving their slaves' family connections, but such men and women were a distinct minority. Without legal protection and subject to the master's whim, the slave family was always at risk.

Yet the slave family did not crumble before the slaveholders' formidable power. During the long years of bondage, slave families transmitted African culture from the old world to the new, socialized the young, succored the old, buffered the slaves' relations with their masters and mistresses, and united relatives who were forced to live apart because of the circumstances of their enslavement. Slaves addressed each other as brother and sister, uncle and aunt, conferring the status of kin on men and women who were unrelated by blood or marriage. Slaves made familial and communal relationships one, thereby strengthening their hand against their owners' impositions.

As masters applied their stamp to the domestic life of the slave quarter, slaves struggled to maintain the integrity of their families. The battlegrounds were numerous, from the choice of spouse, the sanctity of marriage, the rearing of children, and the care of the aged. For those who survived slavery, the intensity of the struggle over family life and its deep import was not soon forgotten.

If slave marriages lacked legal standing, they nevertheless bore great significance to slaves—and sometimes to slaveholders as well. Nothing demonstrated this more fully than the slaves' investment in their wedding ceremony. Tempie Herndon Durham, who had been a slave in North Carolina, remembered well the day she married Exter Durham. Still, indicative of the obstacles slavery imposed on marriage, Exter Durham could not spend much time with his new bride. Belonging to a different owner, he had to return to his home plantation the next day.

When I growed up I married Exter Durham. He belonged to Marse Snipes Durham who had de plantation 'cross de county line in Orange County. We had a big weddin'. We was married on de front po'ch of de big house. Marse George killed a shoat an' Mis' Betsy had Georgianna, de cook, to bake a big weddin' cake all iced up white as snow wid a bride an' groom standin' in de middle holdin' han's. De table was set out in de yard under de trees, an' you ain't never seed de like of eats. All de niggers come to de feas' an' Marse George had a dram for everybody. Dat was some weddin'. I had on a white dress, white shoes an' long white gloves dat come to my elbow, an' Mis' Betsy done made me a weddin' veil out of a white net window curtain. When she played de weddin ma'ch on de piano, me an' Exter ma'ched down de walk an' up on de po'ch to de altar Mis' Betsy done fixed. Dat de pretties' altar I

"Exter done made me a weddin' ring. He made it out of a big red button wid his pocket knife." Tempie Herndon Durham, formerly a slave in North Carolina; pictured in Durham, North Carolina. (See pages 123–25.)

ever seed. Back 'gainst de rose vine dat was full of red roses, Mis' Betsy done put tables filled wid flowers an' white candles. She done spread down a bed sheet, a sho nuff linen sheet, for us to stan' on, an' dey was a white pillow to kneel down on. Exter done made me a weddin' ring. He made it out of a big red button wid his pocket knife. He done cut it so roun' an' polished it so smooth dat it looked like a red satin ribbon tide 'roun' my finger. Dat sho was a pretty ring. I wore it 'bout fifty years, den it got so thin dat I lost it one day in de wash tub when I was washin' clothes.

Uncle Edmond Kirby married us. He was de nigger preacher dat preached at de plantation church. After Uncle Edmond said de las' words over me an' Exter, Marse George got to have his little fun: He say, "Come on, Exter, you an' Tempie got to jump over de broom stick backwards; you got to do dat to see which one gwine be boss of your househol'." Everybody come stan' 'roun to watch. Marse George hold de broom 'bout a foot high off de floor. De one dat jump over it backwards an' never touch de handle, gwine boss de house, an' if bof of dem jump over without touchin' it, dey won't gwine be no bossin', dey jus' gwine be 'genial. I jumped fust, an' you ought to seed me. I sailed right over dat broom stick same as a cricket, but when Exter jump he done had a big dram an' his feets was so big an' clumsy dat dey got all tangled up in dat broom an' he fell head long. Marse George he laugh an' laugh, an' tole Exter he gwine be bossed 'twell he skeered to speak less'n I tole him to speak. After de weddin' we went down to de cabin Mis' Betsy done all dressed up, but Exter couldn' stay no longer den dat night kaze he belonged to Marse Snipes Durham an' he had to [go] back home. He lef' de nex day for his plantation, but he come back every Saturday night an' stay 'twell Sunday night. We had eleven chillun. Nine was bawn befo' surrender an' two after we was set free. So I had two chillun dat wuzn' bawn in bondage. I was worth a heap to Marse George kaze I had so manny chillun. De more chillun a slave had de more dey was worth. Lucy Carter was de only nigger on de plantation dat had more chillun den I had. She had twelve, but her children was sickly an' mine was muley strong an' healthy. Dey never was sick.[1]

While Tempie Herndon Durham's owner joined in the wedding festivities, other masters would have nothing to do with such ceremonies; some actively opposed them. Mathew Jarrett recalled a significant distinction in the words that pronounced slave couples man and wife, one that reflected the tenuous circumstances of their union.

We slaves knowed that them words wasn't bindin'. Don't mean nothin' lessen you say "What God done jined, cain't no man pull asunder." But dey never would say dat. Jus' say, "Now you married."[2]

As Caroline Johnson Harris remembered, slave couples on her plantation did not seek approval of their owners for marriage; instead, they consulted a respected elder in the slave community. Mixing a folk tradition with Christian belief, the ceremony she described was tempered with an awareness that any bond created by slaves could be broken by the owner.

Didn't have to ask Marsa or nothin'. Just go to Ant Sue an' tell her you want to git mated. She tell us to think 'bout it hard fo' two days, 'cause marryin' was sacred in de eyes of Jesus. Arter two days Mose an' I went back an' say we done thought 'bout it an' still want to git married. Den she called all de slaves arter tasks to pray fo' de union dat God was gonna make. Pray we stay together an' have lots of chillun an' none of 'em git sol' way from de parents. Den she lay a broomstick 'cross de sill of de house we gonna live in an' jine our hands together. Fo' we step over it she ast us once mo' if we was sho' we wanted to git married. 'Course we say yes. Den she say, "In de eyes of Jesus step into Holy land of mat-de-money." When we step 'cross de broomstick, we was married. Was bad luck to tech de broomstick. Fo'ks always stepped high 'cause dey didn't want no spell cast on 'em—Ant Sue used to say whichever one teched de stick was gonna die fust.[3]

Andrew Jackson Gill, whose mother and father had resided on two different estates in the same Mississippi neighborhood, emphasized the importance of visiting to his parents' courtship and the maintenance of their family life after marriage.

I was born right cheah 'cross de road a piece, 82 years ago. My name is Andrew Jackson Gill. Gill was de name of de man who owned my daddy. My mammy belonged to dis gen'man by de name of Marster Gill. He has a large plantation 'bout a mile down de road frum Missus Rosa.

Mammy an' daddy wa'nt never lawful' wedded. Dey don't do dat in dem days. My daddy, he done see Mammy one time he come a visitin' wid Marster Gill, an' when he got home he say: "Marster Gill, I sho' does like dat li'l gal over heah at Missus Rosa's. She sho' am purty. Yas Suh!" An' by George he wa'nt messin' roun' loosin' no time fo' he done got Marster Gill's an' Missus Rosa's sanction to take my mammy fer his wife. My daddy, he was a fine man an' treated us chullun jus' dandy. He stay wid Marster Gill, an' mammy stay wid Missus Rosa, but evr' Wednesday an' Saturday night was visitin' time fer de colored folks, an' he come see mammy den. Dere was in de course of time—he! he! he! he!, Lord 'a Mercy!—eight of us chullun. I was de second chile an' Missus Rosa, she sho' done take a shine to me. She kep' me up at de Big House an' I done all de special things she wanted done 'cause she knows I do 'em up right. I used to ride right wid her on de back of her hoss when she go out to 'speck de fields an' sech. It was my special duty to climb down off de hoss an' open an' shut de gates fer her. Yas Suh! She sho' was a mighty fine lady. Her husband was dead an' all her chullun' was away. I don't rightly recollec' how many chullun' she had. Missus Rosa was a doctor woman, an' she run dat plantation all by herself. Us colored folks would step right lively when she speak up an' say, "Do dis an' do dat." She was kin' an' good, but she sho' don't stan' no foolishness.

Mammy an' de res' of de colored folks, dey live out in de Quarters in separate cabins of dey own. Dey job was to he'p Missus Rosa in de fields, an' takin' keer of de cattle an' sech.

On Wednesday an' Saturday all de niggers what wanted to visited 'roun'. Some would ask fer a permission slip whereby it say—"dis cheah nigger so an' so is permitted to visit over at so an so," an' de good Lord he'p a nigger what took it in his haid to go messin' 'roun' lessen he have his permission slip. I 'member one time a young buck in our Quarters was mighty desperate in love wid a gal over at Marster Gills. Missus Rosa done tol' him, she say,—"Ned, dat gal' ain't no good, an' you'd bes' pick you out a nice, sweet gal right in your own Quarters." But Ned, he headstrong an' mighty powerful' in love, so one Saturday night he slip off frum de Quarters widout no permission slip. Well, suh, all dem niggers down in de Quarters done tol' him not to go but he wont listen. An dat nigger wa'nt gone half an hour fo' he come back, wid Marster Gill a leadin' him. All dem niggers in de Quarters come out an' stan' 'roun' wid dey mouth wide open an' dey eyes a rollin'. A doodle bug comin' outten his hole couldn' have made less soun'. Missus Rosa, she come out an' say "Ned, I'se sorry, but you deserve jes' what you're gonna' git!" An' he got it, hard an' heavy, wid de whip. Yas Suh! Missus Rosa listen to reason but she hard when she wanta be.

On Wednesday an' Saturday nights dey was a ban' of eight white men called de Patterollers who would ride 'roun' de country side an' iffen dey foun' a nigger runnin' loose widout no permission slip, dey catch him up an' see dat he gets a good whupping.[4]

> Slaveholders depended on slaves to reproduce their labor force. While most masters were content to let nature take its course and allow slaves to choose their own partners, a few intervened to promote relationships they believed would be most remunerative to them, pairing men and women as they might pair breeding stock. Such meddling created powerful dilemmas for slaves, particularly for young women. Rose Williams was little more than a child at age sixteen when her owner forced her into a relationship with an unwanted partner.

Dere am one thing Massa Hawkins does to me what I can't shunt from my mind. I knows he don't do it for meanness, but I allus holds it 'gainst him. What he done am force me to live with dat nigger, Rufus, 'gainst my wants.

After I been at he place 'bout a year, de massa come to me and say, "You gwine live with Rufus in dat cabin over yonder. Go fix it for livin'." I's 'bout sixteen year old and has no larnin', and I's jus' igno'mus chile. I's thought dat him mean for me to tend de cabin for Rufus and some other niggers. Well, dat am start de pestigation for me.

I's took charge of de cabin after work am done and fixes supper. Naw, I don't like dat Rufus, 'cause he a bully. He am big and cause he so, he think everybody do what him say. We'uns has supper, den I goes here and dare talkin', till I's ready for sleep and den I gits in de bunk. After I's in, dat nigger come and crawl in de bunk with me 'fore I knows it. I says, "What you means, you fool nigger?" He say for me to hush de mouth. "Dis am my bunk, too," he say.

"You's teched in de head. Git out," I's told him, and I puts de feet 'gainst him and give him a shove and out he go on de floor 'fore he knew what I's doin'. Dat nigger jump up and he mad. He look like de wild bear. He starts for de bunk and I jumps quick fer de poker. It am 'bout three feet long and when he comes at me I lets him have it over de head. Did dat nigger stop in his tracks I's say he did. He looks at me steady for a minute and you's could tell he thinkin' hard. Den he go and set on de bench and say, "Jus' wait. You thinks it am smart, but you's am foolish in de head. Dey's gwine larn you somethin'."

"Hush yous big mouth and stay 'way from dis nigger, dat all I wants," I say, and jus' sets and hold dat poker in de hand. He jus' sets, lookin' like de bull. Dere we'uns sets and sets for 'bout an hour and den he go out and I bars de door.

De nex' day I goes to de missy and tells her what Rufus wants and missy say dat am de massa's wishes. She say, "Yous am de portly gal and Rufus am de portly man. De massa wants you-uns for to bring forth portly chillen."

I's thinkin' 'bout what de missy say, but say to mysef, "I's not gwine live with dat Rufus." Dat night when him come in de cabin, I grabs de poker and sits on de bench and says, "Git 'way from me, nigger, 'fore I busts yous brains out and stomp on dem." He say nothin' and git out.

De nex' day de massa call me and tell me, "Woman, I's pay big money for you and I's done dat for de cause I wants yous to raise me chillens. I's put yous to live with Rufus for dat purpose. Now, if you doesn't want whippin' at de stake, yous do what I wants."

I thinks 'bout massa buyin' me offen de block and savin' me from bein' sep'rated from my folks and 'bout bein' whipped at de stake. Dere it am. What am I's to do? So I 'cides to do as de massa wish and so I yields. . . .

I never marries, 'cause one 'sperience am 'nough for dis nigger. After what I does for de massa, I's never wants no truck with any man. De Lawd forgive dis cullud woman, but he have to 'scuse me and look for some others for to 'plenish de earth.[5]

If forced coupling exemplified a master's power, many former slaves remembered how family ties furnished them with the means for material support. Growing up a slave in Virginia, Frank Bell was surrounded by three generations of kin, who shared work as well as living quarters.

My pappy and my grandpappy wukked for ole Marser's people all dey lives. I 'member grampa well. Starlin Bell was his name. Bout the only thing I 'member bout him. Guess I was a boy going on 6 or 7 years old, long before the war it was. Old Grampa never sayed much. Just went around amumblin' to hisself. One day he sat on de well-stand and called me over to him.

"Come here, son," he say to me, and it was the fust time I recollec' dat he had say something to me what wus a little tot dat ain't nobody paid no 'tention to.

He picked me up and rid me cross his foot wid his knee crossed, holding onto my hands, and riding me up and down.

"Son," he say, "I sho' hope you never have to go through the things your ole grandpa done bin through." Ole Grampa died when he was 118 years old—before de war. Guess I was a boy of 'bout ten then. I 'member ole Marser standin' over the hole where they buried him, readin' somethin' out of a grade big book all solemn-like, an' all de folks was standin' there aweepin' and wailin'.

John Fallons had 'bout 150 servants an' he wasn't much on no special house servants. Put everybody in de field, he did, even de women. Growed mostly wheat on de plantation, an' de men would scythe and cradle while de women folks would rake and bind. Den us little chillun, boys an' girls, would come along an' stack.

Used to wuk in family groups, we did. Now we and my four brothers, never had no sisters, used to follow my mom an' dad. In dat

way one could help de other when dey got behind. All of us would
pitch in and help Momma who warn't very strong. 'Course in dat way
de man what was doin' de cradlin' would always go no faster dan de
woman, who was most times his wife, could keep up. Ole overseer on
some plantations wouldn't let families work together, 'cause dey ain't
gonna work as fast as when dey all mixed up, but Marse John Fallons
had a black foreman, what was my mother's brother, my uncle. Moses
Bell was his name, and he always looked out for his kinfolk, especially
my mother.[6]

> Kinfolk loomed large in Fannie Moore's recollections of her
> girlhood on a South Carolina plantation. Moore especially re-
> membered her mother's love for and protectiveness of her and
> her brothers and sisters.

Nowadays when I heah folks a'growlin an' a'grumblin bout not habbin
this an' that I jes think what would they done effen they be brought up
on de Moore plantation. De Moore plantation b'long to Marse Jim
Moore, in Moore, South Carolina. De Moores had own de same
plantation and de same niggers and dey children for yeahs back. . . .

Marse Jim own de bigges' plantation in de whole country. Jes
thousands acres ob lan'. An de ole Tiger Ribber a runnin' right through
de middle ob de plantation. On one side ob de ribber stood de big
house, whar de white folks lib and on the other side stood de
quarters. . . .

De quarters jes long row o' cabins daubed wif dirt. Ever one in de
family lib in one big room. In one end was a big fireplace. Dis had to
heat de cabin and do de cookin too. We cooked in a big pot hung on a
rod over de fire and baked de co'n pone in de ashes or else put it in de

skillet and cover de lid wif coals. We allus hab plenty wood to keep us warm. Dat is ef we hab time to get it outed de woods.

My granny she cook for us chillens while our mammy away in de fiel. Dey wasn't much cookin to do. Jes make co'n pone and bring in de milk. She hab big wooden bowl wif enough wooden spoons to go 'roun'. She put de milk in de bowl and break it [*the cornpone*] up. Den she put de bowl in de middle of de flo' an' all de chillun grab a spoon.

My mammy she work in de fiel' all day and piece and quilt all night. Den she hab to spin enough thread to make four cuts for de white fo'ks ebber night. Why sometime I nebber to to bed. Hab to hold de light for her to see by. She hab to piece quilts for de white folks too. Why dey is a scar on my arm yet where my brother let de pine drip on me. Rich pine war all de light we ebber hab. My brother was a holdin' de pine so's I can help mammy tack de quilt and he go to sleep and let it drop.

I never see how my mammy stan' sech ha'd work. She stan' up fo' her chillun tho'. De ol' overseeah he hate my mammy, case she fight him for beatin' her chillun. Why she git more whuppins for dat den anythin' else. She hab twelve chillun. I member I see de three oldes' stan' in de snow up to dey knees to split rails, while de overseeah stan' off an' grin.

My mammy she trouble in her heart bout de way they treated. Ever night she pray for de Lawd to git her an' her chillun out ob de place. One day she plowin' in de cotton fiel. All sudden like she let out big yell. Den she sta't singing' an' a shoutin', an' a whoopin' an' a hollowin'. Den it seem she plow all de harder. When she come home, Marse Jim's mammy say: "What all dat goin' on in de fiel? Yo' think we sen' you out there jes to whoop and yell? No siree, we put you out there to work and you sho' bettah work, else we git de overseeah to cowhide you ole black back." My mammy jes grin all over her black wrinkled face and say: "I's saved. De Lawd done tell me I's saved. Now I know de Lawd will sho me de way, I ain't gwine a grieve no more. No matter how much yo' all done beat me an' my chillun de Lawd will show me de way. An' some day we nevah be slaves." Ole granny Moore grab de cowhide and slash mammy cross de back but mammy nebber yell. She jes go gack to de fiel a singin'.

My mammy grieve lots over brothah George, who die wif de fever. Granny she doctah him as bes' she could, evah time she git way from de white folks kitchen. My mammy nevah git chance to see him, 'cept when she git home in de evenin'. George he jes lie. One day I look at him an' he had sech a peaceful look on his face, I think he sleep and jes let him lone. Long in de evenin I think I try to wake him. I touch him on de face, but he was dead. Mammy nebber know til she come at night. Pore mammy she kneel by de bed an' cry her heart out! Ol' uncle Allen, he make pine box for him an' carry him to de graveyard over on de hill. My mammy jes plow and cry as she watch em' put George in de groun'.

My pappy he was a blacksmith. He shoe all de horses on de plantation. He wo'k so hard he hab no time to go to de fiel'. His name war Stephen Moore. Mars Jim call him Stephen Andrew. He was sold to de Moores, and his mammy too. She war brought over from Africa. She never could speak plain. All her life she been a slave. White folks never recognize 'em any more than effen dey was a dog.[7]

> Slaves' work profoundly affected how their children were raised. Because most mothers and fathers toiled from dawn to dusk in the owners' fields, the care of young children often fell to older girls and aged women. Large plantations might have dozens of children in communal care arrangements. In a conversation with John Henry Faulk and an unidentified second interviewer, Laura Smalley described the standard practices on one Texas estate.

LS: Ten' to all the children, ten' to the children. Jus' like, you bring a whole lot of children an' put them down at one house. Well there somebody have to look over them an' ten' to them, that-a-way. Just a house full of little children. And if one act bad, they'd whip him, the ol' woman. An' if the ol' woman didn' ten' to the children they'd whip her too, to make her ten' to the children, she wasn' doing nothing. Well she wasn' a crippley woman like me. An' they'd whip her. An' they had trays, I don' know whether you see a tray. Wooden tray, dug out, oh about that long. An' all of them would get aroun' that tray with spoons. An' just eat. I can recollect that 'cause I ate out of the tray. With spoons you know, and eat, such as like mush or soup or something like that. They'd feed them 'fore twelve o'clock. An' all them children get aroun' there and just eat, eat, eat, eat out of that thing. . . .

JHF: Just like slopping hogs, wasn't it?—

LS: Jus' like a tray, made just like a hog trough. An' clothes, they'd wash them thing and scal' them out for the children. I didn't see them scal' but that what they told me. An' young children eat out of that thing, an' tha's with wood spoon, an' if one reach his spoon over in the other's plate, he gonna hit him. Hit him, knock that there spoon back on his side. An' that was when we was children, wasn' able to ten' to no other children. And jus' sit them down in a corner, an' put this chil' between his leg, an' then hold his han' 'roun' this chil'. Tha's the way he nursed him. Couldn' stan' up with him, couldn' shake him this-a-way in the arm. I can 'member that. I had a brother, he name Wright, an' he jus' would shake that chil', set him in the floor, an—

JHF: He was too little to pick him up.

LS: Yes sir. An' that chil' kick much, he'd fall, kick him over too. An'

the old woman come there an' spank him an' give him the chil'
back in his arm. An' they had certain time to come to them
childrens. . . . A cow out there will go to the calf, you know.
An' they'd have certain time, cow come to his calf at night. Well
they come at ten o'clock everyday to all them babies. Them
what nurse. Them what didn' nurse, they didn' come to them at
all. The ol' lady fed them. When that horn blowed, they blowed
a horn for the mothers, they'd jus' come jus' like cows, jus'
a-running, coming to the children.

JHF: Out of the field.

LS: Out of the field.

Int2: How long did they nurse a baby?—

LS: Ma'am?

JHF: Couple of years? How long would they nurse a baby? Till it was
      big enough to walk I guess?

LS: Yes ma'am, well nine months or something like that. They'd
      nurse them until it get big enough to eat. Till they'd eat. An'
      they'd come an' nurse that baby, ten o'clock in the day—

JHF: Everyday.

LS: Yes ma'am. Ten o'clock in the day an' three o'clock in the day.
      They come to that baby an' nurse it.

JHF: Twice a day.

LS: Yes ma'am, twice a day. Come there an' nurse that baby. She
      couldn' eat you know. But one could eat, he wouldn' come till
      dinner time. But one little one what couldn' eat, they'd come to
      it. That ol' woman had a time in there slopping them children.

                         . . . .

JHF: Now who did the cooking for the plantation?

LS: I don' know what the old woman's name done the cooking. Miss
      C[lara] did tell me here not long ago who done the main

cooking. You know they didn' cook in them kitchen like here. They'd have a off kitchen, off from the house.

JHF: Outside huh?

LS: Yes ma'am. An' they'd pack the vittles to the kitchen. They wasn' cooking in the kitchen, dining room. I was a great big girl when I knowed Miss Betsy an' them had a kitchen an' a dining room mixed together. I was a big ol' girl. They cooked it all outside. Right in the yard, they cooked it out there, an' brought it to the kitchen. When I was a chil'.

JHF: Well they had some of the slaves who worked in the house and then some who worked on the yard. Isn't that right?

LS: No ma'am. They work in the yard, men work in the yard some nights. But them there what work in the kitchen, they didn' have nothing to do in the yard. An' they had one to make up beds. An' one to cook, an' then they had six at the time to make up bed, an' then they go to the fiel'. An' they had a regular nurse, you know. Nurse, you never did see old missus with the baby, never no time. I's like, you'd hire somebody to nurse, but be a grown woman nurse, ten' to that baby. An' you'd keep him, never did carry it to old missus, without it was hungry, night or day. They carry it there to her. You ten' to that baby. That baby slep' with the ol' nurses an' all.

JHF: Huh.

LS: Yes sir. Slep' with them. Didn't have nothing to do. Carry that baby an' sit there until he'd nurse. An' then after he'd nurse, then you carry it back, ten' to it. . . . You go give it to her an' nurse it, don' care how col' it is, an' you carry that baby back on in that bed, that room where you was. An' I know—

JHF: Well did the mistress nurse the baby, or did she have?—

LS: She nurse from the breast.

JHF: Uh huh.

LS: But see, she'd nurse this baby that he would be hungry. Well this
      here nurse would bring it to her. An' let her nurse it, an' then
      when she'd nurse she'd han' it right back, night or day. Had to
      ten' to that baby night an' day, han' it back to her. An' that baby
      was any kin' of sick that nurse had to sit up there at night an'
      ten' to it.[8]

> An elderly ex-slave identified only as "Grammaw" remembered
> how, as her nursing mother's oldest daughter, she helped with
> the care of her younger siblings.

De suckin' mothers was given light wuk. . . . My mother had a track
of two acres to tend. I used to tend her suckin' baby and tote it down
to de fiel' for her to nuss. Den de baby would go to sleep and we'd lay
it down 'twixt de cotton rows and ma would make me holp her. She
kep' a long switch and iffen I didn't wuk fast enuf, she switch me.
When she got through she could quit. Sometimes she was through by
noontime. Den she'd go back to de quarters and iffen it was fruit time,
she'd put up some fruit for mistis. . . .
    I was de oldest. . . . Ma was almost fifteen when I was born.
Having me was what kilt her, I was so big and fat. She had sebenteen
mo' chilluns but it finally got her. She died wid a pain in her stomach
when she was ninety year ole.[9]

> Even as slaves drew strength from the bonds of kinship, family
> life under slavery could be a source of pain and anguish. Caro-
> line Hunter, the daughter of a free black man and a slave
> woman, knew that full well.

I ain' got no education and I don' know when I was born, but I do
know I was born a slave. I was born near Suffolk, Virginia. My moma
was a slave, but my papa was free. I had thirteen chillun, an' all died
but four. One ain' never took breath. I had three brothers to live. My
mama, papa, me an' my three brothers all live in one room back of my
mastah's house. We et, slep an' done ev'ything in jus' dat one room. My
papa didn't stay wid us ve'y long. He left 'cause my massa beat him. It
happen lak dis, honey. Pa love dogs an' kep' one wid him all de time.
One day he was out gatherin' up sheep, an' de dog was wid him.
Somehow, de dog kilt one sheep; papa didn't know it. When massa
found it out he beat my papa till he bled. Papa was free, an' he didn'
think massa had no business beatin' him, so he left an' came to
Norfolk an' jined de army. . . .

Lord, I done been thew somepin'. When I'se five years ole I had to
wuk. I had a job cleanin' silver an' settin' de table. A few years after
dat I was put out in de fiel's to wuk all day. Sometimes I wished I
could run away, but missus useta tell me if we run away to de Yankees
dey'd bore holes in our arms an' put wagon staves through de holes
an' make us pull de wagons like hosses. Dat kep' me f'om leavin', but
some o' de slaves did run, an' yes, honey, when dey did get 'em dey
beat holes in 'em an' put 'em in barrels of brine.

It's hard to believe dat dese things did happen, but dey did 'cause I
live in dat time. I can' never forgit how my massa beat my brothers
cause dey didn' wuk. He beat 'em so bad dey was sick a long time, an'
soon as dey got a smatterin' better he sold 'em. Two of 'em I seen agin
after we was freed, but de oles' one I ain' never seen since. If de massa
couldn' rule you dey would sell you, an' if you got so you couldn' wuk
dey'd take you in a boat dey had an' dump you in de water. . . .

During slavery it seemed lak yo' chillun b'long to ev'ybody but you.
Many a day my ole mama has stood by an' watched massa beat her

chillun 'till dey bled an' she couldn' open her mouf. Dey didn' only beat us, but they useta strap my mama to a bench or box an' beat her wid a wooden paddle while she was naked.[10]

In a society that made protecting wives, mothers, and daughters a hallmark of manhood, the inability of slave men to do so caused enormous pain. Jordan Johnson, born a slave in Virginia in 1848, remembered the ordeal of one man forced to watch his pregnant wife endure a whipping.

Husbands allays went to de woods when dey know de wives was due fo' a whippin', but in de fiel' dey dare not leave. Had to stay dere, not darin' even look like dey didn't like it. Charlie Jones was one slave dat had his wife workin' in de same fiel' wid him. Was plantin' tobacco— he was settin' out an' she was hillin'. Annie was big wid chile an' gittin' near her time, so one day she made a slip an' chopped a young shoot down. Ole man Diggs, de overseer, come runnin' up screamin' at her an' it made her mo' nervous, an she chopped off 'nother one. Ole overseer lif' up dat rawhide an' beat Annie 'cross de back an shoulders 'till she fell to de groun'. An' Charlie he jus' stood dere hearin' his wife scream an' astarin' at de sky, not darin' to look at her or even say a word.[11]

Despite their lack of legal authority over their wives and children, slave men took seriously their responsibilities as husbands and fathers. When Martha Spence was transported from Tennessee to Texas by her owner, her father, the property of another owner, remained behind. The death of her father's owner, however, enabled Spence's owner to purchase her father and reunite the family. After Spence's mother died, her father took over direction of her upbringing.

"[W]hen mawster Burrows died, Mawster Spence bought fathaw, and he came on down to Texas." Martha Spence Bunton, formerly a slave in Tennessee and Texas; pictured at Austin, Texas. (See pages 140–44.)

I was bawn on Mawster John Bell's cotton plantation at Murphfreesboro, Tennessee, dis was on January 1, 1856, right on New Year's day. We belonged to Mawster Bell, but he sold us to Joseph Spence. Dat's why later, I got de name ob Spence, Martha Spence.

Now here, I remembah how when Mawster Spence bought us, we come on down to Texas in wagons, in dem big covered wagons. I kin remembah how we crossed de big Mississippi River on a steamboat. I didn't even have sense enought to be scared ob dat steamboat.

We knowed when we hit Texas, 'cause de mawster was a tellin' us all times, "We had better git off ob de road and pull up alongside ob dem trees and brushes, 'cause a nawther is on de way." When dat nawther struck, weeds and leaves would jes' staht a rollin' along de land. Yo' might not believe me when dem weeds got to tumblin' along dat way, us poor, ignorant little niggers thought dat dey was rabbits. We sure did. We never saw no rabbits in Tennessee, but we had heard dat dere was a lot ob 'em in Texas.

Mawster Spence rode his hoss, and sometimes he'd let us git three days ahead ob him and den he'd catch up wid us. I believe Mistress Spence come along in a richer way, in a coach, or a stagecoach, I believe. I know dat she didn't come along wid us.

Mawster's nephew, William Hamilton, rode along wid us in de covered wagons. De chillun had to walk in de mawnin's while de older folks rode, in de afternoons, de older folks walked and us chillun rode. Ob course, de littlest chillun rode all of de time. Sometimes we took de wrong road and had to turn bock and find de main road.

We come through Louisiana into East Texas. Here sistah Nancy took sick and had a baby. She was married to a slave, John Spence. He was along wid us. Dey called de little baby girl Anna. Mothaw, my other sistahs, Nester, Parthenia, Susan, and me come on down to Austin, where Mawster Spence rented a cotton fahm.

When I was a child, I had to help de other chillun bring de dinner pails to de workers in de fields. We toted buckets dat had meat, cabbage, biscuits and milk in 'em. About twelb o'clock de men would unhitch de mules, and wait fo' us. Dey was hungry and dey got plenty to eat. All ob us got enough to eat.

Fathaw wasn't out in dem fields, 'cause he was owned by Mawster

William Burrows ob Murphfreesboro, Tennessee, and he warn't allowed to come along. But when mawster Burrows died, Mawster Spence bought fathaw, and he came on down to Texas. He den worked out in de fields ob Mawster Billingsley. Mawster Spence had enough hands, so he allowed fathaw to work out.

But fathaw was near us. Den mothaw got a cold and diptheria, and died. We was lak little orphan niggers, but fathaw den come over and took care ob us. He was fathaw and mothaw to us. Muh, dat's whut we called mothaw in dem early days, wasn't wid us no more.

Fathaw, poor soul, was a big bodied man. I remembah how on Sunday mawnin's when we didn't have nothin' to do, he'd git out ob bed in our log cabin, make a big fire, and tell us:

"Jiminy-cripes! yo' chillun stay in yo' beds. I'll make de biscuits."

He would too. I still laugh when I think about dem big rye biscuits dat was so laghe, dat we called 'em "nigger Heels." Dey sure was big biscuits, but dey was good. Some ob dem big biscuits was made out ob black shorts,* but dey was good, too.

We never did git no butter and sometimes, we'd see de little white chillun goin' around eatin' bread dat was buttered and sugared. We got plenty ob other eats: sliced meat, biscuits ob black shorts, roastin' ears in season, plenty of sweet milk and butter-milk, but no butter.

Den we'd ask some ob de chillun; "Joseph, give us a peice ob yo' bread, please."

He'd say, "all right, break off a peice, don't let mothaw see yo' do it, though."

Joseph was de best ob de three Spence boys. Den we'd ask Robert. He'd say, "no I ain't! Yo' go and git yo' some cawnbread."

---

*"Shorts" was a coarse byproduct of wheat milling, consisting of bran, germ, and flour.

De boys' mothaw, Mistress Mag, would whoop us, when we needed it. But she also whooped her chillun, when dey done wrong or wouldn't mind.

Mistress Mag was a big chu'ch member. She'd have prayer meetin's, mawnin' and night. But I got tired listenin' to her. She asked God to make her boys rich and well-to-do. She got her wish. One ob de boys was a jedge, another was a professor, and one ob' 'em is still livin' and he is a big doctor, I believe. I was thinkin' about dat de other day.

One day fathaw found out dat his little chaps, he always called us his chaps, had bugs in dere hair. We had lice. Mistress Mag tried to git us rid ob 'em. One day fathaw went up to mawster Spence, who was always good to us and said, "Mawster Joe, if yo' please, tell Mistress Mag to stop bathin my chaps' heads wid dat lye soap! Mawster Joe, I'se tellin' yo', she'll kill my little niggers. She'll git dere brains out ob dere heads dat way."

And Mawster Spence would nigh always have his way. . . .

Oh, fathaw was good to us. Ob course, he whooped us when we needed it. I believe dat when chillun is bad, dey should git a whoopin'. De proberbs in the Good Book say dat de chillun shall not be spared de rod lest, yea, dey shall not be saved. And dey must be punished and whooped to make 'em mind. I read my Bible lots ob times durin' de week. I believes in de Bible.[12]

Aware of the insecurity of their domestic life, slaves could not take their families for granted. Any number of circumstances might separate husbands from wives and parents from children, because slaveholders' needs always overrode slaves' wishes. Slaves labored to maintain their relationships, often in the face of great risk. Hannah Chapman, whose father lived on a different plantation than she, told of the sacrifices he made to remain in contact with his children.

Any slave that was owned by Bill Easterlin, will tell yo' just like I is dat he fed well, clothed well, an' housed well, but he wuz stern an' could when he sat out to. After being whipped some o' de slaves would hide fer days an' weeks in de woods. Some ob 'em stay hid out mos' all de time. My father and mudder wuz strict on us. How dey could whip! Dey neber would let us go 'round much only ter meetin's. We neber wuz let ter go to frolics or any places ter hab merriment. Dey didn't believe in hit.

When I wuz little I played lak mos' any chile. Us played in de barn and had swings, us lacked tar play run and ketch, marbles an' hid an' seek.

My father wuz sold 'way from us when I wuz small. Dat wuz a sad time fer us. Mars wouldn't sell de mudders 'way from deir chillun so us lived on wid her wid out de fear ob bein' sold. My pa sho' did hate ter leave us. He missed us and us longed fer him. He would often slip back ter us' cottage at night. Us would gather 'round him an' crawl up in his lap, tickled slap to death, but he give us dese pleasures at a painful risk. When his Mars missed him he would beat him all de way home. Us could track him de nex' day by de blood stains.[13]

Vinnie Busby, who had grown up not far from Chapman in Mississippi, related a similar story about her own father.

My pa an' ma wasn't owned by de same masters. My pa wuz owned by Marse Bill Brown who owned a plantation near Marse Easterlin. An' Marse being curious lak he wouldn't let pa come to see ma an' us. At night he would slip over to see us an' ole Marse wuz mos' alwa's on de look out fer everything. When he would ketch him he would beat him so hard 'till we could tell which way he went back by de blood. But pa, he would keep a comin' to see us an' a takin' de beatins.[14]

Concerned that slave men's nocturnal visiting of loved ones disrupted discipline and made the men unfit for work the next day,
owners often took drastic measures to prevent it. Anna Lee, a
former slave in Tennessee, remembered the tribulations of a
man who refused to stop seeing his "woman" on a nearby plantation.

Yes I'se seen slaves in chains there on our farm. And I'se seen one
slave that had to wear a bell for ever so long. I'm telling you child, that
overseer he was sure mean to the slaves. We had to wear chains to the
field just like we were convicts if we were the least bit stubborn. That
slave he had to wear a bell because he got to slipping off at night to
see his woman. The way they fixed that bell on that negro was a big
frame fixed that would fit over his head and shoulders and the bell put
in that frame above the negro's head so he could not reach it to silence
it, but that didn't stop him from going to see his woman. He would get
some of the negroes to stuff that bell full of rags and leaves or
something to keep it from clapping, then he would leave to go see his
woman and she would meet him on the line of the two places under a
big tree and they would stay out all night and then they would not be
no account the next day. They tried every way to stop it as they were
both good hands but they finally had to sell that poor slave and that
slave's new Maser carried him to another state and I'se never did
know whatever became of that poor negro as we never did hear of him
no more.[15]

Of the masters' numerous intrusions in slave family life, none
angered slaves so much—or created as much havoc within
their own families—as the sexual violation of slave women by
slaveowners, their sons, and their agents. The children of
unions between white slaveholding men and slave women

stood as symbols of the illicit relationship, sowing discord between a master and his slaves, the master and his wife, his wife
and the slaves, and among the slaves themselves. Henry Ferry,
who served on a Virginia plantation, recounted the conse-
quences of his owner's visits to the cabin of a slave named
Martha.

Ole Marse John ain't never had no chillun by his wife. His wife was
pow'ful jealous of Martha an' never let her come near de big house,
but she didn't need to 'cause Marsa was always goin' down to the
shacks where she lived. Marse John used to treat Martha's boy, Jim,
jus' like his own son, which he was. Jim used to run all over de big
house, an' Missus didn't like it, but she didn't dare put him out. One
day de Parson come to call. He knew Marse John but didn't know
Missus Mamie. He come to de house an' Jim come runnin' down de
stairs to meet him. He took de little boy up in his arms an' rubbed his
haid, an' when Missus come, tol' her how much de boy look like his
father and mother."Course it favor its father most," de preacher say,
tryin' to be polite, "but in de eyes, de lookin' glass of de soul, I ken see
dat he's his mother's boy." Miss Mamie shooed de child away an' took
de preacher inside. Never did let on it wasn't her chile. Was pow'ful
mad 'bout it, though. Never would let dat boy in de house no' mo'.[16]

Although many children of relationships between master and
slave received privileges denied other slaves, some were stig-
matized and abused by one or both parents and their respective
communities. J. W. Terrill, the son of his owner and a slave in
DeSoto, Louisiana, suffered at his father's hand until he found
succor with a kindly aunt.

My father took me away from my mother when at age of six weeks old
and gave me to my grandmother, who was real old at the time. Jus'

befo' she died she gave me back to my father, who was my mammy's master. He was a old batchelor and run saloon and he was white, but my mammy was a Negro. He was mean to me.

Finally my father let his sister take me and raise me with her chillen. She was good to me, but befo' he let her have me he willed I must wear a bell till I was 21 year old, strapped 'round my shoulders with the bell 'bout three feet from my head in steel frame. That was for punishment for bein' born into the world a son of a white man and my mammy, a Negro slave. I wears this frame with the bell where I couldn't reach the clapper, day and night. I never knowed what it was to lay down in bed and get a good night's sleep till I was 'bout 17 year old, when my father died and my missy took the bell offen me.

Befo' my father gave me to his sister, I was tied and strapped to a tree and whipped like a beast by my father, till I was unconscious, and then left strapped to a tree all night in cold and rainy weather. My father was very mean. He and he sister brung me to Texas, to North Zulch, when I 'bout 12 year old. He brung my mammy, too, and made her come and be his mistress one night every week. He would have kilt every one of his slaves rather than see us go free, 'specially me and my mammy.

My missy was purty good to me, when my father wasn't right 'round. But he wouldn't let her give me anything to et but cornbread and water and little sweet 'taters, and jus' 'nough of that to keep me alive. I was allus hongry. My mammy had a boy called Frank Adds and a girl called Marie Adds, what she give birth to by her cullud husban', but I never got to play with them. Missy worked me on the farm and there was 'bout 100 acres and fifteen slaves to work 'em. The overseer waked us 'bout three in the mornin' and then he worked us jus' long as we could see. If we didn't get 'round fast 'nough, he chain us to a tree at night with nothin' to eat, and nex' day, if we didn't go on the run he hit us 39 licks with a belt what was 'bout three feet long an' four inches wide.

I wore the bell night and day, and my father would chain me to a tree till I nearly died from the cold and bein' so hongry. My father didn't 'lieve in church and my missy 'lieved there a Lord, but I wouldn't have 'lieved her if she try larn me 'bout 'ligion, 'cause my father tell me I wasn't any more than a damn mule. I slep' on a chair and tried to res' till my father died, and then I sang all day, 'cause I knowed I wouldn't be treated so mean. When missy took that bell offen me I thinks I in Heaven 'cause I could lie down and go to sleep. When I did I couldn't wake up for a long time and when I did wake up I'd be scairt to death I'd see my father with his whip and that old bell. I'd jump out of bed and run till I give out, for fear he'd come back and git me.[17]

No event was more disruptive for slave families than the division of slaveholdings by sale, inheritance, or other circumstances. Slaves tried as best they could to influence the outcome of such transactions and keep their families together, but rarely with much success. In a heroic effort, Robert Glenn's father, a slave in North Carolina, arranged to purchase his son with the money he had earned in "overwork" payments. But all for naught: Glenn was sold to another and carried out of state.

I was a slave before and during the Civil War. I am 87 years old. I was born Sept.16, 1850. I was born in Orange County, North Carolina near Hillsboro.

I belonged to a man named Bob Hall, he was a widower. He had three sons, Thomas, Nelson, and Lambert. He died when I was eight years old and I was put on the block and sold in Nelson Hall's yard by the son of Bob Hall. I saw my brother and sister sold on this same plantation. My mother belonged to the Halls, and father belonged to the Glenns. They sold me away from my father and mother and I was carried to the state of Kentucky. I was bought by a Negro speculator by the name of Henry Long who lived not far from Hurdles Mill in Person County. I was not allowed to tell my mother and father goodbye. I was bought and sold three times in one day.

My father's time was hired out and as he knew a trade, he had by working overtime saved up a considerable amount of money. After the speculator, Henry Long, bought me, mother went to father and pled with him to buy me from him and let the white folks hire me out. No slave could own a slave. Father got the consent and help of his owners to buy me and they asked Long to put me on the block again. Long did so and named his price but when he learned who had bid me off he backed down. Later in the day he put me on the block and named another price much higher than the price formerly set. He was asked by the white folks to name his price for his bargain and he did so. I was again put on the auction block and father bought me in, putting up the cash. Long then flew into a rage and cursed my father saying, "you damn black son of a bitch, you think you are white do you? Now just to show you are black, I will not let you have your son at any price." Father knew it was all off, mother was frantic but there was nothing they could do about it. They had to stand and see the speculator put me on his horse behind him and ride away without allowing either of them to tell me goodbye. I figure I was sold three times in one day, as the price asked was offered in each instance. Mother was told under threat of a whupping not to make any outcry when I was carried away. He took me to his home, but on the way he stopped for refreshments, at a plantation, and while he was eating and drinking, he put me into a room where two white women were spinning flax. I was given a seat across the room from where they were working. After I had sat there awhile wondering where I was going and thinking about mother and home, I went to one of the women and asked, "Missus when will I see my mother again?" She replied, "I don't know child, go and sit down." I went back to my seat and as I did so both the women stopped spinning for a moment, looked at each other, and one of them remarked. "Almightly God, this slavery business is a horrible thing. Chances are this boy will never see his mother again." This remark nearly killed me, as I began to fully realize my situation. Long, the Negro trader, soon came back, put me on his horse and finished the trip to his home. He kept me at his home awhile and then traded me to a man named William Moore who lived in Person County. Moore at this time was planning to move to Kentucky which he soon did, taking me with him. My mother found out by the "Grapevine telegraph" that I was going to be carried to Kentucky. She got permission and came to see me before they carried me off. When she started home I was allowed to go part of the way with her but they sent two Negro girls with us to insure my return. We were allowed to talk privately, but while we were doing so, the two girls stood a short distance away and watched as the marster told them when they left that if I escaped they would be whipped every day until I was caught. When the time of parting came and I had to turn back, I burst out crying loud. I was so weak from sorrow I could not walk, and the two girls who were with me took me by each arm and led me along half carrying me.[18]

A slaveholder's death often meant division for even well-established slave families, who were parceled out among heirs and creditors. The death of their mistress sent Mattie Dillworth and her sister to the auction block, where they were separated forever.

My name is Mattie Dillworth; but my marster called me Martha Ann; I wuz born a slave in Boyle county, Kentucky; my mother's named wuz Clara Knox; she died when I wuz a chile, an' wuz buried in Kentucky on de plantation with a peach tree for a head board; I b'longed to de McLains; my master's name wuz Reuben an' hiz wife wuz named Betsy; I b'longed to Miss Betsy, fur dey owned they property separate—she owned her'n and he owned his'n; dey wuz very rich an' lived on a big plantation in a big two story, or three story house; dey had lots of slaves, an' dey lived by dey own say-so.

I stay'd in de house to wait on Miss Betsy an' de gals; I had to stan' behin' Miss Betsy's chair; I had good clothes, but I didn't war no shoes, an' my feets iz got corns on dem today, fum standin'.

De house had a parlor an' a do' bell—an' here's whar I cum in; when de bell wud ring I had to go to de do' an' receive de cumpny; and sho dem to de parlor an' den go upstairs an' 'nouce who dey wanted to see; dey cum in dey horse an' carriages.

Sum time my ole mistus wu'd whup me; she kep a cow hide whup in de closet and she wu'd make me git hit; but I wu'd take so long to fin' hit she wou'd git mad; I jus' didn't want to fin' hit. The overseer didn't never whup me, and no body else, but ole Mistus. I stay'd in de house an' didn't have no hard wuk to do' if enny body had sed ennything to me 'bout workin' in de fields I'd uv slapped 'em in de face. I sho wu'd. . . .

Bimeby Miss Betsy died an' az I sed, she had her own property an' Master Reuben had to sell her property to settle wid de chilluns; dey tuk us an' put us in what dey called "de trader's yard" whar de visitors an' de speculators c'ud see us, an' den dey set a day fer to sell us; I wuz on de back po'ch when dey tol' me to cum to de block; de man puts me up on de block an' ses: "Here's a little girl 12 years old she's got de scofula (scrofula) but she's young an' will out gro' hit." Dey put

my sister on de block the same day dey did me, an' dey sol' her in
anudder direction, up de country, an' I aint never seen her to dis day.
Didn't no body buy me; I 'spose dey wuz skeered uv de scofula; dem
dat dey c'dn't sell in Kentucky, the trader decided to tak' to Mississippi
to see ef he c'ud sell; dey put us in a big 6 horse stage coach, an' bro't
us to Grenada, an' put us in a hotel 'til dey cu'd set a day to trade us
off; I wuz sol' at Coffeeville to Mr. Murry Fly; he borrowed the money
fur to buy me an' los' hiz home tryin' to pay for me; I helped in de
kitchen 'till Marster had to go to de war; I made a crop for him on hiz
fahm; hit wuz twixt Coffeeville an' Oakland.[19]

> Mary Ferguson's childhood on the Eastern Shore of Maryland
> was changed forever on the eve of the Civil War, when her
> owner sold her to slave traders. Without so much as a chance to
> say goodbye to her parents and siblings, she was taken and re-
> sold in Georgia, hundreds of miles away.

In 1860 I wuz a happy chile. I had a good ma an a good paw; one older
bruther an one older suster, an a little bruther an a baby suster, too. All
my fambly wucked in de fields, 'ceptin me and de two little uns, which
I stayed at home to mind. . . .

It wuz durin' cotton chopping time dat year (1860), a day I'll never
fergit, when de speckulataws bought me. Ma come home from the fiel'
'bout haf atter 'leven dat day an cooked a good dinner, I hopin her. O, I
never has forgot dat last dinner wid my fokes! But, some-ow, I had
felt, all de mawnin, lak sumpin was gwineter hapin'. I could jes feel it
in my bones! An' sho nough, bout de middle of the even', up rid my
young Marstar on his hoss, an' up driv two strange white mens in a
buggy. Dey hitch dere hosses an' cum in de house, which skeered me.
Den one o' de strangers said, "git yo clothers, Mary; we has bought you

frum Mr. Shorter." I c'mmenced cryin' an' beggin' Mr. Shorter to not let 'em take me away. But he say, "yes, Mary, I has sole yer, an' yer must go wid em."

Den dese strange mens, whose names I ain't never knowed, tuk me an' put me in de buggy an' driv off wid me, me hollarin' at de top o' my voice an' callin' my Ma! Den dem speculataws begin to sing loud—jes to drown out my hollerin'.

Us passed de very fiel' whar paw an' all my fokes wuz wuckin', an' I calt out as loud as I could an', as long as I could see 'em, "good-bye, Ma!" "good-bye, Ma!" But she never heared me. Naw, suh, dem white mens wuz singin' so loud Ma could'n hear me! An' she could'n see me, caze dey had me pushed down out o' sight on de floe o' de buggy.

I ain't never seed nor heared tell o' my Ma an' Paw, an' bruthers, an' susters from dat day to dis.

My new owners took me to Baltymore, whar dey had herded tergether two two-hoss wagon loads o' Niggers. All o' us Niggers was den shipped on a boat to Savannah, an' frum dar us wuz put on de cyars an' sent to Macon.

In Macon, us wuz sold out, and Doctor (W. R.) Little, of Talbotton, bought me at oxion (auction) an' tuck me home wid 'im. Den I wuz known as Mary Little, instid of Mary Shorter.[20]

> The ever-present threat of sale kept slaves ever-vigilant. When news of a slave trader's approach or an owner's plan to migrate reached the quarter, there was often nothing left to do but pray.

The master bought slaves from the slave traders what use to travel around the country. Sometimes he go to the big markets and buy a few. He didn't sell many himself. But when the slaves got a feeling there was going to be an auction they would pray. The night before the sale they would pray in their cabins. They didn't pray loud but they prayed long and you could hear the hum of voices in all the cabins down the row.[21]

> The westward expansion of cotton cultivation in the Lower South increased the vulnerability of slave families to separation by sale or their owner's relocation. During the nineteenth century, ten of thousands of slaveholders moved west in search of new opportunities, carrying with them or purchasing hundreds of thousands of slaves. The effect of westward migration on slave family life was nothing short of disastrous, as Josephine Howard learned at a early age. Born a slave on Tim Walton's plantation near Tuscaloosa, Alabama, Howard saw her father left behind when Walton moved with his slaves to Texas. Howard's mother and grandmother had endured the middle passage from Africa; her mother and she lived through an overland passage nearly as wrenching. She never saw her father again.

Lawd have mercy, I been here a thousand year, seems like. 'Course I ain't been here so long, but it seems like it when I gits to thinkin' back. It was long time since I was born, long 'fore de war. Mammy's name was Leonora and she was cook for Marse Tim Walton what had de plantation at Tuscaloosa. Dat am in Alabamy. Papa's name was Joe Tatum and he lived on de place 'jinin' ourn. Course, papa and mamy wasn't married like folks now, 'cause dem times de white folks jes' put slave men and women together like hosses or cattle.

Dey allus done tell us it am wrong to lie and steal, but why did de white folks steal my mammy and her mammy? Dey lives clost to some water, somewheres over in Africy, and de man come in a little boat to de sho' and tell dem he got presents on de big boat. Most de men am out huntin' and my mammy and her mammy gits took out to dat big

Sarah Douglas, formerly a slave in Alabama, with her husband, Sam.

boat and dey locks dem in a black hole what mammy say so black you can't see nothin'. Dat de sinfulles' stealin' dey is.

De captain keep dem locked in dat black hole till dat boat gits to Mobile and dey is put on de block and sold. Mammy is 'bout twelve year old and dey am sold to Marse Tim, but grandma dies in a month and dey puts her in de slave graveyard.

Mammy am nuss gal till she git older and den cook, and den old

W. L. Bost, formerly a slave in North Carolina.

Marse Tim puts her and papa together and she has eight chillen. I reckon Marse Tim warn't no worser dan other white folks. De nigger driver sho' whip us, with de reason and without de reason. You never knowed. If dey done took de notion dey jes' lays it on you and you can't do nothin'.

One mornin' we is all herded up and mammy am cryin' and say dey gwine to Texas, but can't take papa. He don't 'long to dem. Dat de lastes' time we ever seed papa. Us and de women am put in wagons but de men slaves am chained together and has to walk.

Siney Bonner, formerly a slave in Alabama.

Marse Tim done git a big farm up by Marshall but only live a year dere and his boys run de place. Dey jes' like day papa, work us and work us. Lawd have mercy, I hear dat call in de mornin' like it jes' jesterday. "All right, everybody out, and you better git out iffen you dont' want to feel dat bullwhip 'cross you back."

My gal I lives with don't like me to talk 'bout dem times. She say it

Richard and Drucilla Martin, formerly slaves in Tennessee.

Lucinda Davis, formerly a slave in Indian Territory and Texas.

ain't no more and it ain't good to think 'bout it. But when you has live in slave times you ain't gwine forgit dem, no, suh![22]

> Separated from his mother as a young boy in South Carolina, Caleb Craig still dreamed about her as an old man.

When I born? Christmas eve, 1851. Where 'bouts? Blackstock, S.C. Don't none of us know de day or de place we was born. Us have to take dat on faith. You know where de old Bell house, 'bove Blackstock, is? Dere's where I come to light. De old stagecoach, 'tween Charlotte and Columbia, changed hosses and stop dere but de railroad busted all dat up.

My mammy name Martha. Marse John soon give us chillun to his daughter, Miss Marion. In dat way us separated from our mammy. Her was a mighty pretty colored woman and I has visions and dreams of her, in my sleep, sometime yet. My sisters would call me Cale but her never did. Her say Caleb every time and all de time. Marse John give her to another daughter of his, Miss Nancy, de widow Thompson then, but afterwards her marry a hoss drover from Kentucky, Marse Jim Jones. I can tell you funny things 'bout him if I has time befo' I go.

Us chillun was carried down to de June place where Miss Marion and her husband, Marse Ed P. Mobley live. It was a fine house, built by old Dr. June. Marse Ed bought de plantation, for de sake of de fine house, where he want to take Miss Marion as a bride.

Dere was a whole passel of niggers in de quarter, three hundred or maybe more. I didn't count them, 'cause I couldn't count up to a hundred but I can now. Ten, Ten, double ten, forty-five, and fifteen. Don't dat make a hundred? Sho' it do.[23]

After young Mingo White had been sold away from his mother and father, other slaves accepted responsibility for nurturing him. His adoptive "mammy" became the only mother he knew. Years later, however, his birth mother returned, unleashing a rush of complex emotions.

I was born in Chester, South Carolina, but I was mos'ly raised in Alabama. . . . When I was 'bout fo' or five years old, I was loaded in a wagon wid a lot mo' people in 'hit. Whar I was boun' I don't know. Whatever become of my mammy an' pappy I don' know for a long time.

I was tol' there was a lot of slave speculators in Chester to buy some slaves for some folks in Alabama. I 'members dat I was took up on a stan' an' a lot of people come 'roun' an' felt my arms an' legs an' chist, an' ast me a lot of questions. Befo' we slaves was took to de tradin' post Ol' Marsa Crawford tol' us to tell eve'ybody what ast us if we'd ever been sick to tell 'em dat us'd never been sick in our life. Us had to tell 'em all sorts of lies for our Marsa or else take a beatin'.

I was jes' a li'l thang; tooked away from my mammy an' pappy, jes' when I needed 'em mos'. The only caren' that I had or ever knowed anything 'bout was give to me by a frein' of my pappy. His name was John White. My pappy tol' him to take care of me for him. John was a fiddler an' many a night I woke up to find myse'f 'sleep 'twix' his legs whilst he was playin' for a dance for de white folks. My pappy an' mammy was sold from each yuther too, de same time as I was sold. I use' to wonder if I had any brothers or sisters, as I had always wanted some. A few years later I foun' out I didn't have none. . . .

De nex' time dat I saw my mammy I was a great big boy. Dere was a 'oman on de place what ever'body called mammy, Selina White. One day mammy called me an' said, "Mingo, your mammy is comin'." I said,

Charlie Crump, formerly a slave in North Carolina, with an unidentified girl.

"I thought dat you was my mammy." She said, "No I ain't your mammy, yer mammy is 'way way from here." I couldn't believe dat I had anudder mammy and I never thought 'bout hit any mo'. One day I was settin' down at de barn when a wagon come up de lane. I stood 'roun' lack a chile will. When de wagon got to de house, my mammy got out an' broke and run to me an' th'owed her arms 'roun' my neck an' hug an' kiss me. I never even put my arms 'roun' her or nothin' of de sort. I

Angeline Lester, formerly a slave in Georgia.

jes' stood dar lookin' at her. She said, "Son ain't you glad to see your mammy?" I looked at her an' walked off. Mammy Selina call me an' tol' me dat I had hurt my mammy's feelin's, and dat dis 'oman was my mammy. I went off an' studied and I begins to 'member thangs. I went to Selina an' ast her how long it been sence I seen my mammy. She tol' me dat I had been 'way from her since I was jes' a li'l chile. I went to my mammy an' tol' her dat I was sorry I done what I did an' dat I would lack for her to fergit an' forgive me for de way I act when I fust saw her. After I had talked wid my real mammy, she told me of how de family had been broke up an' dat she hadn't seed my pappy sence he was sold. My mammy never would of seen me no mo' if de Lawd hadn't a been in de plan.[24]

CHAPTER

IV.

SLAVE CULTURE: "honest and fair service to the Lord and all mankind everywhere"

AFRICAN-AMERICAN CULTURE IN SLAVERY EVOLVED IN THE shadow of the masters' rule, but it was no simple reflection of the European-American culture of the owning class. Instead, it represented the slaves' deep resentment of their exploitation and attested to their aspiration for a better life founded on freedom.

On the eve of the Civil War, the slave society of the South had been more than two centuries in the making. Few slaves had personal memories of Africa, and the vast majority spoke English and worshipped the Christian God. Yet, owing to the African heritage of their forebears and their experience in bondage, slaves developed a distinctive set of beliefs and practices that were manifested in art, cuisine, dance, music, religion, and patterns of work and leisure. This cultural repertoire—articulated in ethical imperatives and conceptions of appropriate social relations—was both a resource for coping with a world they could not control and a product of their ongoing conflict with their owners. The slaves' cosmology, sacred and secular, revealed more than just a desire to escape the oppressive confines of the masters' rule; it also articulated an ideal of their own making, to give "honest and fair service to the Lord and all mankind everywhere."

Slaves fashioned their beliefs in the interstices of long days and weeks of debilitating toil, in the narrow slices of time they could claim as their own—late at night, Sundays and (if they were fortunate) Saturday evenings, and holidays such as Christmas and the Fourth of July. Often slave culture received its fullest expressions in slave cabins and in furtive places such as brush-arbor churches, clandestine schools, and other hideaways that lay beyond the wary gaze of slaveholders and their agents. At the same time, slave culture also took shape under the owners' noses: field chants and work songs were as distinctive a product of African-American life in slavery as religious spirituals, and the masters's fields were as much realms of African-American life as they were the property of European-American society. Indeed, the African-American culture of the slaves exerted a profound influence on the European-American culture of their owners and other white Southerners, as evidenced in music, cuisine, folk medicine, linguistic patterns, and other cultural forms.

Out of lives marked by hard work and oppression, Southern slaves developed a culture that prized the joyful moments to be found in even the most mundane existence, steadfastness in the face of worldly trial, and faith in the ultimate triumph of the right. It helped sustain slaves through their long captivity and prepared them to strive for a better life when freedom came at last.

> The slaves' distinctive culture developed from the slaves' distinctive experience, at the center of which was work. Recalling her youth in Tennessee, Rachel Cruze suggested how she and

her fellow slaves found pleasure and creative satisfaction not only in organized amusements such as corn-huskings and Christmas festivities but also in going about their workaday lives.

Ole Major's farm was on right level ground, but there were hills all around. The house was white and lay right along the road, with a porch running its full length both at the front and back. The front porch was a real fine one, with broad steps and nice-turned spindles, and at the time and where old Major used to sit there was a tea rose growing right up to the top of the porch. The other was the dirt porch, and the women in the kitchen used to sit there when they would be preparing vegetables for dinner.

The creek over which the spring house was built came to us from high up over the hill, and before it struck the lower level of the farm the water passed through two caves, one much higher than the other, so that the water, being shielded from sun and dust, was cold and sparkling. Sometime in summer, when some big doings meant the killing of sheep or hogs, the fresh meat would be place in the upper cave and covered with walnut leaves, and it would keep there just as though it were in a refrigerator. All the neighbors 'round about used it at times.

The spring house stood close to the big house, and here was kept the butter, cream and milk and such like that had to be kept cool. There were shelves built in it to accommodate the food in case of heavy rains. Apples and other fruits were often kept in the upper part.

My colored grandmother cooked for the hands down at the quarters. When she wanted vegetables she just sent some one up into the master's garden for it, and if she wanted meat or lard she went over to the smokehouse where every fall ole Major stored 100 to 120 hogs. There never was no stint in the food given ole Major's people.

Miss Nancy had a hen house up near the big house where she kept the chickens for the family, and then there was another group around the barn, for the hands. Sometimes Miss Nancy's chickens wouldn't get as nice and fat as the ones down at the barn; then she would go down and get some of them.

The material for the cotton clothes worn on the farm in summer was woven right in our own kitchen. We bought the raw cotton usually, but sometimes we would grow a small patch. Then we would card it, spin it and weave on the big loom in the kitchen. I have spun many a broach. They take it off and wind it on a reel, and make a great hank of thread—there would be four cuts in a hank. They would first size the thread by dipping it in some solution, and then, when it was dry, they would dye it. Dye stuffs would be gotton from the barks and roots of different trees, and with these we would be able to make red, brown and black dyes. We would then weave it into jeans, a heavy cotton for men's coats and pants, or the lighter linsey for women's clothes.

Counterpanes and coverlids were made of wool. Yes, we raised sheep—by the hundreds. The raw wool was first sent to the mill to be carded, then we would spin it into a thread, to be dyed just as the cotton was. The wool, too, would be woven into jeans for the heavier winter clothing for the men and into linsey-woolsey for the women's warmer dresses.

I can still hear the lam-lam-lamlam, lam-lam-lamlam of the big loom.

We grew flax, too, and made plough lines out of it. I reckon that was before the leather harness had come in . The flax field was so pretty. The long shoots, no thicker than a pencil, would bloom—the purtiest little pink and white flowers—and when the wind would sweep over the field it would ripple and wave like silk. When the seed appeared it was carefully picked—flax seed seemed to be precious—then, the flax would be cut down and left to dry where it fell. When the sun had dried it the outside skin would crack, and then they'd scutch it and it would fly out like feathers. Then they'd wind it on a big ball, and it would then be spun into thread by the flax wheel.

Many slaves had a wife on a neighboring farm, and Miss Nancy was always good about seeing that the men quit work at 12 o'clock on Saturday; then they'd get their selves cleaned up and go to visit their wives until Sunday night. She always sent along with each man, as a present to his wife, food of some kind. Sometimes it would be meat, or butter, or sweet potatoes, or maybe grapes—but something always sent with the man for his wife. Miss Nancy said she didn't want anyone feeding her niggers. If any of the men had truck patches they were welcome to work these on Saturday afternoons.

Saturday afternoons and Sunday nights were the times the young fellows looked about for likely mates. Gainan Macabee, who owned a large farm across the river, had a great number of lively-looking girl slaves, and all the young men in the neighborhood would make it their business to get over there if possible. Gainan he watched his girls closely—used to sit on a chair between his two houses where he could see everything—and if a skinny reedy-sort of nigger made his appearance among the young people Gainan would call him over and say, "Whose nigger are you?" The boy would tell him. Gainan would look him over and say, "Well, that's all right, but I don't want you comin' over to see my gals. You ain't good stock." And it would just be too bad for that nigger if Gainan caught him there again.

But when he saw a well-built, tall, husky man in the crowd Gainan would call him and say, "Whose nigger are you?" And when he was told he'd say, "Well, that's all right. You can come over and see my gals anytime you want. You're of good stock". . . . .

But there are heaps of pleasant thing to look back on. The week before Christmas was always a lively one, what with dances and corn huskin's in the neighborhood. I've seen many a corn huskin' at ole Major's farm when the corn would be piled as high as the house. Two sets of men would start huskin' from opposite sides of the heap. It would keep one man busy just getting the husks out of the way, and the corn would be thrown over the husker's head and filling the air like birds. The women usually had a quilting at those times, so they were pert and happy.

About midnight the huskin' would be over and plenty of food would make its appearance—roast sheep and roast hogs and many other things—and after they had their fill they would dance till morning. Things would continue lively in the neighborhood until New Year's Day, and then they got down to work—as it was that time the yearly cleaning and repairing of the farm took place.[1]

> Communal activities brought together slaves who lived and worked apart. As a privileged house servant in Mississippi, Prince Johnson spent most of his working hours in the Big House. Nevertheless, he joined the field slaves and his owner's family in the year-end festivities that marked the completion of the harvest, the birth of Jesus, and the beginning of the new year.

Nobody worked after dinner on Saturday. We took that time to scrub ourselves and our houses so as to be ready for inspection Sunday morning. Some Saturday nights we had dances. The same old fiddler played for us that played for the white folks. And could he play! When he got that old fiddle out you couldn't keep your foots still. When Christmas came that was the time of all times on that old plantation.

They don't have no such as that now. Every child brought a stocking
up to the big house to be filled. They all wanted one of Old Miss'es
stockings cause now she weighted near on to three hundred pounds.
Candy was put in piles for each person. When their names were called
they walked up and got it, and everything there was for him besides.
We didn't work on New Year's day. We could go to town or anywhere
we liked, but we didn't have no kind of celebration. The most fun a
person can have is at a "corn shucking." You have two captains and
they each choose the ones they want on their side. Then the shucking
begins. The last one I attended, the side I was on beat by three barrels.
We put our Captain on our shoulders and rode him up and down while
every body cheered and clapped their hands like the world was
coming to an end. You can't make mention of nothing good that we
didn't have to eat after the "shucking." I studies about those days now.
The big parties at the white folks house, and me all dressed up with
tallow on my face to make it shine, serving the guests.[2]

> Special occasions were marked by special rituals of leisure and
> communal engagement, but slaves also found pleasurable mo-
> ments in their nonworking hours year-round. James Bolton,
> who had been a slave in Arkansas, remembered the ordinary
> forms of recreation as well as the extraordinary ones.

What sort er tales did they tell 'mongst the slaves 'bout the Norf fo' the
war? To tell the trufe, they diden' talk much lak they does now 'bout
them sort er things. None er our nigger ever runned away, an' we
diden' no nuthin' 'bout no Norf, twel long atter freedom done come.
We visited 'roun' each others cabins at night. Ah did hyar tell 'bout the
patterollers. Folkses said that effen they cotched niggers out at night,
they 'ud give 'em "What Paddy gave the drum."

Atter supper we used to gather 'roun' an' knock tin buckets an' pans. We beat 'em like drums. Some used they fingers, an' some used sticks fer to make the drum soun's, an' mos'en allus somebuddy blowed on quills. Quills was a row er whistles made outen reeds or sometimes they made 'em outen bark. Evvy whistle in the row was a diffunt tone, an' you could play any kine er tune yer wants effen you had a good row o' quills. They sho' did soun' sweet.

Spring plowin' an' hoein' times we wukked all day Saddays, but mos 'em genully we laid offa wuk at twelve o'clock Sadday. That was dinner time. Sadday nights we played an' danced; sometimes in the cabins an' sometimes in the yahds. Effen we diden' have a big stack er fat kin'lin wood lit up to dance by, sometimes the mens an' 'omens would carry torches o' kin'lin' wood whilst they danced, an' it sho' was a sight to see. We danced the "Turkey Trot," an' "Buzzard Lope," an' how we did love to dance the "Mary Jane"! We would git in a ring an' when the music started we would begin wukkin' our footses, while we sung, "You steal mah True Love, an' Ah Steal You'en."

We never did no wuk on Sundays on our plantation. The chu'ch was 'bout nine miles from the plantation an' we all walked thar. Anybuddy too old an' feeble to walk the nine miles jes' stayed home. Kyazen Marster diden' 'low his mules used none on Sunday. All along the way niggers from other plantations 'ud jine us, an' sometimes fo' we git to the chu'ch house, they wud be forty or fifty slaves comin' erlong the road in a crowd. Preachin' genully lasted twell 'bout thee o'clock. In summer time we had dinner on the groun' at the chu'ch. How-some-ever we diden' have no barbecue like they does now. Evvybuddy cooked nuff on Sadday an' fetched it in baskets.

Chris'mas, we allus had plenny good sumtin' teat an' we all get tergether an' had lots er fun. We runned up to the big 'ouse early

Chris'mas mawnin' an' holler out, "Mawnin', Chris'mas Gif'!" Then they
give us plenny er Sandy Claus, an' 'ud go back to our cabins to have
fun twel New Years Day. We knowed Chris'mas was over an' gone
when New Years Day come, kyazen we got back to wuk that day, atter
frolickin' all Chris'mas week.

We would sing an' pray Easter Sunday and on Easter Monday we
frolicked an' danced all day long.

'Bout the mos' fun we had was at cawn shuckin's whar they put the
cawn in long piles, an' call in the folkses from the plantations nigh
'roun' to shuck it. Sometimes fo' er five hunnert head er niggers 'ud be
shuckin' cawn at one time. When the cawn all done been shucked,
they'd drink the likker the marsters give 'em, an' then frolic an' dance
from sundown to sunup. We started shuckin' cawn 'bout dinner time
an' tried to finish by sundown so we could have the whole night fer
frolic. Some years we 'ud go to ten er twelve cawn shuckin's in one
year.[3]

> As much as slaveholders saw their plantations and farms as im-
> permeable kingdoms, slaves loved to visit neighboring relatives
> and friends. Still, as Tom Holland remembered, the most inno-
> cent visit to see a wife or girlfriend was fraught with danger.

If we went off without a pass we allus went two at a time. We slipped
off when we got a chance to see young folks on some other place. The
patterrollers cotched me one night and, Lawd have mercy me, they
stretches me over a log and hits thirty-nine licks with a rawhide
loaded with rock, and every time they hit me the blood and hide done
fly. They drove me home to massa and told him and he called a old
mammy to doctor my back, and I couldn't work for four days. That

never kep' me from slippin' off 'gain, but I's more careful the next time.

We'd go and fall right in at the door of the quarters at night, so massa and the patterrollers thinks we's real tired and let us alone and not watch us. That very night we'd be plannin' to slip off somewheres to see a Negro gal or our wife, or to have a big time,'specially when the moon shine all night so we could see. It wouldn't do to have torch lights. They was 'bout all the kind of lights we had them days and if we made light, massa come to see what we're doin', and it be jus' too bad then for the stray Negro![4]

> The dangers of clandestine visiting gave special meaning to those times when the patrols were relaxed and slaves could pass freely about the countryside. Green Cumby, who grew up in Texas, remembered corn-shucking as one such moment.

De best time was when de corn shuckin' was at hand. Den you didn't have to bother with no pass to leave de plantation, and de patter rolls didn't bother you. If de patter rolls cotch you without de pass any other time, you better wish you dead, 'cause you would have yourself some trouble.

But de corn shuckin, dat was de gran' times. All de marsters and dere black boys from plantations from miles 'round would be dere. Den when we got de corn pile high as dis house, de table was spread out under de shade. All de boys dat 'long to old marster would take him on de packsaddle 'round de house, den dey bring him to de table and sit by he side; den all de boys dat 'long to Marster Bevan from another plantation take him on de packsaddle 'round and 'round de house, allus singin' and dancin', den dey puts him at de other side de table, and dey all do de same till everybody at de table, den dey have de feast.[5]

> Music was central to festive occasions like corn-huskings, but it was also interwoven into everyday life. Harriet Jones, whose slave family had been carried from North Carolina to Texas long before the Civil War, remembered the role of song and dance.

Come Christmas, Miss Ellen say, "Harriet, have de Christmas tree carry in and de holly and evergreens." Den she puts de candles on de tree and hangs de stockin's up for de white chillen and de black chillen. Nex' mornin', everybody up 'fore day and somethin' for us all, and for de men a keg of cider or wine on de back porch, so dey all have a li'l Christmas spirit.

De nex' thing am de dinner, serve in de big dinin' room, and dat dinner! De onlies' time what I ever has sich a good dinner am when I gits married and when Miss Ellen marries Mr. Johnnie. After de white folks eats, dey watches de servants have dey dinner.

Den dey has guitars and banjoes and fiddles and plays old Christmas tunes, den dat night marse and misses brung de chillun to de quarters, to see de niggers have dey dance. 'Fore de dance dey has Christmas supper, on de long table out in de yard in front de cabins, and have wild turkey or chicken and plenty good things to eat. When dey all through eatin', dey has a li'l fire front de main cabins where de dancin' gwine be. Dey moves everything out de cabin 'cept a few chairs. Next come de fiddler and banjo-er and when dey starts, de caller calls. "Heads lead off," and de first couple gits in middle de floor, and all de couples follow till de cabin full. Next he calls, "Sashay to de right, an do-si-do." Round to de right dey go, den he calls, "Swing you partners,"

and dey swing dem round twice, and so it go till daylight come, den he
sing dis song:

> It's gittin' mighty late when de Guinea hen squall,
> And you better dance now if you gwine dance a-tall
> If you don't watch out, you'll sing 'nother tune,
> For de sun rise and cotch you, if you don't go soon,
> For de stars gittin' paler and de old gray coon
> Is sittin' in de grapevine a-watchin' de moon.

Den de dance break up with de Virginny Reel, and it de end a happy
Christmas day. De old marse lets dem frolic all night and have nex'
day to git over it, 'cause its Christmas.[6]

> During long hours in the field, singing would bolster the slaves'
> collective efforts while providing an opportunity to comment
> on their lives and labor. Fannie Berry described the psychologi-
> cal and practical functions of slave work songs and after-hours
> dancing in the slave quarters "back of the big house."

I recollec' how Miss Sarah Ann hired out a bunch of niggers to de
railroad dat dey was buildin' thew de woods. Dey come down an' hired
all de niggers dat was 'roun'. Dat's how de do de wuk. Dey hire niggers
in one place an' use dem to cut down de timber an' saw it up in de ties,
den dey move on an' hire niggers hundreds of 'em in the de next place.

Well, when de railroad come to Appomatox dey hire de niggers and
Miss Sarah Ann hired her'n to 'em too. An' chile, you order hear dem
niggers singin' when dey go to wuk in de mornin'. Dey all start acomin'
from all d'rections wid dey ax on dey shoulder, an' de mist an' fog be
hangin' over de pines, an' de sun jes' breakin' cross de fields. Den de
niggers start to sing

A col' frosty mo'nin',
De niggers mighty good,
Take yo' ax upon yo' shoulder,
Nigger, TALK to de wood.

An' de woods jes' ringin' wid dis song. Hundreds of dem jes' asingin' to beat de ban'. Dey be lined up to a tree, an' dey sing dis song to mark de blows. Fust de one chop, den his pardner, an' when dey sing TALK dey all chop together; an' perty soon dey git de tree ready to fall an' dey yell "Hi" an' de niggers all scramble out de way quick 'cause you can't never tell what way a pine tree gonna fall. An' sometime dey sing it like dis:

Dis time tomorrow night,
Where will I be?
I'll be gone, gone, gone,
Down to Tennessee.

De niggers sing dis sorrowful, 'cause some niggers have been beat, or whupped, or sole away. Cose Miss Sarah Ann ain't never sole none of her niggers but ole man Derby what had hundreds 'ud sell some of his'n any time ole slavetrader come 'round.

Used to go over to de Saunders place fo' dancin'. Musta been hundred slaves over thar, an' they always had de bes' dances. Mos' times fo' de dance dey had Dennis to play de banjer. Dennis had a twisted arm, an' he couldn't do much work, but he sho' could pick dat banjer. Gals would put on dey spare dress ef dey had one, an' men would put a clean shirt on. Gals always tried to fix up fo' partyin', even ef dey ain't got nothin' but a piece of ribbon to tie in dey hair. Mos' times wear yo' shoes to de dance an' den take 'em off. Dem ole hard shoes make too much noise, an' hurt yo' feet. Couldn't do no steppin' in dem field shoes.

"[D]e corn shuckin', dat was de gran' times. All de marsters and dere black boys from plantations from miles 'round would be dere." Green Cumby, formerly a slave in Texas; pictured at Abilene, Texas. (See pages 174–75.)

Wasn't none of this sinful dancin' where yo' partner off wid man an woman squeezed up close to one another. Danced 'spectable, de slaves did, shiftin' 'round fum one partner to 'nother an' holdin' one 'nother out at arm's length.

What kind of dances? Well, dey wasn't no special name to 'em. Dere

Harriet Jones

was cuttin' de pigeons wings—dat was flippin' yo' arms an' legs roun'
an' holdin' yo' neck stiff like a bird do. Den dere was gwine to de east,
an' gwine to de west—dat was wid partners an' sometimes dey got to
kiss each other, but dey stan' back an' kiss widout wrappin' no arms
roun' like de young folks do today. An' dere was callin' de figgers an'
dat meant dat de fiddler would call de number an' all de couples got to
cut dat number.

" 'Fore de dance dey has Christmas supper, on de long table out in de yard in front de cabins. . . ." Harriet Jones, formerly a slave in North Carolina and Texas; pictured in Texas, with unidentified women. (See pages 175–76.)

Set de flo'? Dat was—well de couples would do dat in turn. Dey come up an' bend over toward each other at de waist, an' de woman put her hands on her hips an' de man roll his eyes all roun' an' grin an' dey pat de flo' wid dey feet jus' like day was puttin' it in place. Used to do dat bes' on dirt flo' so de feet could slap down hard against it. Sometimes dey would set de flo' alone—either a man or a woman. Den dey would set a glass of water on dey haid an' see how many kinds of steps dey could make widout spillin' de water.

Dancin' on de spot was de same thing as set de flo'—almos'. Jus' mean you got to stay in de circle. De fiddler would take a charred corn-cob an' draw a circle on de flo', den call one arter de odder up an' dance in de circle. Effen yo' feet tetch de edge you is out. Dat was jus' like a cake-walk, 'cause sometime dey bake a cake an' give it to de one dat did de mos' steps on de spot. No, I never did win no cake, but I was purty good at it jus' de same, I reckon.[7]

Born in Louisiana the year the Civil War began, Bob Ledbetter
carried memories of slave songs from his youth into the era of
World War II. Prodded by John and Ruby Lomax, he called some
of them to mind.

JL: Well, tell me, where were you born Uncle Bob?

BL: I was born not far from this place. Up here south, uh, west of
     here. 'Bout five miles.

JL: And how old are you?

BL: Well now, I told you 'bout, oh, they say I'm seventy something,
     two or three. My daddy tol' me I was nineteen years ol' on the
     eighteenth of December. An' tha's all I can go by.

JL: Eighteenth of December when?

BL: Well, 1880.

JL: Yeah. And you don't know to figure how much that makes you
     now?

BL: No sir. I'm a poor figurer.

JL: You told me a story or two about yourself and about your father
     as we came along. What were they?

BL: Well they, mention it so I know what you talking about an' I can
     start it over again I reckon.

JL: Well, was your father a songster like you?

BL: Nothing but ol' hymns. He was regular church man.

JL: Well what kind of songs did you sing when you were young?

BL: Well, I jus' hollered reels, jus' fiddle reels, all the time, my
     singing.

JL: Were you a fiddler youself?

BL: No sir, no sir. I couldn't make no music at all.

JL: Well you could make music with your mouth.

BL: Oh yes sir, I could do that. I sure would do that. Everywhere you
     hears me you hear me singing a song, a reel.

JL: And out in the field what did you do when you were working?

BL: Tha's what I'd do. Hollering, singing reels.

JL: And what was it you sang about, the cotton?

BL: 'Bout little Joe?

JL: Yeah.

BL: Little Joe, my Sam tol' me to pick a little cotton, the boy says don't for the seed's all rotten.

JL: Well now say it just like you did to me in the car and say it louder.

BL: [*sings*]

> My Sam told me to pick a little cotton,
> The boy says don't, the seed's all rotten.
> Get out of the way, ol' Dan Tucker,
> Come too late to get your supper.

I don' remember, I never did sing it.

JL: Well how did you tell me you used to call your sweetheart out at night?

BL: Let me see, I'm near forgot what I was to holler, what sort of holler—

JL: And holler.

BL: Jus' tell me one word of it so I'll know what you talking about.

JL: You said you didn't have any starch or soap.

BL: Yeah. [*sings*]

> No soap, no starch,
> Nobody to wash my clothes,
> Nobody to wash my clothes.

I hate to sing to anybody. My voice, it broke.

JL: Well didn't you say you used to sing that in the field too?

BL: Yeah I sing that in the fiel' too. Yes sir.

JL: Would your sweetheart be out there in the field?

BL: No, she'd be 'joining. 'Joining fields you know.

JL: Uh huh. Well what was some of the other old field hollers that you used to have?

BL: [*sings*]

> I'm going home.
>
> I'm going home.
>
> I'm going home.

That was one of them.

JL: Well when you wanted to summon a boy from across the creek way far off, how would you notify him?

BL: I just holler that holler, you hear me a-hollering. An' he'd answer me way over yonder.

JL: Well what was the holler?

BL: That same thing I was singing.

> No soap, no starch,
>
> Nobody to wash my clothes,
>
> Nobody to wash my clothes.

That same ol' holler. An' he'd answer me way out at his field.

RL: What'd he say?

BL: Well he'd sing the same thing.

JL: And how would he sing it? Sing it like he did.

BL: [*sings*]

> No soap, no starch,
>
> Nobody to wash my clothes,
>
> Nobody to wash my clothes.

An' if he took a notion then he'd say: [*sings*]

> I'm going home.
>
> I'm going home.
>
> I'm going home.

I knowed that he's coming soon as he got supper. At the white folk kitchen I looking for him.[8]

Vinnie Brunson spoke of the larger meaning of slave songs both during slave times and after.

De Bible tells how de angels shouted in heaven, so dat is where dey get de scriptures fer de dance dat is called de "Shout." De ones dat do dis does not sing, dey jes dance, dey songs are sung by de congregashun. In most cases de "shout" is done at de end of de services.

In de shoutin' song de best singers git to gether an start de song, hit moves slow at fust den gits faster an louder, as dey sing dey jine hands an make a circle, den somebody git happy an jumps out in de middle of de circles an goes to dance to de time of de singing an de clappin' of hands and feet, others jine her as de spirit moves dem, till dey all make a ring dat circles roun' an roun'. De folks in de congregashun jine de singin' an keepin' de time by pattin' de hands an feet an' hit makes a big noise an praise service.

As one crowd git's tired an quits, another starts up 'till dey all has a chance to take part in de praise service of de dance shout. De spiritual songs is sung in time to de kind of service hit is efn hit is a meetin song hit is sung fast an if hit is a funeral hit is sung slow. Dey sing "Swing Low Sweet Chariot" a heap at de praise song, an' at de funerals bof.   (Praise song fast.)

Swing low, Sweet chariot, Comin' fer ter carry me home.
Swing low, sweet chariot, comin' fer ter carry me home.
I looked over Jordan an' what did I see,
Comin' fer to carry me home?

A band of angels comin' after me,

Comin' fer to carry me home.

(Funeral slow)

Swing-low, sweet chariot, coming fer to carry me home,

Swing l-o-w, s-w-e-e-t–char-iot, C'omin' fer to carry me home.

Yes'm de nigger used to sing to nearly everything he did. Hit wuz des de way he 'spressed his feelin's an hit made him relieved, if he wuz happy, hit made him happy, if he wuz sad hit made him feel better, an so he des natcherly sings his feelin's.

De timber nigger he sings as he cuts de logs an keeps de time wid his axe. De wimmen sing as dey bend over de washtub, de cotton choppers sing as he chops de cotton. De mother sing as she rocks her baby to sleep. De cotton picker sing as he picks de cotton, an dey all sing in de meetin's an at de baptizin' an' at de funerals.

Hit is de niggers mos' joy, an his mos comfort w'en he needs all dese things. Dey sing 'bout de joys in de nex' world an de trouble in dis. Dey first jes sung de 'ligious songs, den dey commenced to sing 'bout de life here an w'en dey sang of bof' dey called dem de "Spirituals." De ole way to sing dem wuz to keep time wid the clappin of de han's an pattin' of de feet.

Dey sing dem in different ways for different occasions, at a meetin' w'en dey shouts dey sing hit joyful, an w'en they sing de same song at a funeral dey sing it slow an moanful, w'en dey sing de same song in de fiel's hit is sung, if dey work fas', quick, if dey is tired hit is sung slow. If hit is sung at Chrismas, den hit is sung gay an happy.

De days of slavery made de nigger live his life over in de "spirituals," most of de real ole time slaves are gone, jes a few maybe who were boys den, but dar song lives on wif bof' de white an de black folks, we forgets de sorrows an remembers de happy days jes like in de songs.[9]

Most planters issued their slaves a weekly ration of food, composed mainly of corn meal and pork, the staples of the Southern diet. But slaves aspired to more interesting fare. James Bolton recalled how slaves enriched their diet—and cured what ailed them—by tapping the bounty of the woods and streams.

Maw she went up to the big 'house wunst a week to git the 'lowance or vittuls. They 'lowanced us a week's rations at a time. Hit were genully hawg meat, cawn meal an' some times a little flour. Maw, she done our cookin' on the coals in the fire place at our cabin. We had plenty er 'possums, an' rabbits, an' fishes, an' some times we had wile tukkeys an' partridges. Slaves woan 'spozen to go huntin' at night, an' evvybuddy know you kyan' ketch no 'possums 'ceppin at night. Jes the same, we had plenny 'possums, an' no buddy ax' how we cotch 'em. Now 'bout them rabbits! Slaves woan lowed to have no guns an' no dawgs er they own. All the dawgs on our plantation b'longed to mah employer, Ah means, to mah marster, an' he 'lowed us to use his dawgs to run down the rabbits. Nigger mens an' boys 'ud go in crowds, sometimes as many as twelve at one time, an' a rabbit ain' got no chanct 'ginst a lot er niggers an' dawgs, when they light out fer to run 'im down. Whut wile critters we wannid to eat an' coulden' run down, we was right smart 'bout ketchin' in traps. We cotch lots er wile tukkeys an' partridges in traps an' nets. Long Crick runned thoo' our plantation an' the river woan' no fur piece off. We sho' did ketch the fishes, mos'ly cats, an' perch, an heaps an' heaps of suckers. We cotch our fishes mos'en genually with hook an' line, but the cyarpenters on our plantation knowed how to make basket traps that sho' nuff did lay in the fishes. Gawd only knows how long it had been since this ole nigger pulled a big shad outer the river. Ain' no shads been cotch in the river 'round' hyar in so long ah disremembahs when."

We diden' have no gyardens er our own 'roun' our cabins. Mah employer, Ah means, mah marster, had one big gyarden fer our whole plantation, an' all his niggers had to wuk in it when-so-ever he wannid 'em to, then he give 'em all, plenny good gyarden jess for theyselves. They was collarts, an' cabbage, an' turnips, an' beets, an' english peas, an' beans, an' onions, an' they was allus some gyarlic for illments. Gyarlic was mos'ly to kyere wums. They roasted the gyarlic in the hot ashes an' squez the juice outen it, an' made the chilluns take it. Sometimes they made poultices outen gyarlic for the pneumony.

We saved a heap er bark from wile cherry, an' poplar an' black haw, an' slip'ry ellum trees, an' we dried out mullein leaves. They was all mixed an' brewed to make bitters. When-some-ever a nigger got sick, then bitters was good fer, well, Ma'am, they was good far whut ailed 'im. We tuk 'em fer rheumatiz, fer fever, an' fer the mis'ry in the stummick, an' fer mos' all sorts er sickness. Red oak bark tea was good fer so' th'oat.[10]

> In times of shortage, such as during the Civil War, slaves used their ingenuity to make something from nothing. Charley Roberts remembered how slaves on his plantation used smokehouse floorboards for a more palatable fare.

I don't know why, but I remember we didn't have salt given to us, so we went to the smoke house where there were clean boards on the floor where the salt and grease drippings would fall from the smoked hams hanging from the rafters. The boards would be soft and soaked with salt and grease. Well, we took those boards and cooked the salt and fat out of them, cooked the boards right in the bean soup. That way we got salt and the soup was good.[11]

With their owners' permission, slaves sometimes were attended by white physicians in times of serious illness. Normally, though, they did much of their doctoring themselves, often using natural products dispensed by knowledgeable fellow slaves. Julia Henderson, who had been a slave in Georgia, carried an abundance of folk medical lore into freedom.

For snakebite you tie a string jus' as tight as you kin around dere, dat will draw de poison out. You see dat keep de blood from circulatin'. Dey say das good, to dig a hole and bury de foot in it. Tobacco will kill a cotton-worm bite. I know, 'cause dey have bitten me. Tobacco good for bee sting, too. For red bugs, take salty meat grease and hit really will kill 'em, dat beat usin' kerosene! If a blue-gum person bite you, you go mad. I wouldn' let dat person get mad wid me for nuttin'—she bite me and t'would kill me or drive me mad!

Elderberry leaves good for baby rash and de bark good for fever, hit really will cure it. For warts, you take nine grains of corn and pick dat wart until it bleed and take dat corn and git dat blood on dat corn, and wrap it up and drop it in de street. Someone pick it up and dey pick it off your hand. De wart really will go way 'cause I had one and done it. 'Nother way is to steal a Irish potato and put it in yo' pocket. I seen a man done dat but he oughtn't to have let me see him steal it.

For headache, Jimpson weed is good. Jus' take it and beat it up like a poultice and tie it around de head, and t'will cure headache. Dairy vine leaves made into a poultice, hit's really good. A string around de head, knotted in front, will draw out de pain. Salt on de mole of de head will stop headache. If you got headache squeeze de head back and front or put vinegar and salt on brown paper and tie around de head.

Rheumatism kin be cured if you tie a string in knots and put some kerosene on it and turpentine, and tie it around yo' knee. I have done

dis. Hit's good to war brass if you got rheumatism, I had Frank
wearing brass around his wais'.

For kernels I have taken de jawbone of a hog and taken de marrow
and put it on de karnels, unless sometimes it be so big you have to go
to de doctor. I always try what I knows first and if hit don't work, I go
to a doctor. . . .

But ever'thing I have told you I have tried out, . . . and dey is really
good. Das de reason I kin tell it. . . .

For corn on de toe, . . . I have tried kerosene. For star (sty) on de
eye, dey told me to go to a cross-road and say: "Star, Star, go away, if
you please!" It went away. Jus' dat one time I did dat, yes'em, it went
away.

For sore eyes breast milk is good, and salt and water. If you git
onjon (onion) juice in you' eyes, look in de water and dat will draw it
out. I work in onjon two days, and didn' git it in my eyes a-tall.

A person was staying wid me, she had fits. Dey based (bathed) her
in water, pure cold water, and if I wasn' dere, dey would jus' thow it
over her. Das de onlies' thing to do for fits.

For measles, cornshuck tea is good. Mommer, she use dis here goat
pills—made tea out of it and let 'em drink it. It tas' bad but we had to
take what mommer give us. Put sugar in it to keep it from tastin' so
bad.

For mumps, fresh marrow fum de hog's jaw (jowl) will cure 'em.
For swellings you boil mullein and pine tar and rub de swelling. Rusty
nail water didn't help much. For fever and swelling a poultice of cow
manure mixed with water and salt is good.

When I had indigestion, I git me some black draught powder fum de
drug store and takes a pinch of powder for nine mornings. For cramps
I wars a brass ring on my finger or my wrist. Chicken manure tea is
good for scarlet fever, you sweeten' it jus' a little bit. When you get

tetter-rash dus go out dere and ketch de dew and rub it over yo' face
but you don't wash it off. If you got worms, take peach leaves and beat
it in a poultice and bind it around your stomick and it will turn 'em
back downwards. I have done tried dat. Peach leaves is good for
constipation, too. You just cook de sallie (salad) and eat it. I have done
it many a time, hit's fine. You put on de sallie leaves and parboil it, den
take it up and put it in hot grease and fry it. And pokeberry wine is so
pretty, and fine for rheumatism—I already told you 'bout dat
one. . . .

Sulphur in yo' pocket keep you from gettin' it [*small pox*]. You won't
hardly pick up no kind of germs if you got sulphur on you. I always
heard if you hang onjon up in yo' house, it keep down fever, and I have
tried it. When persons got smallpox, buzzard's grease is de bes'—stew
it up in lard and take de fat. . . .

When de half-moon stands straight up in de sky . . . it's draining
water. If it lay down on its back it will be clear a long time. When de
sunset go down behind a cloud it goin' rain and if a whole lot of little
sprangles is round de sun, hit drawing water. Sun-dogs mean rain. I
seen 'em week befo' last. Hit's kind of hazy-lookin', shady white and
red, shaped like a dog. Whirl-winds comin' down de road is sign of
rain.[12]

> Medicines were not the only tonic for what ailed former slaves;
> religion served that purpose, too. Slaves' faith buoyed their spir-
> its and fostered a vision of a better life, both here and in the
> hereafter. Religious meetings were also joyous social occa-
> sions. Clara C. Young recalled how meetings brought together
> slaves from all over her Mississippi neighborhood.

We worked hard in de fiel' all day, but when dark come we would all
go to de quarters an' afte' supper we would set 'roun' an' sing an' talk.

Mos' of de time we had good food to eat 'cause mos' of us had our
gardens, an' de quarters cook would fix what we wanted if we brung it
to her. Durin' de last years 'fo de surrender, we didn' have much to eat
tho' an' made out de best we could.

De mos' fun we had was at our meetin's. We had dem mos' ever'
Sunday an' dey lasted way into de night. De preacher I laked de bes'
was name Mathew Swing. He was a comely nigger, black as night, an'
he sho' could read out of his han'. He neber larned no real readin' an'
writin' but he sho' knowed his Bible and would hol' his han' out an'
mak lak he was readin' an' preach de purtiest preachin' you ever
heered. De meetin's last frum early in de mawnin' 'til late at night.
When dark come, de men folks would hang up a wash pot, bottom
up'ards, in de little brush church-house us had, so's it would catch de
noise an' de oberseer couldn' hear us singin' an' shoutin'. Dey didn'
min' us meetin' in de day time, but dey thought iffen we stayed up ha'f
de night we wouldn' work so hard de nex' day—an' dat was de truf.

You should'a seen some of de niggers get 'ligion. De best way was to
carry 'em to de cemetary an' let 'em stand ober a grave. Dey would
start singin' an' shoutin' 'bout seein' fire an' brimstone; den dey would
sing some mo' an' look plum sanctified.

When us had our big meetin's, dere would allus be some darkies
frum de plantations aroun' to come. Dey would have to slip off 'cause
dey marsters was afraid dey would git hitched up wid some other
black boy er gal on de other plantation an' den dey would either have
to buy or sell a nigger 'fo you could git any work out of him.[13]

During the nineteenth century, as growing numbers of slaves
accepted Jesus Christ, Christianity became a central institution
in the slave community. While slaves, like their white co-
worshippers, embraced Jesus for many reasons, they under-

stood that their owners had their own reasons for promoting Christianity in the quarter. Beverly Jones, who had been a slave in Virginia, recalled that white ministers preached to slaves a gospel carefully tailored to meet the needs of a slaveholding society. It emphasized obedience to earthly masters while placing faith in heavenly ones. Slaves received the catechism skeptically.

On Sundays they would let us go to church up at Sassafras Stage, near Bethel. Was the fust church for niggers in these parts. Wasn' no white church; niggers built it an' they had a nigger preacher. 'Couse they wouldn't let us have no services lessen a white man was present. Most times the white preacher would preach, then he would set dere listenin' while the colored preacher preached. That was the law at that time. Couldn' no nigger preacher preach lessen a white man was present, an' they paid the white man what attended the colored services. Niggers had to set an' listen to the white man's sermon, but they didn' want to 'cause they knowed it by heart. Always took his text from Ephesians, the white preacher did, the part what said, "Obey your masters, be good servant."

Can' tell you how many times I done heard that text preached on. They always tell the slaves dat ef he be good, an' worked hard fo' his master, dat he would go to heaven, an' dere he gonna live a life of ease. They ain' never tell him he gonna be free in Heaven. You see, they didn't want slaves to start thinkin' 'bout freedom, even in Heaven.[14]

Richard Carruthers remembered how slaves interpreted a white preacher's injunction against theft.

If they didn't provishun you right on Saturday night, you jus' had to slip around and git you a chicken. That was easy enough, but grabbin' a pig was a sure-'nuff problem. You have to cotch him by his snoot so he won't squeal and clomp down tight while you take a knife and stick him till he die. Then you take the hide and insides and put them in a sack and throw them in the crick. Some folks mought call that stealin', but it ain't stealin', is it? When you don't git 'lowanced right, you has to keep right on workin' in the field and no nigger like to work with his belly groanin'. No ma'am, the good Lord won't call that stealin', now will he?

When the white preacher come to the plantation to preach to us niggers, he pick up his Bible and claim he gitting the text right out fo'm the good book, and he preach: "The good Lord say: 'Don't you niggers steal chickens fo'm your missus. Don't you niggers steal your marster's hogs.'" And that would be all he preach.[15]

> The skeptical view of their owners' religion produced an incisive critique of slavery. Jeff Calhoun described how one slave, himself a plantation preacher, countered his owner's accusation of theft with his own understanding of biblical doctrine.

Uncle Billy wuz our preachah and de garden tendah, Uncle Billy got in trouble once. He didn't like collads and de missus had three big fine collads in de garden and she all time after Billy to take good care of dese collads. So'es one Sattidy night aftah church Billy slips out and cuts dem down. De next mornin de cook wuz sent to de garden fer vegetables and some of dese collads fer de mistress but de wuz gone, de cook hurries to de house and tells de missus. She tells marster, he come in mad and say who done dis, de girl dat is de cook says Billy done it case he don't like collards. He says to get Billy to come here. Billy come to de house marster says Billy you preachah? Billy say yas sah. He says, Billy you'se cut dem collads, Billy says yas sah, I'se got some greens. He says now Billy you preachah, git me de Bible and he reads, Thou shall not steal, den he handed Billy de Bible and sayd read dis. [H]e shore hates to, but Marster makes him do it, den he shore tares loose on Billy bout stealin. [F]inally Billy says now marster I can show you in de Bible where I did not steal. [H]e tells Billy to find it and Billy finds it and reads, "You shall reap when you laborth." Marster sayd to Billy get to hell outn here.[16]

> Shang Harris of Augusta, Georgia, turned the tables on the
> slaveholders' concern about larceny among slaves.

Dey talks a heap 'bout de niggers stealin'. Well, you know what was de fust stealin' done? Hit was in Afriky, when de white folks stole de niggers jes' like you'd go get a drove o' hosses and sell 'em. Dey'd bring a steamer down dere wid a red flag, 'cause dey knowed dem folks liked red, and when dey see it dey'd follow it till dey got on de steamer. Den when it was all full o' niggers dey'd bring 'em over here and sell 'em.[17]

> Dissatisfied with the preaching of the white ministry and eager
> to worship in their own way, slaves frequently retreated to hid-
> den churches of their own making. Often these were little more
> than clearings in the woods, but the advantages were manifest.
> Religious gatherings at such sanctuaries, Silvia King remem-
> bered, sometimes lasted well into the night.

Mos' dat I 'members 'bout church in slavery time wuz w'en de w'ite folkses 'ud take us to dere church. Us sot in de back ob de church an' atter de big dinner on de groun', den in de afternoon, us git preached to

Mary Armstrong, formerly a slave in Missouri.

by de w'ite man. Some ob de sarbants, mos'ly de ole ones 'ud preach
ter us. An' den de black folks 'ud git off, down in de crick bottom, er in
a thic'et, an' sing an' shout an' pray. Don't know why, but de w'ite
folks sho' didn't like dem ring shouts de cullud folks had. De folks git
in er ring an' sing an' dance, an' shout; de dance is jes' a kinder shuffle,
den hit gits faster, an' faster as dey gits wa'amed up; an' dey moans an'

Martha Bradley, formerly a slave in Alabama.

shouts; an' sings, an' claps, an' dance. Some ob em gits 'zausted an'
dey drop out, an' de ring gits closer. Sometimes dey sing an' shout all
night, but at der brake ob day, de nigger gotter git ter de cabin an' git
'bout he buizness fer de day. Come brek fus an' old Marster, he gotter
know whar eberyone ob de sarbants is, an' tell 'em of de tasks fer de
day. De w'ite folks say de ring shout make de nigger loose he haid an'
dat he git all 'cited up an' be good fer nuffin' fer a week.[18]

Richard Carruthers explained the lengths slaves went to in order to pray on their own.

Us niggers used to have a prayin' ground down in the hollow and
sometime we come out of the field, between 11 and 12 at night,
scorchin' and burnin' up with nothin' to eat, and we wants to ask the
good Lawd to have mercy. He puts grease in a snuff pan or bottle and

Richard Toler, formerly a slave in Virginia.

Ank Bishop, formerly a slave in Alabama.

make a lamp. We takes a pine torch, too, and goes down in the hollow
to pray. Some gits so joyous they starts to holler loud and we has to
stop up they mouth. I see niggers git so full of the Lawd and so happy
they draps unconscious.

I kep' a eye on the niggers down in the cotton patch. Sometime they
lazy 'round and if I see the overseer comin' from the big house I sings
a song to warn 'em, so they not git whupped, and it go like this:

Hold up, hold up, American Spirit!
Hold up, hold up, H-O-O-O-O-O-O-O![19]

Young Fountain Hughes and his fellow slaves held religious
meetings not at a dedicated church building or a brush arbor,
but in one of the worshippers' homes. Speaking with Hermond
Norwood, Hughes particularly remembered the singing that
was an integral part of serving the Lord.

HN: You're not getting tired are you Uncle Fountain?
FH: No, no I ain't. I'm jus' same as at home. Jus' like I was setting in
       the house. An' I was thinking 'bout how we served the Lord
       when I come along, a boy.
HN: How was that?
FH: We would go to somebody's house. We didn' have no houses
       like they got now. We had these what they call log cabin. An'
       they have maybe one ol' colored man would be there, maybe
       he'd be as old as I am. An' he'd be the preacher. Not as old as I
       am now, but, he'd be the preacher, an' then we all sit down an'
       listen at him talk about the Lord. Well, he'd say, well, I wonder,
       sometimes you say I wonder if we'll ever be free. Well, some of
       them would say, we gonna go as' the Lord to free us. So they'd
       say, we gonna sing "One Day Shall I Ever Reach Heaven and
       One Day Shall I Fly." An' they would sing that for about a hour.
       Then next one they'd get up an' say let's sing a song, "We Gonna
       Live on Milk and Honey, Way By and By." Oh I can hear them
       singing now but I can't repeat it like I could in them days. But
       some day when I'm not hoarse, I could sing it for you, but I'm
       too hoarse now. An' then we'd sing, "I'm A-Gonna Sing Aroun'
       the Altar." Oh, I wish I could sing it for you, "I'm Gonna Sing
       Aroun' the Altar."

HN: Well I wish you could too.

                        . . . .

FH: Now, I heard, people here now sing about "Roll Jordan Roll."
       Well that's a ol' time, that's what the ol' people use' to sing in ol'
       back days.
HN: Is that "Roll Jordan Roll?"
FH: Yeah. But they don't sing it like the ol' people use' to sing it in
       them day. They sing it quite different now. An' another one they
       sing, "By an' By When the Morning Come." Well they sing that
       different too. But they're getting the ol' people's song. I hear
       them come over the radio. I know them all jus' as good as they,
       but they sing them different.
HN: Have different names to some of them, huh?
FH: Yes. Well they cut them off shorter an' all like that.[20]

> Fearful of the subversive potential of the slaves' self-organized
> religious meetings—or merely annoyed at how they left slaves
> tired and unfit for work—many owners prohibited them. Slave
> preachers were viewed with extra suspicion, and patrollers
> kept an eye out for clandestine gatherings. Ishrael Massie, him-
> self a minister, recalled the dangers black ministers faced in
> Virginia.

No, dar wuz no church fer de slaves in dem days. We went to de white
folks church to carry dinner an', after dat white preacher finish
preachin' to de white folks, he would take us niggers down in de
bushes under a tree. Dar he would preach one hour to us niggers. Ole
man Josiah Bailey wuz dis preacher—der ol'est one in Greenville
County. He had another one to come an' help him sometimes. His

Mary Rice, formerly a slave in Alabama.

name wuz preacher Owens. When Josiah Bailey died I wuz working wid his son-in-law, Collier.

Paterrollers? Yas, dar wuz plenty of 'em. I done bin to a many, many meetin' whar dey come.

In dese meetin's de preacher didn't know a letter in a book but, ya know, he preached his kind of doctrine. Dar wasn't no Bible in dem days 'cept what de white folks had an' dey won't gwine let de nigger

John Cole, formerly a slave in Georgia.

see hit—even ef he could read. Dar wuz no gwine to school. Nuthin'
of dat sort. De ole mistess started learnin' us slave chillun. As soon as
ole marster foun' hit tout, he stopped her from learnin' niggers
anything.

Lemme tell ya dis happenin' at a meetin'. Ole preacher would come
in bringing—ha, ha, ha—a long knot of lightwood. Ha! Ha! Ha! An'
he'd stick hit close to de fir' so dat de fiah draw pitch out hit. When de
paterrolers knock at de dow, 'twas already hot. Ya see, dis preacher

Fannie Moore, formerly a slave in South Carolina.

would run to the fiah place, git him a light an' take dat torch an' wave
hit back an' fo'th so dat de pitch an' fiah would be flyin' every which a
way in dese paterrollers faces—you know dat burnt 'em. Out de dow
niggers go every which a way in de dark. Dar wuz a mighty scramble
an' scuffle. Ya see, paterrollers wuz mostly after de preacher 'cause he
wuz de leader of de meetin' an' ef dey caught 'im, he knowd dar wuz a
beatin' fer 'im. De Captian of my crowd wuz Jim Bennett. Chile, he'd

slip dem shoes off an' run like de devil. I kin see him now! As far as ya'd seed him dat torch wuz a-wavin'. Ole pat a-runnin' in one direction an' he'd be in another—light misleadin'. Sometimes, yas, dey would ketch 'im but hit seldem. Dem whar didn't run out would praise God in de way we knowd. Honey, we had answer from dem prayers. God knowd in dem days we wuz servin' him best we knowd how.[21]

Laura Smalley related to John Henry Faulk a story, possibly told to her by her mother, about a slave whose clandestine praying earned him a whipping from his owner.

JHF: Did the slaves have church?

LS: I never 'member no church. Mama said, all the church they would have, be a tub, a tub of water sitting jus' like this thing is, an' that would catch your voice. An' they would have church aroun' that tub, all of them get aroun' the tub.

JHF: The old master didn' want them having church.

LS: Didn' want them having no church. No, they didn' have no church. An' ol' master come along, one of them was there, having church 'roun' the tub, an' he was down praying. An' ol' master come in, he jus' a-praying, he come in, he did, an' tol' him get up from there. He didn' get up, he jus' a-praying. An' the ol' master commence to whipping him. He quit praying an' then ask the Lord have mercy on ol' master. Say ol' master sure would hit him with a bull whip. He's holler have mercy on ol' master. Until ol' master whipped him an' he kep'—wouldn' get up, you know, when a person hit you, you flinch. He just praying for ol' master. Ol' master step back and said, "I'm good min' to kick you naked." The nigger never did stop praying. He had to go off an' leave him praying, 'cause he wouldn' stop. Well that was through the Lord, you know. That cause that.

JHF: Yeah, the Lord works a lot of things.

LS: Yes sir. 'Cause the Lord suffered him to stay down there an' get that whipping an' pray. You know, jus' keep a-praying.[22]

The slaves' religion embodied a moral code that would guide those who reached the promised land of freedom, just as it had guided their ancestors through slavery. Alice Sewell, who had been a slave in Alabama, articulated the slaves' deepest aspirations.

Dey didn't 'low us to sing on our plantation 'cause if we did we just sing ourselves happy and git to shouting and dat would settle de work, yes mam.

Day did 'low us to go to church on Sunday about two miles down de public road, and dey hired a white preacher to preach to us. He never did tell us nothing but be good servants, pick up old marse and old misses' things about de place, and don't steal no chickens or pigs and don't lie 'bout nothing. Den day baptize you and call dat, you got religion. Never did say nothing 'bout a slave dying and going to heaven. When we die, dey bury us next day and you is just like any of de other cattle dying on de place. Dat's all 'tis to it and all 'tis of you. You is just dead dat's all. De old lady dat raised my mother, she was a black mammy. She done all de burying of de niggers, said de funeral sayings by herself. She knew it by heart. . . .

We used to slip off in de woods in de old slave days on Sunday evening way down in de swamps to sing and pray to our own liking. We prayed for dis day of freedom. We come from four and five miles away to pray together to God dat if we don't live to see it, do please let our chillun live to see a better day and be free, so dat dey can give honest and fair service to de Lord and all mankind everywhere. And we'd sing "Our little meetins 'bout to break, chillun we must part. We got to part in body, but hope not in mind. Our little meetin's bound to break." Den we used to sing "We walk about and shake hands, fare you well my sisters I am going home."[23]

> Slaveholders usually allowed their slaves to receive a measure of verbal religious instruction, but "book learning" was another matter. The laws of most slave states forbade teaching slaves to read and write, and, even where the law was silent, slaveholders made their opposition clear. Still, a handful of slaves— perhaps 5 percent of the population—secured the rudiments of literacy by the eve of the Civil War. Mandy Jones remembered how slaves in his Mississippi neighborhood learned their ABCs and then clandestinely taught other slaves.

I 'members what dey done in slave times, I was a chile but I used to set an' lissen to 'em talk. De slaves would run away sometimes, an' hide out in de big woods. Dey would dig pits, an kiver the spot wid bushes an' vines, an' mebbe lay out fer a whole year. An' dey had pit schools in slave days too. Way out in de woods, dey *was* woods den, an' de slaves would slip out o' de Quarters at night, an go to dese pits, an some niggah dat had some learnin' would have a school. De way de cullud folks would learn to read was from de white chillun. De white chilluns thought a heap of de cullud chilluns, an' when dey come out o' school wid deir books in deir han's, dey take de cullud chilluns, an' slip off somewhere an' learns de culled chilluns deir lessons, what deir teacher has jes' learned dem. Dere was a yaller slave man named Gunn, an' his young marster taught him so good, dat atter awhile he taught a pit school hisself. Dis Gunn had a boy named Henry, who learned in his daddy's pit school, an' atter de S'render, Henry Gunn had a school for de cullud chilluns. He was my onlies' teacher, but I didn' learn much, I was too big to go to school, 13 years ole, but I had to work in de fiel! We learned firs' de A B C's, den l-o-g, log, d-o-g, dog, jes' like dat, yo knows how it goes, de Blueback speller. Dey doan have 'em no more, I doan see dese cullud chilluns now, totin' em wid deir books. Henry Gunn an' his father were all yaller, an' his sisters too. I doan no what nation dey was, dey might a been Artesians, dey all come from up de Mobile Rd. I jes' didn' get to go to school much, you see I got to be a big girl right atter de S'render an' had to work in de fiel's.[24]

CHAPTER

V.

SLAVES NO MORE: CIVIL WAR AND THE COMING OF FREEDOM

ET IN MOTION BY THE SLAVEHOLDERS' DESIRE TO PRE-serve slavery, the Civil War ended with the liberation of four million American slaves. Although their owners sought to keep them ignorant of the events that fueled the great conflict, sooner or later slaves came to understand that the war was about them and that their future hinged on its outcome. They identified with the Union cause, equating Northern success with their own liberation, although the Union's paramount leaders initially denied the connection and insisted that they fought only for national unity. Ultimately, the slaves' view prevailed: by New Year's Day 1863, when President Abraham Lincoln issued the Emancipation Proclamation, the war for Union had indeed become a war for liberty.

Slaves and former slaves played a pivotal role in securing Union victory and destroying slavery. By escaping their owners, they undermined the Confederate war effort; by working inside federal lines, they advanced the Union cause; and by serving in the Union army and navy, they assured the federal army's battlefield triumph. The vast majority of the Union's 200,000 black soldiers and sailors had been slaves. Their enlistment assured their freedom and helped to liberate enslaved relatives, friends, and neighbors.

Yet for every slave who ran away and joined the war for freedom, several remained behind Confederate lines. Mobilization for war profoundly affected the lives of these slaves. When slaveholding men marched off to war—sometimes taking with them body servants, cooks, and valets—they often left their plantations and farms in the hands of old men, women, younger sons, and overseers. The absence of large numbers of white men who had managed Southern agriculture and disciplined slave laborers enabled some slaves to escape bondage and sometimes allowed those who remained to redefine its terms in their favor. Yet the stress of war also induced those who took control of the plantations and farms to ratchet up discipline and work slaves harder and longer than ever before. If the war opened avenues to freedom, it also created new trials for slaves. Slaveholders unable to control their slaves often sold them or "refugeed" them to remote areas for safekeeping, breaking up families and communities. Like their owners, slaves also suffered from the devastation by the contending armies and from war-induced shortages of food and other necessities.

Freedom came, but it came slowly and unevenly. For most slaves, the prospect for freedom improved as the Union army neared. The arrival of federal soldiers typically spelled the end of bondage in the areas they occupied; conversely, in regions that were remote from blue-clad troops, slaveowners tended to be more successful in holding on to what remained of slavery. In large stretches of the Confederacy, most notably Texas, the freedom promised by Lincoln's proclamation did not become a reality until months after the fighting had ended and the Confederacy had surrendered.

Barney Alford, an ex-slave from Mississippi, recalled the differing response of slaveholders and slaves, first to the prospect of war and then to its reality.

Dey sed de big war wus comin' an' sed de south culdnt be beat, an' men wud cum to de big house an' stan' round under de trees an' prop deir foot up on de roots uf de trees an' dey wud stan' dar an' talk about how quick de war wud be ober.

Sum uf de slaves wud git to gedder at night time, an' go down by de crick an' pray for to be sot free. Sumtimes udder slaves from udder plantations wud cum an' jine in de prayin'. I never went down dar, fur I wus 'sleep at dat time.

One day Marse Edwin rode away on one uf his fine hosses, an' Mistiss, she cried an' cried an' sed he wus gone an' maybe git kilt. Sum uf de slaves wanted ole man Abe to whip de south an' sum uf dem was for de south beatin', but all uf 'em wanted to be sot free. Dey jes' didnt want to wurk under a whup; dey all wanted to be free to cum an' go when dey wanted.

Den one day I heard hoss feet an' I seed de Yankees cumin' up de big road, an' dey cum right up to de gate an' ast my Mistiss to give dem sumthing to eat. She tole dem she had nuffin; dey jes' laughed an' went to de smoke house an' busted open de door an' tuk all our meat an' sugar an' flour an' tuk it wid 'em. Den dey tuck de two fine hosses dat Marse loved so much, but dey bothered nuffin in de big house; an' my Mistiss, she cried an' cried.

But dem Yankees went down to de gin an' sot fire to it wid all dé cotton an' burnt it up. Sum uf de slaves went wid dem Yankees an' dey tuck two uf ole Marse mules an' day never cum back.

One day ole Marse cum home to stay an' he looked mi'ty sad. One day he rung de big bell an' had all de darkies to cum to de house an' told dem dey wus freed. He tole dem if dey wud stay wid him dat year he wud contract wuf dem; sum uf 'em left right den, an' sum uf 'em stayed on. My mammy stayed on an' I stayed wid her, an' den ole Marse paid me fur sum wurk, but he paid me mi'ty lil'l.

While de war wus going on I had to help shuck corn an' dey put it in bog bags an' put de bags on de mules an' me an' ole Tobe had to ride dem mules way down in Louisiana to a mill an' bring back de meal. We wus gone all day.

Afte' de war wus ober me an' mammy stayed on wid ole Marse fur nigh on to five years, an' he got so he culdnt pay me fur my wurk an' den I went to de Great Eastern saw mill out from Osyka an' hired to Mr. Joe Bridewell, an' he put me to skinnin' logs fore dey went to de saw. He give me a dollar a day, an' I sho' wus happy. I stayed at dat mill an' wurk fur nigh 'bout four years when de mill burnt down.

When de slaves wus sot free, dey had nuffin an' ole Marse didnt give 'em anything. All uf us had a mi'ty hard time.[1]

> When slaveholders and their allies sought to inculcate slaves with pro-Confederate sentiments, slaves received the message skeptically while keeping their own counsel. William H. Adams, a "spiritualist preacher and healer" in the 1930s, remembered how slaves in his Texas neighborhood reacted to the teachings of a white preacher more than seventy years before.

De slaves didn' have no church den, but dey'd take a big sugar kettle and turn it top down on de groun' and put logs roun' it to kill de soun'. Dey'd pray to be free and sing and dance.

When war come dey come and got de slaves from all de plantations and tuk 'em to build de breastworks. I saw lots of soldiers. Dey'd sing a song dat go something like dis:

"Jeff Davis rode a big white hoss,
Lincoln rode a mule;
Jeff Davis is our President,
Lincoln is a fool."

I 'member when de slaves would run away. Ole John Ballinger, he had a bunch of dogs and he'd take after runaway niggers. Sometimes de dogs didn' ketch de nigger. Den ole Ballinger, he'd cuss and kick de dogs.

We didn' have to have a pass but on other plantations dey did, or de paddlerollers would git you and whip you. Dey wus de poor white folks dat didn' have no slaves. We didn' call 'em white folks dem days. No, suh, we called dem "Buskrys."

Jus' fore de war, a white preacher he come to us slaves and says: "Do you wan' to keep you homes whar you git all to eat, and raise your chillen, or do you wan' to be free to roam roun', without a home, like de wil' animals? If you wan' to keep you homes you better pray fer de South to win. All dey wan's to pray for de South to win, raise the hand." We all raised our hands 'cause we was skeered not to, but we sho' didn' wan' de South to win.

Dat night all de slaves had a meetin' down in de hollow. Ole Uncle Mack, he gits up and says: "One time over in Virginny dere was two ole niggers, Uncle Bob and Uncle Tom. Dey was mad at one 'nuther and one day dey decided to have a dinner and bury de hatchet. So dey sat down, and when Uncle Bob wasn't lookin' Uncle Tom put some poison in Uncle Bob's food, but he saw it and when Uncle Tom wasn't lookin', Uncle Bob he turned de tray roun' on Uncle Tom, and he gits

de poison food." Uncle Mack, he says: "Dat's what we slaves is gwine
do, jus' turn de tray roun' and pray for de North to win."

After de war dere was a lot of excitement 'mong de niggers. Dey
was rejoicin' and singin'. Some of 'em looked puzzled, sorter skeered
like. But dey danced and had a big jamboree.[2]

> Sold away from her parents as a child, Katie Phoenix lived a
> solitary life as the sole slave of her mistress. Having little con-
> tact with other slaves, she initially saw the war through her se-
> cessionist owner's eyes. Later, she reached a different
> conclusion.

Mrs. Harris lived alone in a big house. I was the only slave she had.
There was no other children, white or black. Once, I remembers her
granddaughter comes and dat was the first time I knew there was
another child in the world than me. I had a idea I weren't a child: I
thought I was just littler, but as old as grown-ups. I didn't know people
had grown up from children.

It didn't seem as how I had the straight of nothing. I knew I was
unhappy, but I thought everythin' was like dat. I didn't knowed there
was happiness for nobody—me, nor nobody. When I got whipped I
thought that was jus' a part of being alive. I didn't take it like it was my
special punishment jus' comin' to me.

I slep' in Mrs. Harris' own room on de floor. It was a dark, big house.
I now guesses she was scared to be alone asleep, but maybe it was
cose she had a fire in de room, I slep' by de fire, but in de summer I
slep' in her room too.

When de war broke I didn't know what it was for. Mrs. Harris had
three sons that was living some place away, and they went to war. Mrs.
Harris was hatin' the North and I was hatin' the North too. I thought
the North was kind of like a spider in a dream that was going to come

and wipe away de house and carry me off. When I heard about Santa
Clause that was goin' to come down the chimney, I screamed. I gets a
poker and wasn't goin' to let him in. Everythin' was like a tangled
dream jus' opposite to what I found out later it was. I believes now
Mrs. Harris liked to get me thinkin' weren't like they was. . . .
    I 'members when the end of the war came. Mrs. Harris set up a
cryin'. I cries harder than she does. I didn't know what worser was to
befall, but I thinks it was dangerous to breathe. Then I hears some
slaves shoutin' glad cose they was free. I didn't know what 'free'
meant, and I askes Mrs. Harris if I was free. She says I was free but
was goin' to repent of it. But she told me she wasn't going to whip me
any more; and she never did, cose my father came and took me away.[3]

> Owners sensed the slaves' desire for freedom, even though the
> slaves rarely dared to express it directly. Susan Snow, who had
> been a slave in Mississippi, recollected how her singing of a
> childhood ditty revealed more than she realized about the views
> of her fellow slaves.

I was born in Wilcox County, Alabama, in 1850. W. J. Snow was my old
marster. He bought my ma from a man named Jerry Casey. Venus was
her name, but dey mos'ly called her "Venie". . . .
    My ma was a black African an' she sho' was wild an' mean. She was
so mean to me I couldn' b'lieve she was my mammy. Dey couldn'
whup her widout tyin' her up firs'. Sometimes my marster would wait
'til de nex' day to git sombody to he'p tie her up, den he'd forgit to
whup 'er. Dey used to say she was a cunger [conjurer] an' dey was all
scared of 'er. But my ma was scared o' cungers, too.
    All de Niggers on de place was born in de fam'ly an' was kin 'cept
my ma. She tol' me how dey brought her from Africa. You know, like
we say "President" in dis country, well dey call him "Chief" in Africa.

Seem like de Chief made 'rangements wid some men an' dey had a big goober grabbin' for de young folks. Dey stole my ma an' some more an' brung 'em to dis country.

I don't 'member nothin' 'bout havin' no pa. You know, honey, in dem days husbands an' wives didn' b'long to de same folks. My ma say her husband was so mean dat after us lef' Alabama she didn' want to marry no more. . . .

I was raised in Jasper County. Marster bought lan' from ever'body 'roun' 'til he had a big plantation. He had niggers, horses, mules, cows, hogs, an' chickens. He was a rich man, den. . . .

I got more whuppin's den any other Nigger on de place, 'cause I was mean like my mammy. Always a-fightin' an' scratchin' wid white an' black. I was so bad Marster made me go look at de Niggers dey hung to see what dey done to a Nigger dat harm a white man.

I's gwine tell dis story on myse'f. De white chillum was a-singin' dis song:

> Jeff Davis, long an' slim,
> Whupped old Abe wid a hick'ry limb.

> Jeff Davis is a wise man, Lincoln is a fool,
> Jeff Davis rides a gray, an' Lincoln rides a mule.

I was mad anyway, so I hopped up an' sung dis one:

> Old Gen'l Pope had a shot gun,
> Filled it full o'gum,
> Killed 'em as dey come.

> Called a Union band,
> Make de Rebels un'erstan'
> To leave de lan',
> Submit to Abraham."

Old Mis' was a-standin' right b'hin' me. She grabbed up de broom an' laid it on me. She made *me* submit. I caught de feathers, don't you forgit it.

I didn't know it was wrong. I'd hear'd de Niggers sing it an' I didn' know dey was a-singin' in dey sleeves. I didn' know nothin' 'bout Abe Lincoln, but I hear'd he was a-tryin' to free de Niggers an' my mammy say she want to be free.

De young folks used to make up a heep o' songs, den. Dey'd decompose dey own songs an' sing 'em.[4]

> When Andy Anderson's owner joined the Confederate army, he left his Texas plantation in charge of an overseer who instituted a stricter regimen than the slaves had ever known. Initially pleased to be sold away from the place, Anderson soon discovered that he had exchanged one bad situation for another.

De war breaks and dat make de big change on de massa's place. He jines de army and hires a man call' Delbridge for overseer. After dat, de hell start to pop, 'cause de first thing Delbridge do is cut de rations. He weigh out de meat, three pound for de week, and he measure a peck of meal. And 'wern't enough. He half starve us niggers and he want mo' work and he start de whippin's. I guesses he starts to edumacate 'em. I guess dat Delbridge go to hell when he died, but I don't see how de debbil could stand him.

We'uns am not use' to sich and some runs off. When dey am cotched there am a whippin' at de stake. But dat Delbridge, he sold me to Massa House, in Blanco County. I's sho' glad when I'm sold, but it am short gladness; 'cause here be another man what hell be too good for. He gives me de whippin' and de scars am still on my arms and my back, too. I'll carry dem to my grave. He sends me for firewood and when I gits it loaded, de wheel hits a stump and de team jerks and dat

breaks de whippletree. So he ties me to de stake and every half hour
for four hours, dey lays ten lashes on my back. For de first couple
hours de pain am awful. I's never forgot it. Den I's stood so much pain
I not feel so much and when dey takes me loose, I's jus' 'bout half
dead. I lays in de bunk two days, gittin' over dat whippin', gittin' over
it in de body but not de heart. No, suh, I has dat in de heart till dis
day.[5]

> The war opened opportunities for slaves to escape bondage,
> especially when the Union army was stationed nearby. But run-
> ning away remained a dangerous and difficult undertaking.
> John Finnely, who had been a slave in northern Alabama,
> weighed the consequences carefully before fleeing to the feder-
> als at the age of about twelve. His subsequent wartime experi-
> ences included a stint of Union military labor and an encounter
> with a famous Tennessean in Nashville.

De war am started den for 'bout a year, or somethin' like dat, and de
Fed'rals am north of us. I hears de niggers talk 'bout it, and 'bout
runnin' 'way to freedom. I thinks and thinks 'bout gittin' freedom, and
I's gwine run off. Den I thinks of de patter rollers and what happen if
dey cotches me off de place without de pass. Den I thinks of some
joyment sich as de corn huskin' and de fights and de singin' and I don't
know what to do. I tells you one singin' but I can't sing it:

> De moonlight, a shinin' star,
> De big owl hootin' in de tree;
> O, bye, my baby, ain't you gwineter sleep,
> A-rockin' on my knee?

> Bye, my honey baby,
> A-rockin' on my knee,

Baby done gone to sleep,
Owl hush hootin' in de tree.

She gone to sleep, honey baby sleep,
A-rockin' on my, a rockin' on my knee.

Now, back to de freedom. One night 'bout ten niggers run away. De
next day we'uns hears nothin', so I says to myself, "De patters don't
cotch dem." Den I makes up my mind to go and I leaves with de chunk
of meat and cornbread and am on my way, half skeert to death. I sho'
has de eyes open and de ears forward, watchin' for de patters. I steps
off de road in de night, at sight of anything, and in de day I takes to de
woods. It takes me two days to make dat trip and jus' once de patters
pass me by. I am in de thicket watchin' dem and I's sho' dey gwine
search dat thicket, 'cause dey stops and am a-talkin' and lookin' my
way. Dey stands dere for a li'l bit and de one comes my way. Lawd
A-mighty! Dat sho' look like de end, but dat man stop and den look
and look. Den he pick up somethin' and goes back. It am a bottle and
dey all takes de drink and rides on. I's sho' in de sweat and I don't
tarry dere long.

De Yanks am camped nere Bellfound and dere's where I gits to.
'Magine my 'sprise when I finds all de ten runaway niggers am dere,
too. Dat am on a Sunday and on de Monday, de Yanks puts us on de
freight train and we goes to Stevenson, in Alabama. Dere, us put to
work buildin' breastworks. But after de few days, I gits sent to de
headquarters at Nashville, in Tennessee.

I's water toter dere for de army and dere am no fightin' at first but
'fore long dey starts de battle. Dat battle am a 'sperience for me. De
noise am awful, jus' one steady roar of de guns and de cannons. De
window glass in Nashville am all shoke out from de shakement of de
cannons. Dere am dead mens all over de ground and lots of wounded

and some cussin' and some prayin'. Some am moanin' and dis and dat
one cry for de water and, God A-mighty, I don't want any sich 'gain.
Dere am men carryin' de dead off de field, but dey can't keep up with
de cannons. I helps bury de dead and den I gits sent to Murphysboro
and dere it am jus' de same.

You knows when Abe Lincoln am shot? Well, I's in Nashville den and
it am near de end of de war and I am standin' on Broadway Street
talkin' with de sergeant when up walk a man and him shakes hands
with me and says. "I's proud to meet a brave, young fellow like you."
Dat man an Andrew Johnson and him come to be president after Abe's
dead.[6]

> Thomas Cole, separated from his mother in the aftermath of his
> master's death, dreamed as a teenager of escaping slavery, per-
> haps through the aid of Harriet Tubman or other leaders of the
> Underground Railroad. But the "free states" were a long way
> from his home in northern Alabama. The war drew freedom
> closer and gave Cole the opportunity to realize his long-planned
> exodus. Stealing away in late 1862 or early 1863, Cole headed
> north, but he never reached the free states. Taken up by Union
> soldiers in Tennessee, he was put to work as a military laborer
> and later joined the Union army, in which capacity he wit-
> nessed some of the conflict's bloodiest battles.

I might as well begin far back as I remember and tell you all about
myself. I was born over in Jackson County, in Alabama, on August 8,
1845. My mother was Elizabeth Cole, her bein' a slave of Robert Cole,
and my father was Alex Gerrand, 'cause he was John Gerrand's slave. I
was sposed to take my father's name, but he was sech a bad, ornery,
no-count sech a human, I jes' taken my old massa's name. My mother
was brung from Virginny by Massa Dr. Cole, and she nussed all his six

chillen. My sister's name was Sarah and my brother's name was Ben
and we lived in one room of the big house, and allus had a good bed to
sleep in and good thing to eat at the same table, after de white folks
gits through.

I played with Massa Cole's chillen all de time, and when I got older
he started me workin' by totin' wood and sech odd jobs, and feedin' de
hawgs. Us chillen had to pick cotton every fall. De big baskets weigh
about seventy-five to a hundred pounds, but us chillen put our pickin's
in some growed slave's basket. De growed slaves was jes' like a mule.
He work for grub and clothes, and some of dem didn't have as easier a
time as a mule, for mules was fed good and slaves was sometimes half
starved.

But Massa Cole was a smart man and a good man with it. He had
'spect for the slaves' feelin's and didn't treat dem like dumb brutes,
and 'lowed dem more privileges dan any other slaveholder round dere.
He was one of de best men I ever knows in my whole life and his wife
was jes' like him. Dey had a big, four-room log house with a big hall
down the center up and down. De logs was all peeled and de chinkin'
a diff'rent color from de logs and covered with beads. De kitchen am a
one-room house behin' de big house with de big chimney to cook on.
Dat where all de meals cooked and carry to de house.

In winter massa allus kill from three to four hundred hawgs, de two
killin's he done in November and January. Some kill and stick, some
scald and scrape, and some dress dem and cut dem up and render de
lard. Dey haul plenty hick'ry wood to de smokehouse and de men
works in shifts to keep de smoke fire goin' sev'ral days, den hangs do
meat in de meathouse. First us eat all de chitlin's, den massa begin
issuin' cut-back bones to each fam'ly, and den 'long come de spareribs,
den de middlin' or a shoulder, and by dat time he kill de second time
and dis was to go all over 'gain. Each fam'ly git de same kind of meat

each week. Iffen one git a ham, dey all git a ham. All de ears and feet was pickle and we eats dem, too. If de meat run out 'fore killin' time, us git wild turkeys or kill a beef or a goat, or git a deer.

Massa let us plant pumpkins and have a acre or two for watermelons, iffen us work dem on Saturday evenin's. Dere a orchard of 'bout five or six acres peaches and apples and he 'low us to have biscuits once a week. Yes, we had good eatin' and plenty of it den.

Massa had one big, stout, healthy lookin' slave 'bout six foot, four inches tall, what he pay $3,000 for. He bought six slaves I knows of and give good, old-time 'ligion, and us all go to shoutin' and has a good time. Dis gen'ration too dig'fied to have de old-time 'ligion.

When baptizin' comes off, it almost like goin' to de circus. People come from all over and dey all singin' songs and everybody take dere lunch and have de good time. Massa Cole went one time and den he git sick, and next summer he die. . . .

I thinks to myself, dat Mr. Anderson, de overseer, he'll give em dat cat-o-nine tails de first chance he gits, but makes up my mind he won't git de chance, 'cause I's gwine run off de first chance I gits. I didn't know how to git out of dere, but I's gwine north where dere ain't no slaveowners. In a year or so dere am 'nother overseer, Mr. Sandson, and he give me de log house and de gal to do my cookin' and sich. Dere am war talk and we 'gins gwine to de field earlier and stayin' later. Corn am haul off, cotton am haul off, hawgs and cattle am rounded up and haul off and things 'gins lookin' bad. De war am on , but us don't see none of it. But 'stead of eatin' cornbread, us eats bread out of kaffir corn and maize. We raises lots of okra and dey say it gwine be parch and grind to make coffee for white folks. Dat didn't look good either. Dat winter, 'stead of killin' three or four hundred hawgs like we allus done befo', we only done one killin' of a hundred seventy-five, and dey not all big ones, neither. When de meat supply runs low, Mr. Sandson sends some slaves to kill a deer or wild hawgs or jes' any kind of game. He never sends me in any dem bunches but I hoped he would and one day he calls me to go and says not to go off de plantation too far, but be sho' bring home some meat. Dis de chance I been wantin' so when we gits to de huntin' ground, de leader to scatter out, and I tells him, me and 'nother man goes north and make de circle round de river and meet 'bout sundown. I crosses de river and goes north. I's gwine to de free country, where dey ain't no slaves. I travels all dat day and night up de river and follows de north star. Sev'ral times I think de blood houn's am trailin' me and I gits in de big hurry. I's so tired I couldn't hardly move, but I gits in a trot.

I's hopin' and prayin' all de time I meets up with dat Harriet Tubman woman. She de cullud women what takes slaves to Canada. She allus travels de underground railroad, dey calls it, travels at night and hides out in de day. She sho' sneaks 'em out de South and I thinks she's de brave woman.

I eats all de nuts and kills a few swamp rabbits and cotches a few fish. I builds de fire and goes off 'bout half a mile and hides in de thicket till it burns down to de coals, den bakes me some fish and rabbit. I's shakin' all de times, 'fraid I'd git cotched, but I's nearly starve to death. I puts de rest de fish in my cap and travels on dat night by de north star and hides in a big thicket de nex' day and along evenin' I hears guns shootin'. I sho' am scart dis time, sho' 'nough. I's scart to come in and scart to go out, and while I's standin' dere, I hears two mens say, "Stick you hands up, boy, What you doin?" I says, "Uh-uh-uh, I dunno. You ain't gwine take me back to de plantation, is you?" Dey says, "No. Does you want to fight for de North?" I says I will, 'cause dey talks like northern men. Us walk night and day and gits in Gen Rosecran's camp and dey thunk I's de spy from de South. Dey asks me all sorts of questions and says dey'll whip me if I didn't tell 'em what I's spyin' 'bout. Fin'ly dey 'lieves me and puts me to work helpin' with de cannons. I feels 'portant den, but I didn't know what was in front of me or I 'spects I'd run off 'gain.

I helps set dem cannons on dis Chickamauga Mountain, in hidin' places. I had to go with a man and wait on him and dat cannon. First thing I knows, bang, bang, boom, things has started, and guns am shootin' faster dan you can think, and I look 'round for de way to run. But dem guns am shootin' down de hill in front of me and shootin' at me, and over me and on both sides of me. I tries to dig me a hole and git in it. All dis happen right now, and first thing I knows, de man am kickin' me and wantin' me to help him keep dat cannon loaded. Man, I didn't want no cannon, but I has to help anyway. We fit till dark and de Rebels git more men dan us, so Gen. Rosecran sends de message to Gen. Woods to come help us out. When de messenger slips off, I sho' wish it am me slippin' off, but I didn't want to see no Gen. Woods. I jes' wants to git back to dat old plantation and pick more cotton. I'd been willin' to do mos' anything to git out that mess, but I done told Gen. Rosecran I wants to fight de Rebels and he sho' was lettin' me do it. He wasn't jes' lettin' me do it, he was makin' me do it. I done got in dere and he wouldn't let me out.

White folks, dere was men layin' wantin' help, wantin' water, with blood runnin' out dem and de top or sides dere heads gone, great big holes in dem. I jes' promises de good Lawd if he jes' let me git out dat mess, I wouldn't run off no more, but I didn't know den he wasn't gwine let me out with jes' dat battle. He gwine give me plenty more, but dat battle ain't over yet, fer nex' mornin' de Rebels 'gins shootin' and killin' lots of our men, and Gen. Woods ain't come, so Gen. Rosecran orders us to 'treat, and didn't have to tell me what he said, neither. De Rebels comes after us, shootin', and we runs off and leaves dat cannon what I was with settin' on de hill, and I didn't want dat thing nohow.

We kep' hotfootin' till we gits to Chattanooga and dere is where we stops. Here comes on dem Rebel generals with de big bunch of men and gits right at top of Look Out Mountain, right clost to Chattanooga, and wouldn't let us out. I don't know jes' how long, but a long time. Lots our hosses and mules starves to death and we eats some de hosses. We all like to starve to death ourselves. Chattanooga is in de bend de Tennessee River and on Look Out Mountain, on de east, am dem Rebels and could keep up with everything we done. After a long time a Gen. Thomas gits in some way. He finds de rough trail or wagon road round de mountain 'long de river and supplies and men comes by boat up de river to dis place and comes on into Chattanooga. More Union men kep' comin' and I guess maybe six or eight generals and dey gits ready to fight. It am long late in Fall or early winter.

Dey starts climin' dis steep mountain and when us gits three-fourths de way up it an foggy and you couldn't see no place. Everything wet and de rocks am slick and dey 'gins fightin'. I 'spect some shoots dere own men, 'cause you couldn't see nothin', jes' men runnin' and de guns roarin'. Fin'ly dem Rebels fled and we gits on Look Out Mountain and takes it.

Dere a long range of hills leadin' 'way from Look Out Mountain, nearly to Missionary Ridge. Dis ridge 'longside de Chicamauga River, what am de Indian name, meanin' River of Death. Dey fights de Rebels on Orchard Knob hill and I wasn't in dat, but I's in de Missionary Ridge battle. We has to come out de timber and run 'cross a strip or openin' up de hill. Dey sho' kilt lots our men when we runs 'cross dat openin'. We runs for all we's worth and uses guns or anything we could. De Rebels turns and runs off and our soldiers turns de cannons round what we's capture, and kilt some de Rebels with dere own guns.

I never did git to where I wasn't scart when we goes into de battle. Dis de last one I's in and I's sho' glad, for I never seed de like of dead and wounded men. We picks dem up, de Rebels like de Unions, and doctors dem de bes' we could. Then I seed all the sufferin', I hopes I never lives to see 'nother war. Dey say de World War am worse but I's too old to go.

I sho' wishes lots of times I never run off from de plantation. I begs de General not to send me on any more battles, and he says I's de coward and sympathizes with de South. But I tells him I jes' could't stand to see all dem men layin' dere dyin' and hollerin' and beggin' for help and drink of water, and blood everywhere you looks. Killin' hawgs back on de plantation didn't bother me none, but dis am diff'rent.

Fin'ly de General tells me I can go back to Chattanooga and guard de supplies in camp dere and take care de wounded soldiers and prisoners. A bunch of men is with me and we has all we can do. We gits de order to send supplies to some general and it my job to help load de wagons or box cars or boats. A train of wagons leaves sometimes. We gits all dem supplies by boat, and Chattanooga am de 'stributing center. When winter comes, everybody rests awhile and waits for Spring to open. De Union general sends in some more cullud soldiers. Dere ain't been many cullud men, but de las' year de war dere am lots. De North and de South am takin' anything dey can git to win de war.

When Spring breaks and all de snow am gone, and de trees 'gins puttin' out and everything 'gins to look purty and peaceable-like, makin' you think you ought to be plowin' and plantin' a crop , dat when de fightin' starts all over 'gain, killin' men and burnin' homes and stealin' stock and food. Den dey sends me out to help clear roads and build temp'rary bridges. We walks miles on muddy gound, 'cross rivers, wadin' water up to our chins. We builds rafts and pole briges to git de mules and hosses and cannons 'cross, and up and down hills, and cuts roads through timber.

But when dey wants to battle Gen. Thomas allus leaves me in camp to tend to supplies. He calls me a coward, and I sho' glad he thunk I was. I wasn't no coward, I jes' couldn't stand to see all dem people tore to pieces. I hears 'bout de battle in a thick forest and de trees big as my body jes' shot down. I seed dat in de Missionary Ridge battle, too.

I shifts from one camp to 'nother and fin'ly gits back to Chattanooga. I bet durin' my time I handles 'nough ammunition to kill everybody in de whole United States. I seed mos' de mainest generals in de Union Army and some in de Rebel Army.[7]

> The war gave George Johnson's father, Joe, an opportunity of "pullin' a good one on his ol' master." A slave wagoner in northern Missouri, Joe Johnson had crossed the border to the free state of Iowa many times, but always returned because of his family. With the beginning of the war, he worried that this proximity to freedom would lead to his sale south. So one day, Johnson packed up his entire family and followed a familiar route—this time to freedom.

You see my dad used to haul grit to the mills all the time, most genally he had to cross the Iowa line,—that was a free state, but no one was worryin' 'bout him gettin' 'way, cause they trusted him, an' course there was all his family he'd be leavin'.

Well, then when they was forming sides for the Civil War father got wind of it that they was going to send as many of the slaves as they could further south. I reckin 'twas cause they thought 'twould be too easy for most of 'em to get away, if they staid too near the boarder of the free state line. Well, my father and another one of the slaves on the place, each one of 'em had a horse of his own. So, early one morning they dumped all of us in the wagon. There was my father and mother, and brothers and sisters, an' the other man an ' his wife an' family. Well they covered us up just like they would if we was a load of grit to keep it from gettin' wet when it rained. Well, when we got to the state line it was good day light. At the line there was a bunch of rebels standin' 'roun' an' all of 'em knowed father. Father said he got so nervous as he was drivin' through. One of the rebels said, "'Nother load of grit, hey, Joe?"

"Yeo ouh," ocd ho and on ho wont.

Well, when the ol' master discovered they had run off he come over in Iowa, after us but father had gone an' tole the union men what he'd done, and when the ol' master showed up, they told him he'd better get back cross that line. We landed in Mount Pleasant, Iowa. That's where I was brought up.[8]

> Jack Maddox gained his freedom within federal lines, but not before he had spent considerable time as a military laborer for the Confederacy in Louisiana. In that capacity, he witnessed the cruelties of war in the combat deaths of white acquaintances and the brutal killing of a Confederate deserter.

'Bout time war com 'long, I 'member them days plain. My brother and me went to haul salt from Grand Saline, in Texas. Then I's sont with mules and more niggers to work on breastworks. I heared the battle of Vicksburg, and that was somthin' to hear, Gawd knows!

Goin' home I stopped by Mrs. Anderson's place. She had a boy named Bob who deserted and was hidin' at home. Some 'federate soldiers come and say they'll burn the house down lessen he comes out. So he came out and they tied him with a rope and the other end to a saddle and went off with him trottin' 'hind the hoss. His mammy sont me followin' in the wagon. I followed thirteen mile. After a few miles I seen where he fell down and the drag signs on the ground. Then when I come to Hornage Creek I seen they'd gone through the water. I went across and after a while I found him. But you couldn't tell any of the front side of him. They'd drug the face off him. I took him home.

When I got to Tyler I seen Yankee prisoners they took at Mansfield. Richard Burns and Jimmie Lock was there. But after that when I jined the Federals I seen them all again, 'cause they 'scaped out in wheelbarrows, covered with shavin's.

I hadn't been back home long when Jedge got mad and ties my shirt over my head and beats me bloody raw, so I ran away and jined the Federals. We walked through the woods a long time, maybe two weeks, and found them by Monticello, in Arkansas. They give us hardtack and sowbelly and the first coffee I ever drank. It was June 25 and I stayed with that bunch till December of that same year. It was 1865. I went with them to San Antonio and a man named Menger had a hotel and give me a job and a glass of lager beer. First time I ever had any of that. My job was to haul down to the Yankee camp at San Pedro Springs, right by San Antonio.[9]

> George Kye, as a slave in Arkansas, also found a route to free-
> dom that ran through Confederate lines. Serving as a substitute
> for his master, Kye drove a wagon with a "sesesh" (secessionist)
> regiment until federal soldiers informed him he was as free as
> the owner on whose behalf he served.

I was born in Arkansas under Mr. Abraham Stover, on a big farm about twenty miles north of Van Buren. I was plumb grown when the Civil War come along, but I can remember back when the Cherokee Indians was in all that part of the country. . . .

When the War come along I was a grown man, and I went off to
serve because old Master was too old to go, but he had to send
somebody anyways. I served as George Stover, but every time the
sergeant would call "Abe Stover," I would answer "Here."

They had me driving a mule team wagon that Old Master furnished.
I went with the Sesesh soldiers from Van Buren to Texarkana and
back a dozen times or more. I was in the War two years, right up to the
day of freedom. We had a battle close to Texarkana and another big
one near Van Buren, but I never left Arkansas and never got a scratch.

One time in the Texarkana battle I was behind some pine trees and
the bullets cut the limbs down all over me. I dug a big hole with my
bare hands before I hardly knowed how I done it.

One time two white soldiers named Levy and Briggs come to the
wagon train and said they was hunting slaves for some purpose. Some
of us black boys got scared because we heard they was going to Squire
Mack and get a reward for catching runaways, so me and two more lit
out of there.

They took out after us and we got to a big mound in the wood and
hid. Somebody shot at me and I rolled into some bushes. He rid up and
got down to look for me but I was on t'other side of his horse and he
never did see me. When they was gone we went back to the wagons
just as the regiment was pulling out and the officer didn't say nothing.

They was eleven negro boys served in my regiment for their
masters. The first year was mighty hard because we couldn't get
enough to eat. Some ate poke greens without no grease and took
down and died.

How I knowed I was free, we was bad licked, I reckon. Anyways, we
quit fighting and a Federal soldier come up to my wagon and say:
"Whose mules?" "Abe Stover's mules," I says, and he tells me then,
"Let me tell you, black boy, you are as free now as old Abe Stover his

own self!" When he said that I jumped on top of one of them mules'
back before I knowed anything![10]

On the homefront as well as the battlefront, war created new
opportunities and new anxieties for slaves. Isaac Adams, born a
slave in southern Louisiana, recalled some of the changes that
accompanied the war in a Confederate area that fell under
Union occupation in 1862.

The first I knowed about the War coming on was when Mr. Sack had a
whole bunch of whitefolks at the Big House at a function. They didn't
talk about anything else all evening and then the next time they come
nearly all their menfolks wasn't there—just the womenfolks. It wasn't
very long till Mr. Sack went off to Houma with some other men, and
pretty soon we knew he was in the War. I don't remember ever seeing
him come home. I don't think he did until it was nearly all over.

Next thing we knowed they was Confederate soldiers riding by
pretty nearly every day in big droves. Sometimes they would come and
buy corn and wheat and hogs, but they never did take any anyhow,
like the Yankees done later on. They would pay with billets, Young
Missy called them, and she didn't send them to git them cashed but
saved them a long time, and then she got them cashed, but you
couldn't buy anything with the money she got for them.

That Confederate money she got wasn't no good. I was in Arcadia
with her at a store, and she had to pay seventy-five cents for a can of
sardines for me to eat with some bread I had, and before the War you
could get a can like that for two cents. Things was even higher then
than later on, but that's the only time I saw her buy anything.

When the Yankees got down in that country the most of the big men
paid for all the corn and meat and things they got, but some of the

little bunches of them would ride up and take hogs and things like that and just ride off. They wasn't anybody at our place but the womenfolks and the negroes. Some of Mr. Sack's women kinfolks stayed there with Young Mistress.

Along at the last the negroes on our place didn't put in much stuff—jest what they would need, and could hide from the Yankees, because they would get it all took away from them if the Yankees found out they had plenty of corn and oats.

The Yankees was mighty nice about their manners, though. They camped all around our place for a while. There was three camps of them close by at one time, but they never did come and use any of our houses or cabins. There was lots of poor whites and Cajuns that lived down below us, between us and the Gulf, and the Yankees just moved into their houses and cabins and used them to camp in.

The negroes at our place and all of them around there didn't try to get away or leave when the Yankees come in. They wasn't no place to go, anyway, so they all stayed on. But they didn't do very much work. Just enough to take care of themselves and their whitefolks.

Master Sack come home before the War was quite over. I think he had been sick, because he looked thin and old and worried. All the negroes picked up and worked mighty hard after he come home, too.

One day he went into Arcadia and come home and told us the War was over and we was all free. The negroes didn't know what to make of it, and didn't know where to go, so he told all that wanted to stay on that they could just go on like they had been and pay him shares.

About half of his negroes stayed on and he marked off land for them to farm and made arrangements with them to let them use their cabins, and let them have mules and tools. They paid him out of their shares, and some of them finally bought the mules and some of the land. But about half went on off and tried to do better somewheres else.

I didn't stay with him because I was jest a boy and he didn't need me at the house anyway.

Late in the War my Pappy belonged to a man named Sander or Zander. Might been Alexander, but the negroes called him Mr. Sander. When pappy got free he come and asked me to go with him, and I went along and lived with him. He had a share-cropper deal with Mr. Sander and I helped him work his patch. That place was just a little east of Houma, a few miles.[11]

Slaveowners strove to insulate slaves from the corrosive effects of the war, but with only limited success. Owners who lived far from Union troops stood the best chance of holding on to their slaves, for slavery collapsed wherever Northern soldiers marched. The master and mistress of Mary Anderson managed to delay the moment of truth until late in the war, when they declared their slaves free moments before the Yankees reached their North Carolina plantation. The newly freed people celebrated the occasion.

The war was begun and there were stories of fights and freedom. The news went from plantation to plantation and while the slaves acted natural and some even more polite than usual, they prayed for freedom. Then one day I heard something that sounded like thunder and missus and marster began to walk around and act queer. The grown slaves were whisperin to each other. Sometimes they gathered in little groups in the grove. Next day I heard it again, boom, boom, boom. I went and asked missus "is it going to rain?" She said, "Mary go to the ice house and bring me some pickles and preserves." I went and got them. She ate a little and gave me some. Then she said, "You run

along and play." In a day or two every body on the plantation seemed
to be disturbed and marster and missus were crying. Marster ordered
all the slaves to come to the great house at nine o'clock. Nobody was
working and slaves were walking over the grove in every direction. At
nine o'clock all the slaves gathered at the great house and marster and
missus came out on the porch and stood side by side. You could hear a
pin drap everything was so quiet. Then marster said, "good morning,"
and missus said, "Good morning, children." They were both crying.
Then marster said, "Men, women and children, you are free. You are
no longer my slaves. The Yankees will soon be here."

Marster and missus then went into the house got two large arm
chairs put them on the porch facing the avenue and sat down side by
side and remained there watching. In about an hour there was one of
the blackest clouds coming up the avenue from the main road. It was
the Yankee soldiers, they finally filled the mile long avenue reaching
from marster's house to the main Louisburg road and spread out over
the mile square grove. The mounted man dismounted. The footmen
stacked their shining guns and begun to build fires and cook. They
called the slaves, saying, "You are free." Slaves were whooping and
laughing and acting like they were crazy. Yankee soldiers were
shaking hands with the Negroes and calling them Jim, Dinah, Sarah
and asking them questions. They busted the door to the smoke house
and got all the hams. They went to the ice house and got several
barrels of brandy, and such a time. The Negroes and Yankees were
cooking and eating together. The Yankees told them to come on and
join them, they were free. Marster and missus sat on the porch and
they were so humble no Yankee bothered anything in the great house.
The slaves were awfully excited. The Yankees stayed there, cooked,
ate, drank and played music until about night, then a bugle began to
blow and you never saw such getting on horses and lining up in your

life. In a few minutes they began to march, leaving the grove which was soon as silent as a grave yard. They took marster's horses and cattle with them and joined the main army and camped just across Cypress Creek one and one half miles from my marster's place on the Louisburg Road.[12]

> The hard-driving Arkansas planter-physician who owned Katie Rowe warned his slaves that, no matter what the outcome of the war, they would not gain their freedom: he would see them dead before they would be free. Yet it was he, not they, who did not live to see their freedom.

I can set on de gallery, whar de sunlight shine bright, and sew a powerful fine seam when my grandchillun wants a special purty dress for de school doings, but I ain't worth much for nothing else I reckon.

These same old eyes seen powerful lot of tribulation in my time, and

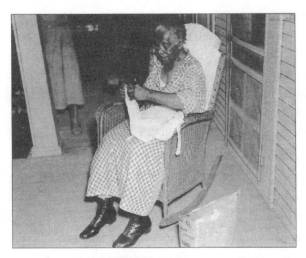

"I never forget de day we was set free!" Katie Rowe, formerly a slave in Arkansas; pictured at Tulsa, Oklahoma. (See pages 235–40.)

when I shets 'em now I can see lots of l'il chillun jest lak my
grandchillun, toting hoes bigger dan dey is, and dey pore little black
hands and legs bleeding whar dey scratched by de brambledy weeds,
and whar dey got whuppings 'cause dey didn't git out all de work de
overseer set out for 'em.

I was one of dem little slave gals my own self, and I never seen
nothing but work and tribulation till I was a grown up woman, jest
about.

De niggers had hard travelling on de plantation whar I was born and
raised, 'cause old Master live in town and jest had de overseer on de
place, but iffen he had lived out dar hisself I speck it been as bad,
'cause he was a hard driver his own self.

He git biling mad and when de Yankees have dat big battle at Pea
Ridge and scatter de 'Federates all down through our country all
bleeding and tied up and hungry, and he jest mount on his hoss and
ride out to de plantation whar we all hoeing corn.

He ride up and tell old man Saunders—dat de overseer—to bunch
us all up round de lead row man—dat my own uncle Sandy—and den
he tell us de law!

"You niggers been seeing de 'Federate soldiers coming by here
looking purty raggedy and hurt and wore out," he say, "but dat no sign
dey licked!"

"Dem Yankees ain't gwine git dis fur, but iffen dey to you all ain't
gwine git free by 'em, 'cause I gwine free you befo' dat. When dey git
here dey going find you already free, 'cause I gwine line you up on de
bank of Bois d' Arc Creek and free you wid my shotgun! Anybody miss
jest one lick wid de hoe, or one step in de line, or one clap of dat bell,
or one toot of de horn, and he gwine be free and talking to de devil
long befo' he ever see a pair of blue britches!"

Dat de way he talk to us, and dat de way he act wid us all de time.

We live in de log quarters on de plantation, not far from Washington, Arkansas, close to Bois d' Arc Creek, in de edge of de Little River bottom.

Old Master's name was Dr. Isaac Jones, and he live in de town, whar he keep four, five house niggers, but he have about 200 on de plantation, big and little, and old man Saunders oversee 'em at de time of de War. Old Mistress name was Betty, and she had a daughter name Betty about grown, and then they was three boys, Tom, Bryan, and Bob, but they was too young to go to de War. I never did see 'em but once or twice 'til after de War.

Old Master didn't go to de War, 'cause he was a doctor and de onliest one left in Washington, and purty soon he was dead anyhow.

Next fall after he ride out and tell us dat he gwine shoot us befo' he let us free he come out to see how his steam gin doing. De gin box was a little old thing 'bout as big as a bedstead, wid a long belt running through de side of de gin house out to de engine and boiler in de yard. De boiler burn cord wood, and it have a little crack in it whar de nigger ginner been trying to fix it.

Old Master come out, hopping mad 'cause de gin shet down, and ast de ginner, old Brown, what de matter. Old Brown say de boiler weak and it liable to bust, but old Master jump down off'n his hoss and go 'round to de boiler and say, "Cuss fire to your black heart! Dat boiler all right! Throw on some cordwood, cuss fire to your heart!"

Old Brown start to de wood pile grumbling to hisself and old Master stoop down to look at de boiler again, and it blow right up and him standing right dar!

Old Master was blowed all to pieces, and dey jest find little bitsy chunks of his clothes and parts of him to bury.

De wood pile blow down, and old Brown land way off in de woods, but he wasn't killed. . . .

Old man Saunders was de hardest overseer of anybody. He would
git mad and give a whipping some time and de slave wouldn't even
know what it was about. . . .

Many de time a nigger git blistered and cut up so dat we have to git
a sheet and grease it wid lard and wrap 'em up in it, and dey have to
wear a greasy cloth wrapped around dey body under de shirt for
three-four days after dey git a big whipping!

Later on in de War de Yankees come in all around us and camp, and
de overseer git sweet as honey in de comb! Nobody git a whipping all
de time de Yankees dar!

Dey come and took all de meat and corn and 'taters dey want too,
and dey tell us, "Why don't you poor darkeys take all de meat and
molasses you want? You made it and it's your's much as anybody's!"
But we know dey soon be gone, and den we git a whipping iffen we
do. Some niggers run off and went wid de Yankees, but dey had to
work jest as hard for dem, and dey didn't eat so good and often wid de
soldiers.

I never forget de day we was set free!

Dat morning we all go to de cotton field early, and den a house
nigger came out from old Mistress on a hoss and say she want de
overseer to come into town, and he leave and go in. After while de old
horn blow up at de overseer's house, and we all stop and listen, 'cause
it de wrong time of day for de horn.

We start chopping again, and dar go de horn again.

De lead row nigger holler, "Hold up!" And we all stop again. "We
better go on in. Dat our horn," he holler at de head nigger, and de head
nigger think so too, but he say he afraid we catch de devil from de
overseer iffen we quit widout him dar, and de lead row man say maybe he
back from town and blowing de horn hisself, so we line up and go in.

When we git to de quarters we see all de old ones and de chillun up in de overseer's yard, so we go on up dar. De overseer setting on de end of de gallery wid a paper in his hand, and when we all come up he say come and stand close to de gallery. Den he call off everybody's name and see we all dar.

Setting on de gallery in a hide-bottom chair was a man we never see before. He had on a big broad black hat lak de Yankees wore but it din't have no yaller string on it lak most de Yankees had, and he was in store clothes dat wasn't homespun or jeans, and dey was black. His hair was plumb gray and so was his beard, and it come way down here on his chest, but he didn't look lak he was very old, 'cause his face was kind of fleshy and healthy looking. I think we all been sold off in a bunch, and I notice some kind of smiling, and I think they sho' glad of it.

De man say, "You darkies know what day dis is?" He talk kind, and smile.

We all don't know of course, and we jest stand dar and grin. Pretty soon he ask again and de head man say, "No, we don't know."

"Well dis de fourth day of June, and dis is 1865, and I want you all to 'member de date, 'cause you allus going 'member de day. Today you is free, jest lak I is, and Mr. Saunders and your Mistress and all us white people," de man say.

"I come to tell you," he say, "and I wants to be sho' you all understand, 'cause you don't have to git up and go by de horn no more. You is your own bosses now, and you don't have to have no passes to go and come."

We never did have no passes, nohow, but we knowed lots of other niggers on other plantations got 'em.

"I wants to bless you and hope you always is happy, and tell you got all de right and lief dat any white people got," de man say, and den he git on his hoss and ride off.

We all jest watch him go on down de road, and dan we go up to Mr. Saunders and ask him what he want us to do. He jest grunt and say do lak we dam please, he reckon, but git off dat place to do it, less'n any of us wants to stay and make de crop for half of what we make.

None of us know whar to go, so we all stay, and he split up de fields and show us which part we got to work in, and we go on lak we was, and make de crop and git it in, but dey ain't no more horn after dat day. Some de niggers lazy and don't git in the field early, and dey git it took away from 'em, but dey plead around and git it back and work better de rest of dat year.[13]

> As Katie Rowe recognized, the coming of Union troops was a mixed blessing for slaves. In an interview with Hermond Norwood, Fountain Hughes underscored how the same soldiers that liberated him and his fellow slaves also left them short of food and draft animals. Nevertheless, Hughes remained adamant in his preference for even an impoverished freedom over slavery.

HN: Do you remember much about the Civil War?

FH: No, I don' remember much about it.

HN: You were a little young then I guess, huh?

FH: I remember when the Yankees come along an' took all the good horses an' throwed all the meat an' flour an' sugar an' stuff out in the river an' let it go down the river. An' they knowed the people wouldn't have nothing to live on, but they done that. An' that's the reason why I don' like to talk about it. Them people, an' if you was cooking anything to eat in there for yourself, an' if they was hungry, they would go an' eat it all up, an' we didn' get nothing. They'd just come in an' drink up all your milk. Jus' do as they please. Sometimes they be passing by all night long, walking, muddy, raining. Oh, they had a terrible time. Colored people tha's free ought to be awful thankful. An' some of them is sorry they are free now. Some of them now would rather be slaves.

HN: Which had you rather be Uncle Fountain?

FH: Me? Which I'd rather be? You know what I'd rather do? If I thought, had any idea, that I'd ever be a slave again, I'd take a gun an' jus' end it all right away. Because you're nothing but a dog. You're not a thing but a dog. Night never comed out, you had nothing to do. Time to cut tobacco, if they want you to cut all night long out in the field, you cut. An' if they want you to hang all night long, you hang tobacco. It didn' matter 'bout you tired, being tired. You're afraid to say you're tired.[14]

> The war enabled some slaves not only to seize their freedom, but also to reunite divided families. The parents of young Mary Barbour, who had long lived apart in tidewater North Carolina, joined together in their break to freedom, gaining liberty and new security for their domestic life behind Union lines. Barbour recounted the harrowing escape of her parents and siblings to New Bern and Roanoke Island, North Carolina.

I reckon dat I wuz borned in McDowell County, case dat's whar my mammy, Edith, lived. She 'longed ter Mr. Jefferson Mitchel dar, an' my pappy 'longed ter er Mr. Jordan in Avery County, so he said.

For de war, I doan know nothin' much, 'cept dat we lived on a big plantation an' dat my mammy wucked hard, but wuz treated pretty good.

We had our little log cabin off ter one side, an' my mammy had sixteen chilluns. Fas' as dey got three years old de marster sol' 'em till we las' four dat she had wid her durin' de war. I wuz de oldes' o' dese four; den dar wuz Henry an' den de twins, Liza and Charlie.

One of de fust things dat I 'members wuz my pappy wakin' me up in de middle o' de night, dressin' me in de dark, all de time tellin' me tar keep quiet. One o' de twins hollered some an' pappy put his hand ober its mouth ter keep it quiet.

Atter we wuz dressed he went outside an' peeped roun' fer a minute den he comed back an' got us. We snook out o' de house an' long de woods path, pappy totin' one of de twins an' holdin' me by de han' an' mammy carryin' de udder two.

I reckons dat I will always 'member dat walk, wid de bushes slappin' my laigs, de win' sighin' in de trees, and' de hoot owls and whippoorwhills hollerin' at each other frum de big trees. I wuz half asleep an' skeered stiff, but in a little while we pass de plum thicket an' dar am de mules an' wagin.

Dar am er quilt in de bottom o' de wagin, an' on dis dey lays we youngins. An' pappy an' mammy gits on de board cross de front an' drives off down de road.

I wuz sleepy but I wuz skeered too, so as we rides 'long I lis'ens ter pappy an' mammy talk. Pappy wuz tellin' mammy 'bout de Yankees comin' ter dere plantation, burnin' de co'n cribs, de smokehouses an' 'stroyin' eber'thing. He says right low dat dey done took marster Jordan ter de Rip Raps* down nigh Norfolk, an' dat he stol' de mules an' wagin an' 'scaped.

We wuz skeerd of de Yankees ter start wid, but de more we thinks 'bout us runnin' way frum our marsters de skeerder we gits o' de Rebs. Anyhow pappy says dat we is goin' ter jine de Yankees.

We trabels all night an' hid in de woods all day fer a long time, but

---

*A prison.

atter awhile we gits ter Doctor Dillard's place, in Chowan County. I reckons dat we stays dar seberal days.

De Yankees has tooked dis place so we stops ober, an' has a heap o' fun dancin' an' sich while we am dar. De Yankees tells pappy ter head fer New Bern and' dat we will be took keer of dar, so ter New Bern we goes.

When we gits ter New Bern de Yankees takes de mules an' wagin, dey tells pappy something, an' he puts us on a long white boat named Ocean Waves an' ter Roanoke we goes.

Later I larns dat most o' de reffes [*refugees*] is put in James City, nigh New Bern, but dar am a pretty good crowd on Roanoke. Dar wuz also a ole Indian Witch 'oman dat I 'members.

Atter a few days dar de Ocean Waves comes back an' takes all ober ter New Bern. My pappy wuz a shoemaker, so he makes Yankee boots, an' we gits 'long pretty good.[15]

> The Union army's recruitment of black soldiers, beginning in earnest in 1863, marked the transformation of the war for the Union into a war against slavery. It also opened new possibilities for slave men, who could gain freedom by enlisting—or use the threat of enlisting as a means to win privileges from their owners. This was true even in Kentucky, Missouri, and Maryland, Union slave states where the Emancipation Proclamation did not apply. A former Kentucky slave, George Conrad revisited a day from his boyhood (probably in May 1864) when every military-aged slave man left his home plantation to join the federal army.

I was born February 23, 1860 at Connersville, Harrison County, Kentucky. I was born and lived just 13 miles from Parish. My mother's name is Rachel Conrad, born at Bourbon County, Kentucky. My father, George Conrad, was born at Bourbon County Kentucky. My grandmother's name is Sallie Amos, and grandfather's name is Peter Amos. My grandfather, his old Masta freed him and he bought my grandmother, Aunt Liza and Uncle Cy. He made the money by freighting groceries from Ohio to Maysville, Kentucky.

Our Master was named Master Joe Conrad. We sometimes called him "Mos" Joe Conrad. Master Joe Conrad stayed in a big log house with weather boarding on the outside.

I was born in a log cabin. We slept in wooden beds with rope cords for slats, and the beds had curtains around them. You see my mother was the cook for the Master, and she cooked everything—chicken, roasting ears. She cooked mostly everything we have now. They didn't have stoves; they cooked in big ovens. The skillets had three legs. I can remember the first stove that we had. I guess I was about six years old.

My old Master had 900 acres of land. My father was a stiller. He made three barrels of whisky a day. Before the War whisky sold for 12½ ¢ and 13 ¢ a gallon. After the War it went up to $3 and $4 per gallon. When War broke out he had 300 barrels hid under old Master's barn.

There was 14 colored men working for old Master Joe and 7 women. I think it was on the 13th of May, all 14 of these colored men, and my father, went to the Army. When old Master Joe come to wake 'em up the next morning—I remember he called real loud, Miles, Esau, George, Frank, Arch, on down the line, and my mother told him they'd all gone to the army. Old Master went to Cynthia, Kentucky, where they had gone to enlist and begged the officer in charge to let him see all of his boys, but the officer said "No." Some way or 'nother he got a chance to see Arch, and Arch came back with him to help raise the crops.[16]

Ex-slaves' role in winning the war for the Union and destroying slavery was a point of pride among black Americans for generations to come. Julius Jones, who had been a slave in west Tennessee before enlisting in the Union army, related a mythic narrative involving President Lincoln, black soldiers, and the course of the war.

When the war came on, I must have been about fourteen years old. All the men on the place ran off and joined the northern army. I was not old enough to join, so they left me behind with the work to do. We couldn't get much news 'bout what was going on. I didn't know what the white folks heared cause they didn't let no information out. The war had been going on for two years before I seed any real action. I was ploughing in the field when I got the word to take all the mules and hide them in the swamp that the Yankees were coming. After I got them all securely hid out, I walks down to the big road to see the soldiers pass. When they came along, they stopped and made me go to the swamps and bring them every last one of them mules. That was in the year 1863, at that time the southern folks had the Yankees whipped, and they would have won that war if it hadn't been for a great man by the name of Abraham Lincoln. That man held a council right then. He 'greed to take all the colored people. Said if they fought on his side he would set them all free. When them niggers heard that free part, they all joined the army. I fought with them for two years and five months. I wasn't turned loose till 1866 we was mustared out in Baton Rouge, La. and discharged in Memphis, Tenn. We was offered land, but I didn't accept none. Mr. Lincoln was sure a wonderful man. He did what God put him here to do, took boundage off the colored people and set them free. Mr. Lee sure didn't leave no such record behind him. They tells me before he died he had a mule and a nigger

brought before him and he told the folks to protect the mule and to
keep the nigger down.[17]

Spotswood Rice, a skilled and literate Missouri slave who supervised his owner's tobacco plantation, chafed under the re-
strictions and cruelties of slavery. After repeatedly trying to
negotiate a better life for himself and his family in bondage,
Rice finally broke for freedom as a Union soldier. His daughter,
Mary Bell, told Rice's story years after his death.

I so often think of de hard times my parents had in dere slave days,
more than I feel my own hard times, because my father was not
allowed to come to see my mother but two nights a week. Dat was
Wednesday and Saturday. So often he came home all bloody from
beatings his old nigger overseer would give him. My mother would
take those bloody clothes off of him, bathe de sore places and grease
them good and wash and iron his clothes, so he could go back clean.

But once he came home bloody after a beating he did not deserve
and he run away. He scared my mother most to death because he had
run away, and she done all in her power to persuade him to go back.
He said he would die first, so he hid three days and three nights, under
houses and in the woods, looking for a chance to cross the line but de
patrollers were so hot on his trail he couldn't make it. He could see de
riders hunting him, but dey didn't see him. After three days and three
nights he was so weak and hungry, he came out and give himself up to
a nigger trader dat he knew, and begged de nigger trader to buy him
from his owner, Mr. Lewis, because Marse Lewis was so mean to him,
and de nigger trader knew how valuable he was to his owner. De
nigger trader promised him he would try to make a deal with his
owner for him, because de nigger trader wanted him. So when dey

brought father back to his owner and asked to buy him, Mr. Lewis said dere wasn't a plantation owner with money enough to pay him for Spot. Dat was my father's name, so of course that put my father back in de hands of Marse Lewis. Lewis owned a large tobacco plantation and my father was de head man on dat plantation. He cured all de tobacco, as it was brought in from the field, made all the twists and plugs of tobacco. His owner's son taught him to read, and dat made his owner so mad, because my father read de emancipation for freedom to de other slaves, and it made dem so happy, dey could not work well, and dey got so no one could manage dem, when dey found out dey were to be freed in such a short time.

Father told his owner after he found out he wouldn't sell him, dat if he whipped him again, he would run away again, and keep on running away until he made de free state land. So de nigger trader begged my father not to run away from Marse Lewis, because if he did Lewis would be a ruined man, because he did not have another man who could manage de workers as father did. So the owner knew freedom was about to be declared and my father would have de privilege of leaving whether his owner liked it or not. So Lewis knew my father knew it as well as he did, so he sat down and talked with my father about the future and promised my father if he would stay with him and ship his tobacco for him and look after all of his business on his plantation after freedom was declared, he would give him a nice house and lot for his family right on his planation. And he had such influence over de other slaves he wanted him to convince de others dat it would be better to stay with their former owner and work for him for their living dan take a chance on strangers they did not know and who did not know dem. He pleaded so hard with my father, dat father told him all right to get rid of him. But Lewis had been so mean to father, dat down in father's heart he felt Lewis did not have a spot of good in him. No place for a black man.

So father stayed just six months after dat promise and taken eleven of de best slaves on de plantation, and went to Kansas City and all of dem joined the U.S. Army. Dey enlisted de very night dey got to Kansas City and the very next morning de Pattie owners were dere on de trail after dem to take dem back home, but de officers said dey were now enlisted U.S. Soldiers and not slaves and could not be touched.[18]

> Having spent the war on a plantation in east Tennessee, an area traversed by both armies, Rachel Cruze had wartime memories aplenty and a rare gift for story-telling. Few of her tales matched the drama of an encounter between her rather indulgent master, William Holder ("Old Major"), and "Uncle Henry," a slave who enlisted in the Union army and one day returned to the estate in the course of his duties. The drama was intensified because Henry was one of the few slaves whom Holder had whipped before the war.

Ole Major said he'd do his own whipping right bravelike, but he really wasn't very successful at it. First time he tried to whip a slave was before I was born. Mamma told me the story. The slave was an old one who belonged to Miss Nancy, but instead of ole Major punishing him he whipped ole Major. And that was the end of that.

Some years after that a young boy named Sico needed punishment, and old Major set out to hold him by sticking Sico's head between his knees and hitting him with a corn stalk. Sico howled and leaned over and bit him. Then old Major he howled and called to Miss Nancy, "Take dis rascal away—he done bit me."

The third and last time for ole Major was when he set out to lick

Uncle Henry. I called all the men on the farm "Uncle." Uncle Henry was a goodlooking young fellow—carried himself straight as a stick. He had grown up with my father, William, and he was forever getting into trouble with William for stealing William's horse out of the barn at night and riding him all around the county until the pore horse would be nearly dead. William had complained and complained to ole Major and old Major had threatened to tear open Henry's back, but nothing had happened. Finally Henry brought the matter to white heat by riding the horse so hard one long night that it died as it reached its stall next morning.

The whole house then decided Henry must be whipped. William was furious and he saw to it himself that the big piece of perforated leather was fastened to the paddle. When anybody asked him what he was doing he'd mutter, "Pappy's going to lick Henry." After the leather was securely fastened on the paddle, William went over to the pump and wet the leather good. Then he filled a pan with water into which had been poured salt and pepper. This is the way a whipping like this acted; first, the back was beaten with the perforated leather thong, the perforations raising blisters which were smartly broken open with a well-handled buggy whip. Then the salt and pepper water was poured into the cuts to keep the man in lively suffering.

Well, ole Major came out to the barn, and Henry was tied up to a branch, having first been stripped to the waist. William sat by on his hunkers, whittling a piece of wood—he was always whittling. Ole Major raised the paddle and the leather thong came swishing down upon the back of the groaning Henry. A second time it cracked through the air, mingling with the age-old cry of the slave, "Pray, master." This was too much for William, who jumped up and with one slash of his sharp knife cut Henry down.

Henry just lay where he fell and groaned as he held his side. William and ole Major were beside themselves and between them they got Henry up to the house and laid him on a bed in the dining room. Miss Nancy was horrified. "Now I suppose you are satisfied since you've killed him. William run and get Dr. Sneed."

Henry's mother, Julia, had come up from the quarters, and she was frantic. Henry had never ceased groaning and holding his side, and ole Major he'd say, "Now, Henry, you mustn't die."

Dr. Sneed finally arrived and examined Henry thoroughly, then he gravely ordered some medicine to be given regularly, with complete rest. Julia followed the doctor to the door, asking him, "Doctor, is he goin' ter die?" The doctor leaned over and whispered, "Julia, there is not a damn thing the matter with Henry." And, do you know, that Henry laid up there for two weeks, right in the Major's dining room.

Henry had high ideas. Sometimes he'd walk off with old Major's gold-headed cane and strut around the neighborhood with it, putting it back the next morning before the Major was up. He had even been known to steal out with ole Major's overcoat. These, however, were easily forgiven, but, when he stole the preacher's shoes, ole Major solemnly told Miss Nancy, "I'll just have to kill that Henry after all."

The preacher was staying overnight and, as is usual, he left his shoes outside his door at bedtime to be shined. Well, Henry came along and saw the boots and proceeded to put them on for his nightly strut. His feet were much larger than those of the preacher and, by the time morning came, Henry's feet were so swollen he couldn't get the boots off. He tried and tried and, finally giving up, he threw himself on mamma's bed in the kitchen and fell asleep.

Those boots were the first things Miss Nancy saw when she came into the kitchen. Everybody tried to get the boots off but they could not be budged. So ole Major was called. That is when he told Miss Nancy, "I'll just have to kill that Henry."

Miss Nancy started to giggle, "Pears to us de preacher needs a new pair of shoes anyhow. Just look at 'em." Ole Major looked at the shoes and agreed and sent a servant down to his store for a pair. The preacher was more than delighted, and it was decided to let Henry have the old ones. . . .

Ole Major played safe with both sides during the war and, in fact, he and Miss Nancy were kind to both of them. The ole Major had both a Rebel and a Union suit, and he wore whichever seemed to be most fitting at the time. Sometime a spy would come along in advance of an army, and I'd call to ole Major, who was siting on the porch, "Major, here comes a spy," And ole Major he'd start up form his chair and bawl, "Who-o-w-a-at?" If I said, "It's a Johnny," and he was in a Rebel suit, he'd throw out his chest and prepare to greet them; but if I said, "Union," he'd sneak to his room, change into the blue uniform with its red lined cape, and come back out on the porch. As he sat down he'd throw back the corner of his blue cape to show its red lining.

Those were such purty uniforms. These drab uniforms our boys wear now—there's nothing purty about them—but the blue of those Union uniforms was a beautiful bright shade, and all the men had those lovely capes lined in red, and bell pants coming well over the foot. I tell you they were purty. The capes of the officers were decorated so as to distinguish them from the common soldiers.

Ole Major and Miss Nancy gave freely to both sides. Time and again they gave a corn field to the army who happened to be in the neighborhood—and there always seemed to be soldiers around us during those times. One time, after Miss Nancy had given a corn field to the Union boys, some of them went into another field and stole some roastin' ears from that field. The Union officers learned of it and the next morning, on parade, the one who had stolen the corn had the roastin' ears tied to his wrists and arms, and forced to march along with the other men. I was standing on the porch with ole Major, and he said, "See the one who is decorated? That's the one who stole our roastin' ears."

The house was here, and there below was the brook, and up there on a high hill was a field—Ridge Field we called it. Both the Union boys and the Johnnies camped there at times and trained new recruits there. I have seen them in a bayonet drill, when the bayonets would flash so close to the bodies of the men you would say they couldn't help going through them. And I have seen the men going along on their knees, and crawling down towards the brook, as they would have to do in ambush.

If the Rebels had won the war ole Major would have been wealthy. At the beginning of the war he had put the bulk of his money into a seegar box, and he took out a couple of small stones from the foundation of the house and said, "Now, Baby, look sharp and dig a hole inside there large enough to hide this box, and never tell anybody about this money." I was rather afraid to crawl into the darkness under the house but I did as I was told, and nobody ever knew anything about that money but ole Major and I. When the soldiers would say, "Where's the Major's money?" I'd always point to the big iron safe and say, "all the Johnny money is in there." Well, they were not looking for Johnny money, so they never bothered to open it. After the war was over, ole Major had me crawl under the house again and bring out the seegar box filled with money, but it wasn't worth anything. I used to play house with it.

I just seemed to mix up with soldiers most of the time. The Union men were at Fort Macabee, right across the river from us—it was the Holston River, I believe—and they could look right into our farm with their powerful field glasses. No, our farm did not run along the river.

Dr. Sneed's farm was between us and the river. Well, one day a man—a most foolish one—road into our yard on a white horse and proceeded toward the barn. I ran after him to see what he was going to do and, just as I got there, a cannon ball fell a few feet from me, covering the horse and rider and myself with black dirt. The outlooks at the fort across the river had recognized him as a Johnny, but seeing me follow him had thrown the ball wide just to give him warning and to save hitting me. That Johnny, when he got his breath, went lickety split down the road toward the place he had come from. The officer in charge at the fort then sent ole Major a note asking him to keep "that child" out of sight so I wouldn't get hurt.

Those 10th Michigan men at Fort Macabee were great fighters. There were 500 of them there. They were located on a hill on the Macabee farm, so that they could see an enemy coming down the hill a long way off. One time they saw a large army coming down and, knowing their little group could not expect to stand up against that long line on the hill, they sent messengers to Knoxville for reinforcements. Then some of them ran to the bridge crossing the river a little distance up stream from them and set the out side of the bridge on fire, so that by the time the troops got there it was too far gone to be used. The enemy divided its forces, some going down the stream two miles to ford across and the others going back upstream aways to do the same thing.

Well, those Michigan men saw the whole maneuver, and they turned some of their cannons to meet the approach from down stream and the rest to hold the enemy up above. Those cannons were terrible things, holding about a half bushel of powder, and then the gunners would put heavy iron log chains in, and iron pots. They waited until all the enemy down below was in the water and then they let them have the full effect of that awful blast. The river turned red with the slaughter. Then they turned their attention to the others coming downstream and let loose upon them.

The survivors left in a hurry, I tell you, and by the time the messengers returned with reinforcements the enemy had disappeared. We saw it all from the top of a hill near the house, but it was not until I grew up that I realized the full horror of that fight.

Miss Nancy even took care of the soldiers when they got sick. One time somebody told her a Union soldier—he was a twin—was took with fever. She said, "Bring him over to the dirt porch and call Dr. Sneed." The doctor decided a bleeding would let out the fever, and he slit both of the feet of the soldier. I don't know how much blood he let out, but it broke the fever and the boy got better.

Bleeding seemed to be the recognized method of dealing with fevers in those days. Dr. Sneed used to bleed the Major regularly once a year—in the spring. Ole Major would lie down on the bed with both arms extended, and the doctor would puncture the arms on the inside of the elbow joints, and I could see the blood smoking with fever as it left the arm. It always broke the Major's fever.

One day, when I was at the quarters with my colored grandmother, we heard the whine of a rifle in the nearby woods, but we didn't know it for that, and so we went into the woods to investigate. We hadn't gone very far when we came upon a Johnny, sitting upright beside a steaming kettle of stew and dog ham. He had the purtiest potato on his fork, just ready to plump it into his mouth, and there he sat, never turning his eyes, nor telling us what that noise was. But, pretty soon up came a Union sniper and he said, "I'll make him talk," and he gave the Johnny a blow that knocked him right over the ground. We knew then that he was dead because as he fell he still held that same

position. The sniper explained that he had been up in a tree and that
he caught the Johnny right in the back of the neck, paralyzing him.

Dog ham? Why, yes, when they got real hungry they'd kill dogs. He
hadn't even bothered to skin the ham, but had just drawn the skin
back from the meat of the ham and stuck the ham into the boiling
stew. Oh, but I wanted some of that stew! The grease was floating on
top of it as thick as butter. I didn't care at all about the Johnny, it
seems. My mind was all taken up with the stew.

Yes, those soldiers would get so hungry sometimes they'd eat most
anything. Uncle Henry, the young fellow who figured in the whipping
by ole Major, told me that sometimes when they were on forced
marches and perhaps had nothing but parched corn all day, they
would grab an ear of raw corn right out of a horse's mouth and eat it;
and if they came across a chicken they'd kill it, take off a few feathers
and bite into the raw meat of the bird.

Henry came back to the farm once at the head of a dozen soldiers.
He had become a recruiting officer. Now, I think they call it
drafting. . . . [W]hen you were asked to join up a bayonet was
shoved into your back and it stayed there until you were safe in the
fort.

Now ole Major was sitting in his favorite chair on the porch when he
saw Henry coming with those soldiers and he like to fell, he was that
scairt. You see, so many times the slaves had returned to kill their
masters, and poor ole Major thought Henry remembered that
whipping.

But Henry drew the men up in front of ole Major and he said, "This
is my master, Major Holden. Honor him, men." And the men took off
their caps and cheered old Major. And he nearly like to fell
again—such a great big burden was off his shoulders then.

When Henry commanded his men to stack arms, and they all

stacked their guns together in front of ole Major except one soldier, who was the lookout. The others then went into the house to see Miss Nancy; and Miss Nancy sent out to have some chickens killed, and in no time at all those men were all seated around the dining room table having a regular feast. That is, all but the one who had to watch the guns, and he was fed later.[19]

> Near the end of the war, the destructive march of Union General William T. Sherman's army struck terror among Confederates in Georgia and the Carolinas. Thousands of slaveholders fled before the federal advance—sometimes taking their slaves with them, but often leaving them behind. Slaves in the path of Sherman's legions, Lorenza Ezell remembered, improvised a song to celebrate the advent of emancipation and lampoon the flight of the "fugitive masters."

Us plantation was jes' east from Pacolet Station on Thicketty Creek, in Spartanburg County, in South Carolina. Dat near Little and Big Pacolet Rivers on de route to Limestone Springs, and it jes' a ordinary plantation with de main crops cotton and wheat.

I 'long to de Lipscombs and my mamma, Maria Ezell, she 'long to 'em too. Old Ned Lipscomb was 'mongst de oldest citizens of dat county. I's born dere on July 29th, in 1850 and I be 87 year old dis year. Levi Ezell, he my daddy, and he 'long to Landrum Ezell, a Baptist preacher. Dat young massa and de old massa, John Ezell, was de first Baptist preacher I ever heered of. He have three sons, Landrum and Judson and Bryson. Bryson have gif' for business and was right smart of a orator.

Dey's fourteen niggers on de Lipscomb place. Dey's seven of us chillen, my mamma, three uncle and three aunt and one man what

"My old massa run off and stay in de woods a whole week when Sherman men come through." Lorenza Ezell, formerly a slave in South Carolina; pictured at Beaumont, Texas. (See pages 256–58.)

wasn't no kin to us. I was oldest of de chillen, and dey called Sallie and Carrie and Alice and Jabus and Coy and Lafate and Rufus and Nelson.

When Gen'ral Sherman come 'cross de Savannah River in South Carolina, some of he sojers come right 'cross us plantation. All de neighbors have brung dey cotton and stack it in de thicket on de

Lipscomb place. Sherman men find it and sot it on fire. Dat cotton
stack was big as a little courthouse and it took two months' burnin'.

My old massa run off and stay in de woods a whole week when
Sherman men come through. He didn't need to worry, 'cause us took
care of everythin'. Dey a funny song us make up 'bout his runnin' off in
de woods. I know it was make up, 'cause my uncle have a hand in it. It
went like dis:

> White folks, have you seed old massa
> Up de road, with he mustache on?
> He pick up he hat and he leave real sudden
> And I 'lieve he's up and gone.
>
> (Chorus)
> Old massa run away
> And us darkies stay at home.
> It mus' be now dat Kingdom's comin'
> And de year of Jubilee.
>
> He look up de river and he seed dat smoke
> Where de Lincoln gunboats lay.
> He big 'nuff and he old 'nuff and he orter know better,
> But he gone and run away.
>
> Now dat overseer want to give trouble
> And trot us 'round a spell,
> But we lock him up in de smokehouse cellar,
> With de key done throwed in de well.

Right after dat I start to be boy what run mail from camp to camp
for de sojers. One time I capture by a bunch of deserters what was
hidin' in de woods, 'long Pacolet River. Dey didn't hurt me, though, but
dey mos' scare me to death. Dey parole me and turn me loose.[20]

While thousands of slaves seized wartime opportunities to flee the site of their bondage, thousands of others who were in reach of Union lines chose to remain. For some, particularly the very old and very young, the physical rigors of flight were too daunting. Other slaves feared punishment if they were recaptured or reprisals against their relatives and friends if they succeeded. Family connections, which sometimes reached into the owner's family, induced many slaves to forego chances to flee. Cato Carter of Alabama, a privileged slave who was also a nephew of his owner, Oll Carter, stood by his pledge to supervise the plantation in Carter's absence. He stayed even as large numbers of his fellow slaves fled.

When my marster and the other mens on the place went off to the war he called me and said, "Cato, you is always been a 'sponsible man and I leave you to look after the womens and the place. If I don't never come back, I want you to always stay by Miss Adeline." I said, "Befo' God I will, Mr. Oll." He said, "then I can go away peaceable."

We thought for a long time the sojers had the Federals whupped to pieces but they was plenty bad times to go through. I carried a gun and guarded the place at night time. The paddyrollers was bad. I captured them and took them to the house more times than one. They wore black caps and put black rags over their faces and was always skullduggerying around at night. We didn't use torches anymore when we went around at night 'cause we were afeared. We put out all the fires around the house at night time.

The young mens in the grey uniforms used to pass so gay and singing in the big road. Their clothes was good and they looked so fine and we used to feed them the best we had on the place. Miss Adeline would say, "Cato, they is our boys and give them the best this place 'fords." We took out the hams and the wine and we killed chickens for them. That was at first.

"[M]y marster . . . called me and said, 'Cato, you is always been a 'sponsible man and I leave you to look after the womens and the place.'" Cato Carter, formerly a slave in Alabama; pictured at Dallas, Texas. (See pages 259–62.)

Then the boys and mens in blue got to coming that way and they was fine looking mens too and Miss Adeline would cry and she would say, "Cato they is just mens and boys and we got to feed them." We had a pavilion built in the yard like they had at picnics and we fed the Federals on that. Three times the Federals said, We is going to take you with us, to me. Miss Adeline let in to crying and say to the yankee

gentlemen, "Dont take Cato. Many of my Niggers has run away to the
North but Cato is the only man I got by me now. If you take Cato I just
don't know what I will do." I tell them that so long as I live I got to stay
by Miss Adeline and that unless somebody forces me away I ain't
gwine to leave. I say, "I got no complaints to make, I want to stay by
Old Miss til' one of us die." The yankee mens say to Miss Adeline,
"Dont 'sturb yourself Miss we aint gwine to take him nor harm nothing
of yours."

The reason they was alright by us was cause we prepared for them
but with some of the folks they was rough something terrible. They
took off all their horses and their corn.

I have seen the trees bend low and shake all over and heard the roar
and the popping of cannon balls. There was springs round and about
not too far from our place and the sojers used to camp there at one of
the springs and build a fire to cook a mule 'cause they got down to
starvation and when some of the other gorillas would see the fire they
would aim to the fire and many is the time they spiled the dinner for
the sojers. The yankees did it and our boys did it too. There was killing
going on so terrible like people was dogs and some of the old ones
said it was near to the end of time 'cause of folks being so wicked.

Mr. Oll came back and all the others did too but he came back first.
He was all wore out and ragged. He stood on the front porch and
called all the Niggers to the front yard. He said, "Mens and womens
you are today as free as I am. You is free to do as you like 'cause the
damned yankees done 'creed that you are. But they aint a Nigger on
my place that was born here or ever lived here that cant stay here and
work and eat to the end of his days as long as this old place will raise
peas and goobers. Go if you wants or stay if you wants."

Some of the Niggers stayed and some went and some that had run
away to the North came back. They always called real humble like at

the back gate to Miss Adeline and she always fixed it up with Mr. Oll that they could have a place.

Near to the close of the war I seen some of the folks leaving for Texas. They said if the Federals win the war you have to live in Texas to keep the slaves. So plenty of them started driftin' their slaves to the west. They would pass with the womens riding in the wagons and the mens on foot. When some of them come back they said that it took three weeks to walk the way. Some of them took slaves to Texas even after the Federals done 'creed a breaking up.[21]

> Whenever and however it came, emancipation unleashed a torrent of emotions within the slave community. Black people greeted the dawning of freedom with joy, likening their deliverance from slavery to the biblical Jubilee. Years later, Felix Haywood of Texas recalled how the dull routine of plantation life yielded to singing, dancing, and celebration at the moment of freedom.

It's a funny thing how folks always want to know about the War. The war weren't so great as folks suppose. Sometimes you didn't knowed it was goin' on. It was the endin' of it that made the difference. That's when we all wakes up that somethin' had happened. Oh, we knowed what was goin' on in it all the time, 'cause old man Gudlow went to the post office every day and we knowed. We had papers in them days jus' like now.

But the War didn't change nothin'. We saw guns and we saw soldiers, and one member of master's family, Colmin Gudlow, was gone fightin'—somewhere. But he didn't get shot no place but one— that was in the big toe. Then there was neighbors went off to fight. Some of 'em didn't want to go. They was took away (conscription). I'm thinkin' lots of 'em pretended to want to go as soon as they had to go.

Felix Haywood

The ranch went on jus' like it always had before the war. Church
went on. Old Mew Johnson, the preacher, seen to it church went on.
The kids didn't know War was happenin'. They played marbles,
see-saw and rode. I had old Buster, a ox, and he took me about plenty
good as a horse. Nothin' was different. We got layed-onto (whipped)
time on time, but gen'rally life was good—just as good as a sweet
potato. The only misery I had was when a black spider bit me on the

"We knowed freedom was on us, but we didn't know what was to come with it." Felix Haywood, formerly a slave in Texas; pictured at San Antonio, Texas. (See pages 262–67.)

ear. It swelled up my head and stuff came out. I was plenty sick and Dr. Brennen, he took good care of me. The whites always took good care of people when they was sick. Hospitals couldn't do no better for you today. Yes, maybe it was a black widow spider, but we called it the "devil biter."

Sometimes someone would come 'long and try to get us to run up North and be free. We used to laugh at that. There wasn't no reason to *run* up North. All we had to do was to *walk*, but walk *South*, and we'd be free as soon as we crossed the Rio Grande. In Mexico you could be free. They didn't care what color you was, black, white, yellow or blue. Hundreds of slaves did go to Mexico and got on all right. We would hear about 'em and how they was goin' to be Mexicans. They brought up their children to speak only Mexican. . . .

But what I want to say is, we didn't have no idea of runnin' and escapin'. We was happy. We got our lickings, but just the same we get our fill of biscuits every time the white folks had 'em. Nobody knew how it was to lack food. I tell my chillen we didn't know no more about pants than a hawg knows about heaven; but I tells 'em that to make 'em laugh. We had all the clothes we wanted and if you wanted shoes bad enough you got 'em shoes with a brass square toe. And shirts! Mister, them was shirts that was shirts! If someone gets caught by his shirt on a limb of a tree, he had to die there if he weren't cut down. Them shirts wouldn't rip no more'n buckskin.

The end of the war, it come jus' like that—like you snap your fingers. . . .

Hallelujah broke out—

> Abe Lincoln freed the nigger
> With the gun and the trigger;
> And I ain't goin' to get whipped any more.
> I got my ticket,
> Leavin' the thicket,
> And I'm a-headin' for the Golden Shore!

Soldiers, all of a sudden, was everywhere—comin' in bunches, crossin' and walkin' and ridin'. Everyone was a-singin'. We was all walkin' on golden clouds. Hallelujah!

Union forever,

Hurrah, boys, hurrah!

Although I may be poor,

I'll never be a slave—

Shoutin' the battle cry of freedom.

Everybody went wild. We all felt like horses and nobody had made us that way but ourselves. We was free. Just like that, we was free. It didn't seem to make the whites mad, either. They went right on giving us food just the same. Nobody took our homes away, but right off colored folks started on the move. They seemed to want to get closer to freedom, so they'd know what it was—like it was a place or a city. Me and my father stuck, stuck close as a lean tick to a sick kitten. The Gudlows started us out on a ranch. My father, he'd round up cattle, unbranded cattle, for the whites. They was cattle that they belonged to, all right; they had gone to find water 'long the San Antonio River and the Guadalupe. Then the whites gave me and my father some cattle for our own. My father had his own brand, (7 B), and we had a herd to start out with of seventy.

We knowed freedom was on us, but we didn't know what was to come with it. We thought we was goin' to get rich like the white folks. We thought we was goin' to be richer than the white folks, 'cause we was stronger and knowed how to work, and the whites didn't and they didn't have us to work for them anymore. But it didn't turn out that way. We soon found out that freedom could make folks proud but it didn't make 'em rich.

Did you ever stop to think that thinking don't do any good when you do it too late? Well, that how it was with us. If every mother's son of a black had thrown 'way his hoe and took up a gun to fight for his own freedom along with the Yankees, the war'd been over before it began.

But we didn't do it. We couldn't help stick to our master. We couldn't no more shoot 'em than we could fly. My father and me used to talk 'bout it. We decided we was too soft and freedom wasn't goin' to be much to our good even if we had a education.[22]

> Charlotte Brown recalled a similarly jubilant mood among the liberated slaves in her Virginia neighborhood during the first flush of freedom.

De news come on a Thursday, an' all de slaves been shoutin' an' carryin' on till ev'ybody was all tired out. 'Member de fust Sunday of freedom. We was all sittin' roun' restin' an' tryin' to think what freedom meant an' ev'ybody was quiet an' peaceful. All at once ole Sister Carrie who was near 'bout a hundred started in to talkin':

> Tain't no mo' sellin' today,
> Tain't no mo' hirin' today,
> Tain't no pullin' off shirts today,
> Its stomp down freedom today.
> Stomp it down!

An' when she says, "Stomp it down," all de slaves commence to shoutin' wid her:

> Stomp down Freedom today—
> Stomp it down!
> Stomp down Freedom today.

Wasn't no mo' peace dat Sunday. Ev'ybody started in to sing an' shout once mo'. Fust thing you know dey done made up music to Sister Carrie's stomp song an' sang an' shouted dat song all de res' de day. Chile, dat was one glorious time![23]

Wallace Quarterman was a young boy when freedom came, but nearly eighty years later he could still recollect the songs with which slaves marked the progress of the war and emancipation. He shared them in a conversation with three interviewers, including Zora Neal Hurston and Alan Lomax.

WQ: My name is Wallace Quarterman in an' through the state of Georgia. [*gap in recording*] Morning I was toting in breakfas' in the house. An' the big gun shot to Port Royal. . . . The overseer ask me what is that, if that is thunder. I tell 'im I don't know. I know what the Yankees come? An' so he shot three time an' he commence to shoot until the plate commence to rattle on the table. An' he call me an' tol' me to run down in the fiel', an' tell Peter to turn the people loose, that the Yankee come. An' so I run down in the fiel' an' whoop and holler [. . .] an' tol' 'em Mr. G[iggle?] say turn the people loose, because the Yankee come.

AL: And who was Peter?

WQ: The driver. An' so he said that Wallace is lying if he said so, when he said so, then the Yankee be to the landing, they drunk. You understan'. [*recites*]

> Way down south, getting mighty po',
> Cause they use to drink coffee but now they drinking rye.
> If they lef to wave the Union [ban'?] 'o make the rebel understan',
> To leave our lan' for the sake of Uncle Sam.
> Way down south getting might poor,
> Shot at the wildcat an' they see the Rebel run.

I ain't going [over them thing?] again. I've been to war already. Yeah, yeah. An' the people them throw 'way they hoe then. They throwed away they hoe, an' they call we all up, an' give we all freedom 'cause we are jus' as much as free as them. Now you understand. But the Yankees [say?] if we go back to the South they'll help we. Well they didn'. Of course there was so much doubt, an' [it] seems to me that they would have done more, but it so much doubt in the way. They couldn' because the colored people sure [been poor], an' some white people sure [been poor] too. You understan' and they rather help them than help we. I had it twice so far, for the Lord has done for me, I come through all the, up an' downs. . . .

ZNH: After they said you could go free, then what did you do? Did you run on off the plantation that day? Did you leave the plantation that day after they told you to go free?

WQ: Well the master had promise' to give we forty dollars a month in pay. Well lots o' the boys say they ain't want it. They rather go free, you know. Well of course, I get along with him you know. . . . the big boss. An' after the [. . .] then they play. Yeah play. [*sings while playing the washtub bass*]

> One foot one way, one foot the other way,
> One foot all aroun'.
> So big that he couldn't cut a figure
> An' he couldn' go a half way roun'.
> Ole master, run away, and set them darky free
> For you mus' be think
> Thy kingdom a-comin'
> The hour of Jubilee.

So we had a big breaking up right there after it, that's right.[24]

While former slaves in most of the South enjoyed their new freedom, in remote backwaters of the Confederacy many black

people who were entitled to liberty remained enslaved for
months after the war. This was the case in much of Texas,
hardly any of which was occupied by the Union army before the
summer of 1865. Many Texas slaves did not taste the fruits of
freedom until late in the year or even after its end. Susan Merritt's owner refused to liberate his slaves until forced to do so by
a federal official, probably an army officer or an agent of the
newly established Freedmen's Bureau.

I heard 'bout freedom in September, but don't 'member the day. They
was pickin' cotton on the place. A white man ride up to Master's house
on a big white horse. The house boy tells Master that a white man out
the front wants to see him. Master walked to the door and hollers,
"Light, stranger." That's what he allus say when anyone rides up to the
place. It was a Government man. He had a big book and a bunch of
papers and wants to know why Master Watt hadn't turned his negroes
loose. Master told him he was trying to get his crop out. He tole
Master to call the slaves in. Uncle Steven blowed the cow horn that
they used to call the hands in at dinner and all the Negroes come
running cause when that cow horn blowed during the day that meant
"Come to the house, quick." The man read a paper to the slaves telling
them they was free. That's the first we knowed anything about it.
    Master worked them on several months after the man was there.
Master said we was going to get 20 acres of land and a mule, but we
didn't get it. Lots of Negroes was killed after freedom. The slaves was
turned loose in Harrison County right after the war. Negroes in Rusk
county heard about it and lots of them run away from slavery in Rusk
to freedom in Harrison County. Their owners had them "bushwhacked,"
shot down while they was trying to get away. You could see lots of
Negroes hanging to trees in Sabine bottom right after freedom. They
would catch them swimming across Sabine River and shoot them. There
sho' is going to be lots of soul cry against them in Judgment.[25]

The owner of Tempie Cummins intended to keep word of freedom from his slaves, only to be thwarted by Cummins's mother,
a domestic who overheard his scheming and broadcast the
news, at considerable risk to herself.

Mother was workin' in the house, and she cooked too. She say she
used to hide in the chimney corner and listen to what the white folks
say. When freedom was 'clared, marster wouldn' tell 'em, but mother
she hear him tellin' mistus that the slaves was free but they didn't
know it and he's not gwineter tell 'em till he makes another crop or
two. When mother hear that she say she slip out the chimney corner
and crack her heels together four times and shouts, "I's free, I's free."
Then she runs to the field, 'gainst marster's will and tol' all the other
slaves and they quit work. Then she run away and in the night she slip
into a big ravine near the house and have them bring me to her.
Marster, he come out with his gun and shot at mother but she run
down the ravine and gits away with me.[26]

Robert Glenn, who was owned by a Confederate master in Kentucky (a Union state where slavery was finally abolished only in
December 1865), took a circuitous road to freedom. He was legally emancipated by late 1865, after his owner, William Moore,
had renounced the Confederacy and hired Glenn for wages. But
Glenn acted cautiously on his new status, for months taking his
"freedom by degrees" until decisively asserting his independence of Moore.

I was in the field when I first heard of the Civil War. The woman who
looked after Henry Hall and myself (both slaves) told me she heard
marster say old Abraham Lincoln was trying to free the niggers.
Marster finally pulled me up and went and joined the Confederate

"[M]other she hear [her master] tellin' mistus that the slaves was free but they didn' know it and he's not gwineter tell 'em till he makes another crop or two." Tempie Cummins, formerly a slave in Texas; pictured at Jasper, Texas. (See page 271.)

Army. Kentucky split and part joined the North and part the South. The war news kept slipping through of success for first one side then the other. Sometimes marster would come home, spend a few days and then go again to the war. It seemed he influenced a lot of men to join the southern army, among them was a man named Enoch

Moorehead. Moorehead was killed in a few days after he joined the southern army.

Marster Moore fell out with a lot of his associates in the army and some of them who were from the same community became his bitter enemies. Tom Foushee was one of them. Marster became so alarmed over the threats on his life made by Foushee and others that he was afraid to stay in his own home at night, and he built a little camp one and one half miles from this home and he and missus spent their nights there on his visits home. Foushee finally came to the great house one night heavily armed, came right on into the house and inquired for marster. We told him marster was away. Foushee lay down on the floor and waited a long time for him. Marster was at the little camp but we would not tell where he was.

Foushee left after spending most of the night at marster's. As he went out into the yard, when leaving, marster's bull dog grawled at him and he shot him dead.

Marster went to Henderson, Kentucky, the County seat of Henderson County, and surrendered to the Federal Army and took the Oath of Allegiance. Up to that time I had seen a few Yankees. They stopped now and then at marster's and got their breakfast. They always asked about buttermilk, they seemed to be very fond of it. They were also fond of ham, but we had the ham meat buried in the ground, this was about the close of the war. A big army of Yankees came through a few months later and soon we heard of the surrender. A few days after this marster told me to catch two horses that we had to go to Dickenson which was the County seat of Webster County. On the way to Dickenson he said to me, "Bob, did you know you are free and Lincoln has freed you? You are as free as I am." We went to the Freedmen's Bureau and went into the office. A Yankee officer looked me over and asked marster my name, and informed me I was free, and asked me whether or not I wanted to keep living with Moore. I did not know what to do so I told him yes. A fixed price of seventy-five dollars and board was then set as the salary I should receive per year for my work. The Yankees told me to let him know if I was not paid as agreed.

I went back home and stayed a year. During the year I hunted a lot at night and thoroughly enjoyed being free. I took my freedom by degrees and remained obedient and respectful, but still wondering and thinking of what the future held for me. After I retired at night I made plan after plan and built aircastles as to what I would to. At this time I formed a great attachment for the white man, Mr. Atlas Chandler, with whom I hunted. He bought my part of the game we caught and favored me in other ways. Mr. Chandler had a friend, Mr. Dewitt Yarborough, who was an adventurer, and trader, and half brother to my ex-marster, Mr. Moore, with whom I was then staying. He is responsible for me taking myself into my own hands and getting out of feeling I was still under obligations to ask my marster or missus when I desired to leave the premises. Mr. Yarborough's son was off at school at a place called Kilch, Kentucky, and he wanted to carry a horse to him and also take along some other animals for trading purposes. He offered me a new pair of pants to make the trip for him and I accepted the job. I delivered the horse to his son and started for home. On the way back I ran into Uncle Squire Yarborough who once belonged to Dewitt Yarborough. He persuaded me to go home with him and go with him to a wedding in Union County, Kentucky. The wedding was twenty miles away and we walked the entire distance. It was a double wedding, two couples were married. Georgianna Hawkins was married to George Ross and Steve Carter married a woman whose name I do not remember. This was in the winter during the Christmas Holidays and I stayed in the community until about the first of January, then I went back home. I had been thinking for several days

before I went back home as to just what I must tell Mr. Moore and as
to how he felt about the matter, and what I would get when I got
home. In my dilema I almost forgot I was free.

I got home at night and my mind and heart was full but I was
surprised at the way he treated me. He acted kind and asked me if I
was going to stay with him next year. I was pleased. I told him, yes sir!
and then I lay down and went to sleep. He had a boss man on his
plantation then and next morning he called me, but I just couldn't
wake. I seemed to be in a trance or something, I had recently lost so
much sleep. He called me the second time and still I did not get up.
Then he came in and spanked my head. I jumped up and went to work
feeding the stock and splitting wood for the day's cooking and fires. I
then went in and ate my breakfast. Mr. Moore told me to hitch a team
of horses to a wagon and go to a neighbors five miles away for a load
of hogs. I refused to do so. They called me into the house and asked
me what I was going to do about it. I said I do not know. As I said that
I stepped out of the door and left. I went straight to the county seat
and hired to Dr. George Rasby in Webster County for one hundred
dollars per year.[27]

> Tom Robinson's life in slavery began in North Carolina and
> ended—two sales and one long-distance move later—in a re-
> mote part of Texas. Although he long hoped and prayed for free-
> dom, Robinson could scarcely believe it when his owner
> informed him that it had finally come.

Where was I born, ma'am? Why it's my understanding that it was
Catawba County, North Carolina. As far as I remember, Newton was
the nearest town. I was born on a place belonging to Jacob Sigmans. I
can just barely remember my mother. I was not 11 when they sold me
away from her. I can just barely remember her.

But I do remember how she used to take us children and kneel down in front of the fireplace and pray. She'd pray that the time would come when everybody could worship the Lord under their own vine and fig tree—all of them free. It's come to me lots of times since. There she was a'praying, and on other plantations women was a'praying. All over the country the same prayer was being prayed. Guess the Lord done heard the prayer and answered it.

Ole man Sigmans wasn't a bad master. Don't remember so much about him. I couldn't have been 11 when he sold me to Pinkney Setzer. He kept me for a little while and then he sold me to David Robinson. All three of them lived not so far apart in North Carolina. But pretty soon after he bought me old man Dave Robinson moved to Texas. We was there when the war started. We stayed there all during the war. I was set free there.

We lived in Cass County. It was pretty close to the Arkansas border, and 'twasn't far from Oklahoma—as is now. I remember well when they was first gathering them up for the war. We used to hear the cannon often. Was I afraid? To be sure I was scared, right at first. Pretty soon we got used to it. Somebody even made up a song, "Listen to the Home-made Thunder." They'd sing it every time the cannon started roaring.

No, ma'am there never was any fighting right around us. I never really saw any fighting. Old man Dave Robinson was good to me. He didn't have a big farm—just owned me. Treated me almost like I was one of his own children. Course, I had to work. Sometimes he whipped me—but no more than he had to. I was just a child and any child has got to be made to mind. He was good to me, and old Miss was good to me. All my masters was pretty good to me—lots better than the usual run. Which one I like the best. Well, you might know. I kept the name Robinson, and I named my son Dave. You might know which one I think the most of.

One day I was out milking the cows. Mr. Dave come down into the field, and he had a paper in his hand. "Listen to me, Tom," he said, "listen to what I reads you." And he read from a paper all about how I was free. You can't tell how I felt. "You're jokin' me." I says. "No, I ain't," says he. "You're free." "No," says I, "it's a joke." "No," says he, "it's a law that I got to read this paper to you. Now listen while I read it again."

But still I wouldn't believe him. "Just go up to the house," says he, "and ask Mrs. Robinson. She'll tell you." So I went. "It's a joke," I says to her. "Did you ever know your master to tell you a lie?" she says. "No," says I, "I ain't." "Well," she says, "the war's over and you're free."

By that time I thought maybe she was telling me what was right. "Miss Robinson," says I, "can I go over to see the Smiths?"—they was a colored family that lived nearby. "Don't you understand," says she, "you're free. You don't have to ask me what you can do. Run along child."

And so I went. And do you know why I was a'going? I wanted to find out if they was free too. . . . I just couldn't take it all in. I couldn't believe we was all free alike.

Was I happy? Law Miss. You can take anything. No matter how good you treat it—it wants to be free. You can treat it good and feed it good and give it everything it seems to want—but if you open the cage—it's happy.[28]

APPENDIX 1

"Remembering Slavery": The Radio Documentary

Remembering Slavery: African Americans Talk About Their Personal Experiences of Slavery and Emancipation is the companion volume of a two-part radio documentary by the same title. Produced by Jacquie Gales Webb for Smithsonian Productions and Kathie Farnell of the Institute of Language and Culture, the program weaves together excerpts from rare audio recordings of former slaves and dramatic recreations of written narratives by some of the nation's leading actors: Debbie Allen, Clifton Davis, Louis Gossett, Jr., James Earl Jones, Jedda Jones, Melba Moore, Esther Rolle, and John Sawyer. The first episode of "Remembering Slavery" covers ex-slaves' memories of life in slavery, the second their recollections of emancipation and life in freedom. Although there is some overlap between the material in *Remembering Slavery*, the book, and "Remembering Slavery," the audio documentary, each contains substantial amounts of material not included in the other.

The following transcriptions of "Remembering Slavery," taken directly from the original script, are intended to accompany the two episodes of the documentary.

Part One

TONEA STEWART: From Smithsonian Productions and the Institute of Language and Culture: *Remembering Slavery*. Those who survived tell their stories.

[*music*]

My name is Tonea Stewart. When I was a little girl about five or six years old, I used to sit on the garret, the front porch. In the Mississippi Delta the front porch is called the garret. I listened to my Papa Dallas. He was blind and had these ugly scars around his eyes. One day, I asked Papa Dallas what happened to his eyes.

"Well daughter," he answered, "when I was mighty young, just about your age, I used to steal away under a big oak tree and I tried to learn my alphabets so that I could learn to read my Bible. But one day the overseer caught me and he drug me out on the plantation and he called out for all the field hands. And he turned to 'em and said, 'Let this be a lesson to all of you darkies. You ain't got no right to learn to read!' And then daughter, he whooped me, and he whooped me, and he whooped me. And daughter, as if that wasn't enough, he turned around and he burned my eyes out!"

At that instant, I began to cry. The tears were streaming down my cheeks, meeting under my chin. But he cautioned, "Don't you cry for me now, daughter. Now you listen to me. I want you to promise me one thing. Promise me that you gonna pick up every book you can and you gonna read it from cover to cover. You see, today, daughter, ain't nobody gonna whip you or burn your eyes out because you want to learn to read. Promise me that you gonna go all the way through school, as far as you can. And one more thing, I want you to promise me that you gonna tell all the children my story."

Papa Dallas survived slavery and I, I kept my promise. I'm now a university professor, a Ph.D., and an actress. He and many others deserve to have their story told. In the late thirties and early forties, federal and private agencies sent interviewers across the South in an effort to document music and culture. Among those interviewed were African Americans like Papa Dallas who had been born into slavery and lived through the Civil War. Many of the interviews were documented on paper. Some of the interviewers were able to record their voices. In this program you will hear parts of these original recordings and dramatic readings of some of the written transcripts by actors Debbie Allen, Louis Gossett, Jr., Esther Rolle, James Earl Jones, Clifton Davis, and others. And now, former slaves tell you, in their own words, of their lives in bondage, and what it was like to be a slave no more.

FOUNTAIN HUGHES: My name is Fountain Hughes. I was born in Charlottesville, Virginia. My grandfather belonged to Thomas Jefferson. My grandfather was a hundred and fifteen years old when he died. And now I am one hundred and one year old.

TONEA STEWART: The Fountain Hughes interview was recorded in 1941. At that time, he had been living in Baltimore for about forty years.

INTERVIEWER: You talk about how old you are Uncle Fountain. How far back do you remember?

FOUNTAIN HUGHES: Well I'll tell you. Things come to me in spells, you know. I remember things more when I'm laying down than I do when I'm standing or when I'm walking around. Now in my boy days, boys lived quite different from the way they live now. Oh, oh you wore a dress like a woman till I was, I believe ten, twelve, thirteen years old.

INTERVIEWER: So you wore a dress.

FOUNTAIN HUGHES: Yes. I didn't wear no pants, and of course didn't make boys' pants. Boys wore dresses. The womens wearing the pants now and the boys wearing the dresses. Still, [*laughs*]

INTERVIEWER: Who did you work for Uncle Fountain when—?

FOUNTAIN HUGHES: Who'd I work for?

INTERVIEWER: Yeah.

FOUNTAIN HUGHES: When I, you mean when I was slave?

INTERVIEWER: Yeah, when you were a slave. Who did you work for?

FOUNTAIN HUGHES: Well, I belonged to, uh, Burney, when I was a slave. My mother belonged to Burney. But we didn' know nothing. Didn' allow you to look at no book. An' there was some free-born colored people, why they had a little education, but there was very few of them, where we was. An' they all had uh, what you call, I might call it now, uh, jail sentence, was jus' the same as we was in jail. Now I couldn' go from here across the street or I couldn' go through nobody's house 'out I have a note or something from my master. An' if I had that pass, that was what we call a pass, if I had that pass, I could go wherever he sent me. An' I'd have to be back, you know, whoever he sent me to, they, they'd give me another pass an' I'd bring that back so as to show how long I'd been gone. We couldn' go out an' stay a hour or two hours or something like. But they'd give me a note so there wouldn' nobody interfere with me, an' tell who I belong to. An' when I come back, why I carry it to my master an' give that to him, that'd be all right. But I couldn' jus' walk away like the people does now, you know. It was what they call, we were slaves. We belonged to people. They'd sell us like they sell horses an' cows an' hogs an' all like that. Have a auction bench, an' they'd put you on, up on the bench an' bid on you jus' same as you bidding on cattle you know.

INTERVIEWER: Was that in Charlotte that you were a slave?

FOUNTAIN HUGHES: Hmmm?

INTERVIEWER: Was that in Charlotte or Charlottesville?

FOUNTAIN HUGHES: That was in Charlottesville.

INTERVIEWER: Charlottesville, Virginia.

FOUNTAIN HUGHES: Selling women, selling men. All that. Then if they had any bad ones, they'd sell them to the nigger traders, what they called the nigger traders. An' they'd ship them down south, an' sell them down south. But, uh, otherwise if you was a good, good person they wouldn' sell you. But if you was bad an' mean an' they didn' want to beat you an' knock you aroun', they'd sell you what to the, what was call the nigger trader. They'd have a regular, have a sale every month, you know, at the court house. An' then they'd sell you, an' get two hundred dollar, hundred dollar, five hundred dollar.

TONEA STEWART: Robert Glenn's father did his best to keep his family intact. He tried to purchase his son with the money he had earned. The distinguished actor James Earl Jones reads his words.

ROBERT GLENN: I was a slave before and during the Civil War. I am eighty-seven years old. I was born September 16, 1850. I was born in Orange County, North Carolina near Hillsboro. I belonged to a man named Bob Hall. He was a widower. He had three sons: Thomas, Nelson, and Lambert. He died when I was eight years old and I was put on the block and sold in Nelson Hall's yard by the son of Bob Hall. I saw my brother and sister sold on the same plantation. My mother belonged to the Halls, and father belonged to the Glenns. They sold me away from my father and mother and I was carried to the state of Kentucky. I was bought by a Negro speculator by the name of Henry Long who lived not far from Hurdles Mill in Person County. I was not allowed to tell my mother and father good-bye. I was bought and sold three times in one day.

My father's time was hired out and he knew a trade. He had by working overtime saved up a considerable amount of money. After the speculator, Henry Long, bought me, mother went to father and pled with him to buy me from him, and let the white folks hire me out. No slave could own a slave, so father got the consent and help of his owners to buy me and they asked Long to put me on the block again. Long did so and named his price. But when he learned who had bid me off he backed down.

Later in the day he put me on the block and named another price much higher than the price formerly set. He was asked by the white folks to name his price for his bargain and he did so. I was again put on the auction block and father bought me in, putting up the cash. Long then flew into a rage saying, "You think you are white do you? Now just to show you are black, I will not let you have your son at any price."

Father knew it was all off. Mother was frantic, but there was nothing they could do about it. They had to stand and see the speculator put me on his horse behind him and ride away without allowing either of them to tell me good-bye. I figure I was sold three times in one day.

Mother was told under threat of whooping not to make any outcry when I was carried away. He took me to his home, but on the way he stopped for refreshments at a plantation, and while he was eating and drinking, he put me into a room where two white women were spinning flax. I was given a seat across the room from where they were working. After I had sat there awhile wondering where I was going and thinking about Mother and home, I went to one of the women and asked, "Missus, when will I see my mother again?"

She replied, "I don't know, child. Go and sit down."

I went back to my seat and as I did so both the women stopped spinning for a moment, looked at each other, and one of them remarked, "Almighty God, this slavery business is a horrible thing. Chances are this boy will never see his mother again." This remark nearly killed me, as I began to fully realize my situation.

Long, the Negro trader, soon came back, put me on his horse and finished the trip to his home. He kept me at his home awhile and then traded me to a man named William Moore. Moore at this time was planning to move to Kentucky, which he did, taking me with him.

My mother found out by the "grapevine telegraph" that I was going to be carried to Kentucky. She got permission and came to see me before they carried me off. When she started home, I was allowed to go part of the way with her, but they sent two negro girls with us to insure my return. We were allowed to talk privately, but while we were doing so, the two girls stood a short distance away and watched, as the master told them when they left that if I escaped, they would be whipped every day until I was caught.

When the time of parting came and I had to turn back, I burst out crying loud. I was so weak from sorrow I could not walk. The two girls who were with me took me by each arm and led me along half carrying me.

JOSEPHINE SMITH: Now I remember, I remember seeing a heap of slave sales, with them in chains, and the speculators selling and buying them off. I also remembers seeing a drove of slaves with nothing on but a rag betwixt their legs being galloped around before the buyers.

TONEA STEWART: Josephine Smith was ninety-four when interviewed in Raleigh, North Carolina. Her written transcript is read by Ms. Debbie Allen.

JOSEPHINE SMITH: About the worst thing that ever I seed, though, it was, oh, it was a slave woman at Louisburg who had been sold off from a three-week-old baby, and she was being marched to New Orleans. She had walked till she was, oh, about give out, and so weak, weak enough to fall into the middle of the road. She was chained to twenty or thirty other slaves, and they stopped to rest in the shade of a big old oak while speculator et their dinner. The slaves ain't had no dinner.

And as I pass by, this woman begs me in God's name for a drink of water. Oh, I gives it to her, too. I ain't never been so sorry for nobody. It was, it was oh, the month of August, and the sun was, oh, bearing down hot when the slaves and their drivers, and when they leave the shade, they walk for a little piece, and this woman fall out. Fall out. She dies right there at the side of the road, dead, just dead, right there. And right there they buries her, cussing, and they telling me about losing money on her. Oh, Lord, Jesus, Lord. Lord have mercy.

[*music*]

TONEA STEWART: Certain slaves were assigned to care for the children while the mothers worked. Laura Smalley describes this system on her plantation.

LAURA SMALLEY: Jus' like, you know, you bring a whole lot of children you know, an' put them down, you know, at one house. Well, there somebody have to look over them you know an' ten' to them, that-a-way. Just a house full of little children. And if one act bad, you know they'd whip him, they'd whip him too, the ol' woman. An' if the ol' woman didn' ten' to the children they'd whip, they'd whip her too, you know, to make her ten' to the children, she wasn' doing nothing. An' they'd whip her. An' they had trays. An' all of them, you know, would get aroun' that tray with spoons. An' eat, such as like mush or soup or something like that. They'd feed them you know 'fore twelve o'clock. An' all them children get aroun' there and just eat, eat, eat, eat out of that thing. An' that ol' woman, you know, she would ten' to them.

An' they had certain time to come to them childrens. I think about, just like a cow out there will go to the calf, you know. An' you know they'd have certain time, you know, cow come to his calf in, at, at night. Well they come at ten o'clock everyday, ten o'clock to all them babies. Them what nurse you know. Them what didn' nurse, they didn' come to them at all, the ol' lady fed them. When that horn blowed, blowed a horn for the mothers, you know, they'd jus' come jus' like cows, jus' a-running, you know, coming to the children.

TONEA STEWART: In some cases, the parents of slaves were forced to help-lessly witness their children being beaten by the masters. Former slave Caroline Hunter said in her interview:

During slavery it seemed lak yo' chillun b'longed to ev'ybody else but you. Many a day my ole mama has stood by an' watched massa beat her chillun 'til they bled an' she couldn' open her mouf. Dey didn' beat us, but dey

useta strap my mama to a bench or a box and 'beat her
wid a wooden paddle while she was naked.

Throughout the hardships, slave families who were able to stay together
found strength in one another. Growing up a slave in Virginia, Frank Bell
was blessed to be surrounded by parents, grandparents, and others, who
shared work as well as living quarters. Louis Gossett, Jr., portrays Frank
Bell.

FRANK BELL: John Fallons had 'bout 150 servants an' he wan't much on no
special house servants. Put everybody in de field, he did, even de
women. Growed mostly wheat on de plantation, an' de men would
scythe and cradle while de women folks would rake and bind. Den us
little chillun, boys an' girls, would come along an' stack.

Used to wuk in family groups, we did. Now me and my four bothers,
never had no sisters, used to follow my mom an' dad. In dat way, one
could help de other when dey got behind. All of us would pitch in and
help momma who warn't very strong. Course in dat way de man what
was doin' de cradlin' would always go no faster dan de woman, who was
most times his wife, could keep up. Ole overseer on some plantations
wouldn't let families work together. But marse John Fallons had a black
foreman, what was my mother's brother, my uncle. Moses Bell was his
name, and he always looked out for his kinfolk.

JOE MCDONALD: I was raise in the house with him.

INTERVIEWER: Mr. Felix McMillan.

JOE MCDONALD: Mr. Felix McMillan, and uh, they taught me mighty good,
they teach me good.

TONEA STEWART: Joe McDonald of Livingston, Alabama, spent his childhood in the Big House with the white folks. The voice of Joe McDonald.

They said, I remember, says, "Joe?" I say, "Yes sir." "When we are dead and in heaven," they said, "we wants to raise you as an intelligent nigger. We wants you to have good friends like we have got." Say, "You'll never be scratched by good rich, sensible white folks because they can tell who you are by your raising and your compliments. That show that you been raised," he said, "not by the colored but by the white." I washed and ironed. Some days I'd wash a hundred pieces. Some, every morning I'd have five beds to make up, five fires to mix, an' the childrens to dress and churning to do. An' after that, well then I'd have some parts of the day. But I had all that to do every day.

BAILEY CUNNINGHAM: We ate twice a day, about sunup and at sundown.

TONEA STEWART: Mr. John Sawyer as Bailey Cunningham.

BAILEY CUNNINGHAM: All the work hands ate in the cabins and all the children took their soup bowls to the big kitchen and got it full of cabbage soup, then we were allowed to go to the table where the white folks ate and get the crumbs from the table.

FOUNTAIN HUGHES: Now, if, uh, if my master wanted sen' me, he never say, you couldn' get a horse an' ride. You walk.

TONEA STEWART: Fountain Hughes.

FOUNTAIN HUGHES: An' you be barefooted an' col'. That didn' make no difference you wasn' no more than a dog to some of them in them days. You wasn' treated as good as they treat dogs now.

TONEA STEWART: On some plantations beatings were rare or even forbidden. On others, they were unpredictable and dependent upon the temperament of overseers and slave holders. Laura Smalley talks about one of the worst beatings she saw.

LAURA SMALLEY: But they taken that ol' woman, poor ol' woman, carried her in the peach orchard, an' whipped her. An' you know, jus' tied her han' this-a-way, you know, 'roun' the peach orchard tree. I can member that just as well, look like to me I can, and 'roun' the tree an' whipped her. You know she couldn' do nothing but jus' kick her feet, you know, jus' kick her feet. But the, they, they jus' had her clothes off down to her wais', you know. They didn' have her plum naked, but they had her clothes down to her waist. An' every now an' then they'd whip her, you know, an' then snuff the pipe out on her you know, jus' snuff pipe out on her. You know, the embers in the pipe, I don' know whether you ever see a pipe smoking.

INTERVIEWER: Blow them out on her?

LAURA SMALLEY: Uh huh.

INTERVIEWER: Good Lord have mercy.

LAURA SMALLEY: Blow them out on her.

INTERVIEWER: Would she scream?

LAURA SMALLEY: Yeah, I reckon she would. I reckon she did. But you see, we, we, we was dared to go out there, where it was you know. Because uh, our old master would whip us an' then Uncle Saul, Uncle Saul would whip us. You see that was the overseer, Uncle Saul. Her papa was the overseer. Well he had to whip her. He whipped her too. Man he sure did whip her. Well he uh, he uh whipped her so that at night they had to grease her back, grease her back. I don' what kin' of grease they had, but they sure grease her back. At night, you know, that-a-way. They jus' grease her back. An' uh, so after they whipped her so long, so, whipped her then so long that way, they quit. They quit an' give her her dinner. Late that evening they give her her dinner. Lay there and watch [*unintelligible*] she was whipped so bad, you know, she didn' want to eat, you know. If they whip you half a day, you ain't want to eat. Not at all. No.

INTERVIEWER: That's right. [*laughs*]

LAURA SMALLEY: 'Cause a little chil', you can whip a little chil' now, he'll get mad, you know, an' don' want to eat nothing. So Uncle Saul, then he, he was gonna whip my mamma. We had a brother, oldes' brother named Cal, an; he was gonna whip my, my mother's boy who pack water. An' she was gonna fight him. [*laughs*]

INTERVIEWER: Is that right?

LAURA SMALLEY: Yes sir. She was gonna fight him. You see one portion of the people belong to Mr. Bethany, an' one portion you know, belong to, belong to his wife. Wife, you know, jus' like, you know, you'd have a lot of niggers, you know, an' they give you portion of them an' your wife portion of them. Her people give you, people heap of them, an' then your people give you some. Well that makes two parts. You got part an' your wife got a part, you know, of colored folks that-a-way. An' so Miss Adeline wouldn' let my, let uh, Uncle Saul whip her. That was her side, you know. That was one of her niggers. She wouldn' let Uncle Saul whip her, that-a-way. Well then they call her a sassy nigger, sassy 'cause wouldn' let Uncle Saul whip her, about the boy packing water. You know, he pack water, you know. All day an' if Uncle Saul, if they stayed late, you know, an' when they got to the water where Uncle Saul was, the overseer was, he jus' pitch it out, just pitch it out, jus' as fas' as the children could get to him. An' he'd whip them if they let him. Yes, he'd whip them if they let him.

TONEA STEWART: Whipping was not the only form of discipline practiced on plantations. Laura Smalley had a relative who was exempt from the lash, but punished in other ways.

LAURA SMALLEY: Uncle Jesse, you know, he wasn', born, he wasn't, he wasn' one of Mr. Bethany's niggers. He was a Paine, my ol' stepdaddy, yes sir, he was a Paine, yeah, he was a Paine. An, uh, he'd do anything you know, he, he would, they couldn' whip them. Uh uh, couldn' whip them. An' he head, his head was red an' he was red.

INTERVIEWER: Well where did he come from?

LAURA SMALLEY: Well, I think he come from at Louisiana, somewhere. Anyhow, he come from somewhere. I couldn' 'xactly tell where he come from, but my mama come from Mississippi. An' uh, when he, he, he'd back up, you know. I don' know where you all ever see a [unintelligible] fence.

INTERVIEWER: Yes, one of these rail fences.

LAURA SMALLEY: Yes sir, yes sir. Well he'd back up in that, an' they wouldn', they wouldn' whip him. He'd get him a stick an' keep them off. Yes sir. An' uh, he was a great big ol' man, you know, an', an' they, he wouldn' let them whip him, you see, an', and' the master wouldn' let them hurt him 'cause he wouldn' let the, the uh, the, you know, the uh, overseer, you know, they'd whip you. The master would make them whip you what overseed you in the fiel'. An' they wouldn' let him whip him at all, wouldn' no. An' the, the ol' master would tell him rather than to kill him or something like that, don' hurt him. But don't, don't kill him, you know, but whip him. He wouldn' whip him, I tell you. No, he wouldn' whip him. No siree, he wouldn' whip him.

INTERVIEWER: Well how would they, how would they punish him then?

LAURA SMALLEY: Give him an ear of corn. [*laughs*] Give him a ear of corn. Jus' like you know, uh, you, you'd give me a ear of corn an' uh that would be for my, my dinner or my breakfas'. When I come home to dinner, he say to give him a ear of corn, say he shell if off, an' plow along an' eat it, just plow along an' eat it. Night come, they'd give him a ear of corn, an' uh, tha's the way they fed him, you know, punish him you know wouldn' give him nothing to eat. An' say look like he was moving along too slow, too fast with that, you know, too good, too good with that you know, jus' giving him corn, and he's eating it, you know an' drinking water an' going jus' the same. Got so they wouldn' give him none. Give him none. Wouldn' give him nothing, you know but let him drink water, you know. An' uh, he live jus' the same. An' he, an' he live with mama, thirty, thirty-two years, an' before he died, 'fore he died. An' he, an' he never did have a scar on him uh, that, the ol' boss put on him.

TONEA STEWART: You are listening to "Remembering Slavery," from Smithsonian Productions and the Institute of Language and Culture.

[*music*]

TONEA STEWART: The inability of slave men to protect their women and children against the wrath of the master caused enormous pain. In this passage read by Louis Gossett, Jr., Jordan Johnson remembers the anguish of a man forced to watch his pregnant wife endure a whipping.

JORDAN JOHNSON: Husbands always went to de woods when de know de wives was due fo' a whippin', but in de fiel' dey dare not leave. Had to stay dere, not darin' even look like dey didn't like it. Charlie Jones was one slave dat had his wife workin' in de same fiel' wid him. They was plantin' tobacco—he was settin' out an' she was hillin'. Annie was big wid chile an' gittin' near her time, so one day she made a slip an' chopped a young shoot down. Ole man Diggs, de overseer, come runnin' up screamin' at her an' it made her mo' nervous, and she chopped off 'nother one. Ole overseer lif' up dat rawhide an' beat Annie 'cross de back and shoulders till she fell to de groun'. An' Charlie, he just' stood dere hearin' his wife scream an' starin' at de sky, not darin' to look at her or even say a word.

JOHN HENRY FAULK: Well did you ever hear of any slaves being mistreated? That, were there any tales going around in those days about that?

HARRIET SMITH: Uh, nuh huh, uh, yes, I know of times they, when they mistreated people, they did, an' I hear our folks talk you know, about them whipping you know, till they had to grease their back to take the clothes from the, the back.

JOHN HENRY FAULK: Good Lord have mercy.

TONEA STEWART: John Henry Faulk interviewed a woman he knew as Aunt Harriet Smith.

HARRIET SMITH: Them white folks were that-a-way. But them Bunton's sure didn' 'low their colored people be whipped. Sunday in the evening the white folks would let the preacher preach, let our folks go to their church for preaching.

JOHN HENRY FAULK: Well did you go to the white folks' church any?

HARRIET SMITH: Yes. I went to Mountain City to the white folks' church many a time. You see the white folks would have church in the morning, then they'd let the colored people have church at their church in the evening.

JOHN HENRY FAULK: That was during slavery time.

HARRIET SMITH: During slavery time, yes. During slavery time.

JOHN HENRY FAULK: Well would the white preacher tell you to behave yourselves and be—

HARRIET SMITH: Oh yes, they—

JOHN HENRY FAULK: Be good to your master and mistress?

HARRIET SMITH: Yes, that's what they preached.

TONEA STEWART: Spirituality helped many slaves make it though their daily routine of servitude and passivity, but organized religion was a part of their lives only so much as their owners would allow. Laura Smalley.

INTERVIEWER: Well did they have church?

LAURA SMALLEY: No.

INTERVIEWER: Did the slaves have church?

LAURA SMALLEY: I never 'member no church. Mama said, the only church, I didn' 'member that part of it, all the church they would have, be a tub, a tub of water sitting jus' like this thing is, you know, an' that would catch your voice. An' they would, they would have church aroun' that tub, all of them get aroun' the tub, get aroun' the tub.

INTERVIEWER: The old master didn' want them having church.

LAURA SMALLEY: Didn' want them having no church. No, they didn' have no church. An' uh, ol' master come along with one of them, one of them was uh, was there, having church 'roun' the tub, an' he was down praying. An' said he was down there praying, jus' a-praying, ol' master come in, he jus' a-praying, he come in, he did, an' tol' him get up from there. He didn' get up, he jus' a-praying. An' say the ol' master commence to whipping him. He quit praying an' then ask the Lord have mercy on ol' master. Lord have mercy on ol' master. Lord have mercy on ol' master. Ol' master sure would hit him with a bull whip. He's holler have mercy on ol' master. Until ol' master whipped him an' he kep' uh, wouldn' get up, you know, just flinch, you know when a person hit you, you know, you flinch. He just praying for ol' master. Ol' master step back and said, "I'm good min' to kick you naked. I'm good min' to kick you naked." The nigger never did stop praying, you know, he had, he had to go off an' leave him praying. He had to go off an' leave him praying, 'cause he wouldn' stop. Well uh, that was through the Lord, you know. That cause that.

INTERVIEWER: Yeah, the Lord works a lot of things.

LAURA SMALLEY: Yes sir. 'Cause the Lord was, uh suffered him to stay down there an' get that whipping an' pray. You know, jus' keep a-praying. An' I think I'd jumped up, I don' know. Seem like to me I'd jumped up. 'Cause they was whipping me that way, I'd have jumped up.

INTERVIEWER: Well what about getting married. How did they go about marrying the slaves?

LAURA SMALLEY: Well they tol' me they jumped over a brook backwards. [*laughs*] I don' know. They told me they jump over the broom backwards. I don' know.

CAROLINE JOHNSON HARRIS: Didn't have to ask masta or nothin'. Just go to Ant Sue an' tell her you want to git mated.

TONEA STEWART: Esther Rolle as Caroline Johnson Harris.

CAROLINE JOHNSON HARRIS: She tell us to think 'bout it hard 'fo two days, 'cause marryin' was sacred in de eyes of Jesus. Afta two days, Mose an' I went back an' say we done though about it an' still want to git married. Then she called all the de slaves afta tasks to pray for de union dat God was gonna make. Pray we stay together an' have lots of chillun' an' none of 'em git sol' way from de parents. Den she lay a broomstick 'cross de sill of de house we was gonna live in an' join our hands together. Before we step over it she ask us once mo' if we was sho' we wanted to git married. 'Course we say, "Yes." Den she say, "In de eyes of Jesus, step into the holy land of matrimony." When we step 'cross de broomstick, we was married.

It was bad luck to touch the broomstick. Folks always stepped high 'cause dey didn't want no spell cast on 'em. Ant Sue used to say whichever one touched de stick was gonna die first.

TONEA STEWART: Matthew Jarrett objected to the way slave marriages were trivialized by the white masters. He said,

> We slaves knowed that them words wasn't bindin'. Don't mean nothin' lessen you say 'what God done joined, cain't no man pull asunder.' But dey never would say dat. Jus' say, 'now you married.'

INTERVIEWER: What about, uh, Johnny, that, uh, business of, of, uh, taking, having some of the Negroes, the good hands, you know, and good women, good men going off and breeding them like cattle. Do you remember anything about that?

LAURA SMALLEY: No'm. I didn' know any, you see, they wouldn' let children know of that, you know. But I heard it after. After that they'd do that. But see, when we was coming up they wouldn' let us know nothing 'bout like that. But they say that was sure so. You know, jus' like a big fine looking woman, big fine looking man, you know, old boss wants, you know, children from them, you know. They just fasten them up in the house or somewhere, you know, and go on off and leave them in there.

Wan' to breed them like they was hogs or horses something like that I say.

TONEA STEWART: That was Laura Smalley talking about the attempts of certain masters to arrange relationships between slave men and women against their will. Rose Williams had a first-hand experience with this type of situation. Rose is portrayed by Jedda Jones.

ROSE WILLIAMS: There's one thing massa Hawkins does to me what I can't shunt from my mind. I know he don't do it for meanness, but I always holds it against him. What he done was force me to live with that Rufus against my wants. After I been at his place 'bout a year, the massa come to me and say, "You gonna live with Rufus in that cabin over yonder. Go fix it for livin'." I was about sixteen years old and had no learning, and I's just a ignorant child. I thought he meant for me to tend the cabin for Rufus and some other niggas. I took charge of the cabin after work was done and fixes supper. Now, I don't like Rufus, 'cause he a bully. He was big, and cause he so, he think everybody do what him say. We has supper, then I goes here and there talking, till I's ready for sleep, and then I git in the bunk. After I's in, he come and crawl in the bunk with me 'fore I knows it. I says, "What you mean, you fool?" He say for me to hush the mouth. "This is my bunk, too," he say. "You's teched in the head. Git out," I's told him, and I puts the feet against him and give him a shove, and out he go on the floor 'fore he know what I's doing. He jumped up and he mad. Um-hmm. He look like the wild bear. He starts for the bunk, and I jumps quick for the poker. It's 'bout three feet long, and when he comes at me I lets him have it over the head. He stops dead in his tracks. He looks at me steady for a minute, and you could tell he was thinking hard. Then he go and set on the bench and say, "Just wait. You thinks your smart, but you're foolish in the head."

"Hush your big mouth and stay away from me, that's all I wants," I say, and just sets and holds that poker in my hand. He just sets, looking like a bull. Then we sets and sets for 'bout an hour, and then he go away, and I bars the door.

Well, the next day I goes to the missy and tells her what Rufus wants, and missy says that, that those are the massa's wishes. She say, "You're a portly gal, and Rufus is a portly man. The massa wants y'all to bring forth portly children."

I's thinking 'bout what the missy say. I say to myself, "I's not gonna live with that Rufus." That night when he come in the cabin, I grabs the poker and sits on the bench and says, "Git 'way from me 'fore I bust your brains out and stomp on them." He say nothing and get out.

And, uh, the next day the massa call me and tell me, "Woman, I's pay big money for you, and I's done that for the cause I wants you to raise me children. I's put you to live with Rufus for that purpose. Now, if you don't want whipping at the stake, you do want I wants."

Oh, I thinks 'bout massa buying me from the block and saving me from being separated from my folks and I thinks about being whipped at the stake. What am I's to do? So I decides to do as the massa wish, so I yields.

INTERVIEWER: Well did the slaves every try to slip away? They ever try to run off?

LAURA SMALLEY: No, not, not, not on, on the place where we was. I never heared them say they run off over there, run off. Other places I hear them stay in the woods, and uh, so long until they'd wear the clothes off of them, slip up.

TONEA STEWART: Laura Smalley.

Now I heard mama say when she was a girl, when she was a girl, she, she was brought from Mississippi, when she was a girl, that, that, that one ol' woman run off. She did run off. They beat her so she run off. An' every night she slip home, an' somebody'd have her something to eat, something to eat. An' she gets that vittles, an' go on back in the woods, go on back stay in the woods. An' then, you know, jus' uh, they'd tell the others, you know, "Could you see," I don' know what their name, "See so an' so, ever see them?" Say "No." "Well you tell them if they come home, we ain' gonna whip them. We ain' gonna whip them if they come home" Well that be all the way, you know they'd come. Said once this man stayed in the wood so long, tell you his hair on him long like a dog. Well jus' go up, you know, an' stayed in the woods, jus' stayed in the woods. An' they couldn' get him out.

INTERVIEWER: Would any of them run off and get plum free where they, did you ever hear—

LAURA SMALLEY: I'd hear talk of them.

INTERVIEWER: —talking about them?

LAURA SMALLEY: Hear them talk about they going off you know. Going off the places where they's free. [*unintelligible*] what I heared her say. I didn' know that. She say it just like, see it be some white people you know. When some nigger come along, you know an' he jus' get him off you know, take an' carry him off where he wouldn' be no, tell him wouldn' be no slave, or wouldn' be beat up, you know. An' carry him off that-a-way.

BILLY MCCRAE: And I 'member I can tell you some more about slavery time. There was an ol' jail house there, ol' log jail house. An' use to put prisoners in that jail house.

TONEA STEWART: This is the voice of a man the interviewers called Uncle Billy McCrea.

An' we use' to go home to people that worked in the kitchen. We use' to go home and steal bread an' stuff an' poke it through them little bars to the prisoners. An' it was an ol' log jail house. They had hounds. An' they brought them hound in and brought three nigger with them hound, runaway niggers, you know, caught in the wood. And they, right, right across, right at the creek there, they take them niggers and whip them. You hear them niggers hollering an' praying. Then they take them out down there an' put them in jail.

TONEA STEWART: Arnold Gragston's early life was spent helping slaves to freedom across the Ohio River, while he himself, remained in bondage. Clifton Davis reads Arnold Gragston.

ARNOLD GRAGSTON: Most of the slaves didn't know when they were born, but I did. You see, I was born on Christmas morning. It was in, 1840. I was a full grown man when I finally got my freedom. Before I got it though, I helped a lot of others get theirs. Lord only knows how many. Might have been as much as two or three hundred. It was way more than a hundred, I know. But that all came after I was a young man, grown enough to know a pretty girl when I saw one, and to go chasing after her, too. Hee hee hee.

I was born on a plantation that belonged to Mr. Jack Tabb in Mason County, just across the river in Kentucky. Mr. Tabb was a pretty good man, oh, he used to beat us, sure, but not nearly so much as others did. Some of his own kin people, even. But he was kind of funny sometimes. He used to have a special slave who didn't have nothing to do but teach the rest of us. We had about ten on the plantation, and a lot on the other plantation. I learned how to read and write and figure. Mr. Tabb liked us to know how to figure.

But sometimes when he would send for us, and we'd be a long time coming, he'd would ask us where have we been. If we told him we'd been learning to read, he would near beat the daylights out of us—after getting somebody to teach us! I think he did some of that so that the other owners wouldn't, wouldn't say he was spoiling his slaves.

He was funny about us marrying, too. He would let us go a-courting on other plantations, near anytime we liked, if we were good. If we found somebody we wanted to marry and she was on a plantation that belonged to one of his kin folks or friends, he would swap a slave so that the husband and the wife could be together. Sometimes, when he couldn't do this, he would let a slave work all day on his plantation and live with his wife at night on her plantation. Some of the other owners were always talking about his spoiling us.

Mr. Tabb was always especially good to me. He used to let me go all about. I guess he had to. Couldn't get too much out of me, even when he kept me right up under his eyes. Hee hee. I learned fast, too, and I think he kinda liked that. He used to call Sandy Davis, the slave who taught me, "the smartest nigger in Kentucky."

It was 'cause he used to let me go round in the day and night that I came to be the one who carried the running-away slaves across the river. It was funny the way it started, too. I didn't have no idea of ever getting mixed up in any sort of business like that until one special night. I hadn't even thought of rowing across the river myself. But one night I had gone on another plantation courting and the old woman whose house I went to told me she had a real pretty girl there who wanted to go across the river, and would I take her? I was scared and backed out in a hurry. But then I saw the girl, and she was a pretty little thing, brown-skinned and kinda rosy, and looking as scared as I was feeling, so it wasn't long before I was listening to the old woman tell me when to take her and where to leave her on the other side.

I didn't have nerve enough to do it that night, though, and I told them to wait for me until tomorrow night. All the next day I kept seeing Mr. Tabb laying a rawhide across my back, or shooting me, and kept seeing that scared little brown girl back at the house, looking at me with her big eyes and asking me if I wouldn't row her across to Ripley. Soon as dusk settled that night, I was at the old lady's house.

I don't know how I ever rowed the boat across the river. The current was strong, and I was trembling. I couldn't see a thing there in the dark, but I felt that girl's eyes.

Well, pretty soon I saw a tall light, and I remembered what the old lady had told me about looking for that light and rowing to it. I did. And when I get up to it, two men reached down and grabbed her. I started trembling all over again, and praying. Then one of the men took my arm and I just felt down inside of me that the Lord had got ready for me. "You hungry, boy?" is what he asked me, and if he hadn't been holding me, I think I would have fell backward into the river.

That was my first trip; it took me a long time to get over my scared feeling, but I finally did, and soon found myself going back across the river, with two and three people, and sometimes a whole boatload. I got so I used to make three and four trips a month.

A lot of my passengers went on north to other parts of Ohio, or to New York, or Chicago, or Canada. Canada was popular then because all of the slaves thought it was the last gate before you got all the way inside of heaven. I don't think there was much chance for a slave to make a living in Canada, but didn't many of 'em come back. They seem like they rather starve up there in the cold than be back in slavery. I guess you could call me a conductor of the underground railroad. Only we didn't call it that then I don't know as we called it anything. We just knew there was a lot of slaves always wanting to get free.

[*Music*]

TONEA STEWART: The voices, thoughts, and feelings you have just experienced came from people who were born slaves, survived the Civil War, and lived through the Reconstruction. It is easy for us to glorify those who fought or escaped the horrors of slavery. At the same time we must not forget those who silently endured and taught their children how to survive until freedom came. Former slave Tom Robinson said:

> You can take anything. No matter how good you treat it, it wants to be free. You can treat it good and feed it good and give it everything it seems to want, but, if you open the cage, it's happy.

FOUNTAIN HUGHES: Colored people tha's free ought to be awful thankful. An' some of them is sorry they are free now. Some of them now would rather be slaves.

INTERVIEWER: Which had you rather be Uncle Fountain? [*laughs*]

FOUNTAIN HUGHES: Me? Which I'd rather be? You know what I'd rather do? If I thought, had any idea, that I'd ever be a slave again, I'd take a gun an' jus' end it all right away. Because you're nothing but a dog. You're not a thing but a dog.

The end of part one.

Part Two

Montage of overlapping audio clips with music.

TONEA STEWART: Delia Garlic of Montgomery, Alabama, sat on her porch and insisted that she was one hundred years old. She had no good words for slavery days. She said,

> Dem days was hell. I was growed up when de war come an' I was a mother befo' it closed. Babies was snatched from dere mother's breas' an' sold to speculators. Chilluns was separated from sisters an' brothers an' never saw each other ag'in. Course dey cry. You think dey don't cry when dey was sold lak cattle? I could tell you 'bout it all day, but even den you couldn't guess de awfulness of it. It's bad to belong to folks dat own you soul an' body; and dat can tie you up to a tree, wid yo' face to de tree an' yo' arms fastened tight arount' it; who take a long curlin' whip an' cut de blood ever' lick. Oh trustin', trustin' was de only hope of de pore black critters in dem days. Us jest prayed for strength to endure it to de end.

TONEA STEWART: Delia Garlic was interviewed by an employee of the Federal Writers' Project. Beginning in the late 1930s, interviewers collected the memories of thousands of former slaves. In this program, dramatic readings of some of these written interviews are performed by actors James Earl Jones, Louis Gossett, Jr., Debbie Allen, Melba Moore, Clifton Davis, John Sawyer, and myself, Tonea Stewart. Some of the interviews were actually audio recorded by scholars. You will also hear excerpts from these historical recordings that captured the voices of men and women who remembered slavery. Let former slaves tell you, in their own words, of their lives in bondage, and what it was like to be a slave no more.

FOUNTAIN HUGHES: My name is Fountain Hughes. I was born in Charlottesville, Virginia. My grandfather belonged to Thomas Jefferson. My grandfather was a hundred an' fifteen years ol' when he died. An' now I am one hundred an', an' one year old. Tha's enough.

INTERVIEWER: You just go ahead and talk away there. You don't mind, do you, Uncle Fountain?

INTERVIEWER: Who did you work for Uncle Fountain when—

FOUNTAIN HUGHES: Who'd I work for?

INTERVIEWER: Yeah.

FOUNTAIN HUGHES: When I, you mean when I was slave?

INTERVIEWER: Yeah, when you were a slave. Who did you work for?

FOUNTAIN HUGHES: Well, I belonged to, uh, Burney, when I was a slave. My mother belonged to Burney.

Burney died during the way time because, uh, he was afraid he'd have to go to war. But, then now, you, an' in them days you could hire a substitute to take your place. Well he couldn' get a substitute to take his place so he run away from home. An' he took cold. An' when he come back, the war was over but he died. An' then, uh, if he had lived, couldn' been no good. The Yankees just come along an', jus' broke the mill open an' hauled all the flour out in the river an' broke the, broke the store open an' throwed all the meat out in the street an' throwed all the sugar out. An' we, we boys would pick it up an' carry it an' give it to our missus an' master, young masters, until we come to be, well I don' know how ol'. I don' know, to tell you the truth when I think of it today, I don' know how I'm living.

TONEA STEWART: One-hundred-and-one-year-old Fountain Hughes had lived through some of the most trying times in American history. So did Mary Barbour. She was eighty-one years old when she was interviewed in Raleigh, North Carolina. Actress, director, choreographer, and producer, Ms. Debbie Allen interprets the written responses of Mary Barbour.

MARY BARBOUR: One of the first things that I remembers was my pappy waking me up in the middle of the night, dressing me in the dark, all the time telling me to keep quiet. Quiet! One of the twins hollered some, and Pappy put his hand over its mouth to keep it quiet. After we was dressed, he, he went outside and peeped around for a minute, then he, he came back and got us. We sneaked out of the house and along the woods path, pappy toting one of the twins and holding me by the hand and Mammy carrying the other two. I reckons that I will always remember that walk, with the bushes slapping my legs, the wind sighing in the trees, and the hoot owls and whippoorwills hollering at each other from the big trees. I was half asleep but I sure was scared. Woo, scared. But in a little while we pass a, a, a plum thicket and there was the mules and the wagon. There was the quilt in the bottom of the wagon, and on this they lays we younguns. And Pappy and Mammy gets on the board across the front and drives off down the road.

Oh, I was, sure was sleepy, but I was scared, too, so as we rides along, I listens to Pappy and Mammy talk. Pappy was telling mammy about the Yankees coming to their plantation, burning the corn cribs, the smokehouses, and just tearing up, just tearing up, just throwing everything. He says right low that they done took Marster Jordan down near Norfolk, and that he stole the mules and wagon and escaped. We was scared of the Yankees to start with, but the more we thinks about running away from our marsters, the scareder we gets of them rebs. Anyhow, Pappy says that we is going to join the Yankees.

Well, we 'bout travels all night and hid in the woods all day for a long time, but after awhile we gets to Doctor Dillard's place, in Chowan County. I reckons that we stays there several days, several days. The Yankees has took this place, so we stops over, and has a heap of fun, a heap of fun, dancing and such while we we's there. The Yankees tell pappy to head for New Bern and that he would be took care of there, so to New Bern we goes, we goes to New Bern. Um-hmm.

WILLIAM I. JOHNSON, JR.,: In July 1864, my master's regiment captured a gang of Yankee soldiers and brought them into camp to keep them until they could be transferred to Libby Prison in Richmond. We were in camp up near Fredericksburg. At that time the rebels were trying to take Washington.

TONEA STEWART: It was May 28, 1937, when William I. Johnson, Jr., was interviewed. At the time, he was a ninety-seven-year-old retired building contractor. Clifton Davis brings the transcript of his interview to life.

WILLIAM I. JOHNSON, JR.,: I didn't know what the war was all about nor why they were fighting, but when the rebels were out on the battlefield a few pickets were left to guard the prisoners and the servants got a chance to talk to the Yankee prisoners. They explained to us about slavery and freedom. They told us if we got a chance to steal away from camp and got over to the Yankee's side we would be free. They said, "If we win, all you colored folks will be free, but if the rebels win you will always be slaves." These words got into our heads. We got together, five of us, and decided to take the chance one night and we made it. Of course, the rebel pickets knew we were servants in the camp and they probably thought we were going to run an errand for our masters. We carried along plenty of chewing tobacco 'cause we knew the pickets would always like a chew and they didn't ask no questions. After we passed the rebel pickets and got out on the road, every time we would hear horses we would run off the road and into the woods. After the horses would pass we would come out and continue our travel as fast as possible.

We reached Washington the next day and Yankee pickets took us to the military headquarters. The other men enlisted in the fighting regiments, but I was lucky enough to be sent with another group of men to Boston, Massachusetts, where I was assigned to General Butler's division, and to the quartermasters corps, in charge of food and rations.

Down here below Richmond, at a place now called Seven Pines, Negro troops fought one of the fiercest battles of the war against the rebels. The battle lasted seven days. Many men were killed on both sides and when the battle was over only seven pine trees were left standing on the edge of the road where previously there had been a great pine forest. After this battle the place became known as Seven Pines.

Give Us a Flag

Oh Frémont he told them when the war it first begun,
How to save the Union and the way it should be won.
But Kentucky swore so hard and old Abe he had his fears,

Till every hope was lost but the colored volunteers.

McClellan went to Richmond 200,000 brave,

He said keep back the niggers and the Union I will save.

Little Mac he had his way the Union's still in tears,

Now they called for the help of the colored volunteers.

Oh give us a flag all free without a slave,

We'll fight to defend it as our fathers did so brave.

The gallant comp'ny "A" will make the rebels dance,

We'd stand by the Union if we only had out chance.

SARAH DEBRO: The first cannon I heard scared me near about to death. We could hear them going boom, boom. Well, I thought it was thunder, then Miss Polly say, "Listen, Sarah, hear them cannons? Well, they's killing our mens." Then she begun to cry.

TONEA STEWART: Sarah Debro was born somewhere back in the 1850s in Orange County, North Carolina. She was a young girl when the world changed. Melba Moore presents her words.

SARAH DEBRO: Well, I run in the kitchen where Aunt Charity was cooking and told her Miss Polly was crying. She said, "Huh. She ain't crying 'cause the Yankees killing the men; she's crying all that 'cause, 'cause she scared we's going to be set free." Then I got mad and told her Miss Polly wasn't like that.

I remember when Wheeler's calvary come through. They was 'federates, but they was mean as the Yankees. They stole everything they could find and killed a pile of niggers. They come around checking everything, and asking the niggers if they wanted to be free. If they say yes, then they shot them down, but if they say no, they let them alone. They took three of my uncles out in the woods and shot they faces off.

When the war was over, the Yankees was all around the place, just telling the niggers just what to do. They told them that they was free, that they didn't have to slave for the white folks no more. My folks all left marse Cain and went to live in houses that the Yankees built. But they was like poor white folks' houses, little shacks made out of sticks and mud, with stick-and-mud-chimneys. They wasn't like marse Cain's cabins, planked up and warm. They was full of cracks, and they wasn't no lamps and no oil. All the light come from the lightwood knots burning in the fireplace.

Hmm, well, one day, see now, my mammy come to the Big House after me. I didn't want to go, I wanted to stay with Miss Polly. I begun to cry, and Mammy caught ahold of me. I grabbed Miss Polly and held her so tight that I tore her skirt binding loose, and her skirt come falling down about her feets. Miss Polly say, "Let her stay with me, Mammy." But mammy shook her head. "You took her away from me and didn't pay no mind to my crying, so now I's taking her back home. We's free now, Miss Polly. We ain't going to be slaves no more to nobody." And she dragged me away. I can see how Miss Polly looked now today. She didn't say nothing, but she looked hard at Mammy, and her face was white.

TONEA STEWART: Louis Gossett, Jr., reads the words of Tom Hester, a free-born who was bound-out to a plantation owner. While looking after horses and wounded men for the Confederate army, he was captured by the Yankees and began to work for the Union army. He said that he saw Grant and Lee meet under an apple tree when Lee surrendered.

TOM HESTER: Gen'ral Lee tipped his hat fust, an' den' Gen'ral Grant tipped hissen. Gen'ral Lee got offen his horse an' Gen'ral Grant got off hissen. Gen'ral Lee got on a new uniform wid gold braid an' lots of buttons, but Gen'ral Grant got on an old blue coat dat's so dirty it look black. Dey stood dere talkin' bout half an hour; an den dey shake hands an' us what was watchin' know dat Lee done give up. Den Gen'ral Lee got on his horse an' Gen'ral Grant got on hissen, an' Genral Lee tipped his hat, an' Gen'ral Grant tipped hissen, an' Gen'ral Lee rode over to de rebel side, an' Gen'ral Grant rode over to our side, an' de war was over.

De nex' day I went out dere to cut a branch off dat tree, but dere wasn't no sign of it—jus' a hole in de goun'. De soldiers done cut dat apple tree down and taken it fo' souvenees. Yessir, ev'y las' piece of it, even the roots.

TONEA STEWART: On April 9, 1865, Confederate General Robert E. Lee surrendered to the Union army. In December of that year, the Thirteenth Amendment was ratified. It said that slavery shall not exist in the United States.

But, change is uncomfortable for most people. Even when the change is for the better. Transitions will always present new challenges. Esther Rolle portrays Eva Strayhorn.

EVA STRAYHORN: Well, you see, all the colored people in the country, men, women, and children, 'cept mother and her children and the two little children that Hannah left in her care, had gone wid de soldiers to the North where they would be set free. Mother wouldn't leave for she told the soldiers, "My Henry is in the South and I'll never see him again if I leave the old home place, for he won't know where to find me." The officer told her that he was coming back the next day after us and for her to be ready to go. Mother told Miss Tessie that she was going to town and take the oath of peace and they couldn't make her leave. Old Miss told her to go on, so that night she hitched up the oxen and took her children and set out to Dover, Arkansas, twelve miles away, to see the Bureau man and take the oath.

The oath of peace was that you would obey the law and wouldn't harbor no rebel soldiers nor no bushwhackers or do nothing that was wrong or would hinder the cause of the North.

When we got back home we didn't have no home. The very night we left, de bushwhackers, or toe-burners as they was called, come to our house and told Miss Tessie that they wanted her money. She told them she didn't have any but they didn't believe her and told her that they would burn her if she didn't give her money. She kept telling them that she didn't have any money and they took everything they wanted and then jerked the curtains off the windows and piled them up in de middle of the room and the furniture on top of them and set them afire and burned everything except the niggers quarters. It was a pity to burn that big pretty two-story house, but they done it.

Mother and us children went to live on the side of the mountain in a little cabin by ourselves and Miss Tessie went to live with Miss Liza, her daughter. Mother had to keep her oath and she was afraid if she went with Miss Tessie that Master Robert might come home and they would say she had broke her oath and make her leave. One night Mother was spinning and I was carding and everything was just as quiet as we heard somebody tap on the door. We set real quiet and then we heard it again. You dare not speak above a whisper so Mother went to the door and said real low, "Who's there?"

"It's your old master, Bill Newton."

Mother forgot and said louder, "Is that really you, Master Bill, and how did you know where I was?" She opened the door and sure enough it was Master Bill. He had come back to see how we was all gittin' along and found his house burnt. Somebody told him his wife was at Miss Liza's so he went there and she told him where we was. He told mother dat he wanted to go to his brother Nazor's and wait for him there and he would take us to where Father was. She hitched up the oxen and we went down to Uncle Nazor's and one night old master and Miss Tessie slipped in there and got us and took us to Texas. We found father and we was all happy again.

[*music*]

INTERVIEWER: I remember a long time ago you told me about during the big break up, the soldiers came by and uh, riding horseback. And you all were sitting on the fence, you children. Can you remember that?

HARRIET SMITH: Course I can. I've sat on the fence at the time, me an' cousin Lou, an' cousin Sally, an' all of us. Our yard had white picket fence aroun' it. The road went right along by our house like the road goes along by my house.

TONEA STEWART: The voice of Harriet Smith.

We sat on that, stood on that picket fence. All day long we seen them soldiers going back to San Antonio an' different places. Colored soldiers.

INTERVIEWER: Colored soldiers?

HARRIET SMITH: Colored soldiers in droves.

INTERVIEWER: Well what about this girl you told me about there one time.

HARRIET SMITH: Well, Mack Porter was the one that uh, belonged to Mrs. Porter, the one that our white folks' neighbors.

INTERVIEWER: Well I thought she went off with a soldier or something.

HARRIET SMITH: She did. She went off with a soldier. Soldiers come along, we all setting on the fence, an' uh, or standing at the fence, setting an' a colored soldier come along an' ask her did she want to go with him.

INTERVIEWER: Right behind him huh?

HARRIET SMITH: Uh, uh, no, rode a horse to herself.

INTERVIEWER: Is that right?

HARRIET SMITH: That's right. We could ride horses. We could jump on them horses, saddle sometime, ride them sometime. We learn how to do—I could stan' flat-footed on the groun', jump on a horse sideways.

INTERVIEWER: Is that right?

HARRIET SMITH: Tha's right, yeah.

INTERVIEWER: Well you were a rider.

HARRIET SMITH: Yes. All of us, all of we all raised to ride horses. Pa had horses of his own, chickens of his own.

INTERVIEWER: Well now, what happened to Mack Porter after she and this soldier—

HARRIET SMITH: I, she wen' on with him. I never did see her an' hear tell of her no more. She was going toward San Antonio.

INTERVIEWER: Going towards San Antonio.

HARRIET SMITH: Yes. She rode on with them down there.

INTERVIEWER: Well, what did she do? She didn't even tell her mama she was going or anything, huh?

HARRIET SMITH: She didn' have any mother.

INTERVIEWER: Oh, I see.

HARRIET SMITH: Yeah.

INTERVIEWER: And it's all, she'd already been freed hadn't she?

HARRIET SMITH: Yes, yes. That was the time the soldiers was going back you know, after the freedom, back. An' she'd always come over to our house an' stay with us.

BILLY MCCRAE: I would, we all would go out every day, right here in town, to see the Yankees all going back home.

TONEA STEWART: Billy McCrea was recorded in Jasper, Texas, in 1940.

BILLY MCCRAE: I can recollect just as good. They'd jus' have, they'd have, uh, six an' eight mules to a cannon, going through an' bolts on them there, uh, uh cannon, cannon. Then they'd take the wagon, an' have bolts all on them wagon. Now, walk, nothing but them mules, nothing but them mules, an' one man a-riding, riding two mule, we all use to take a look at them. You understand? All day long be crossing, I 'member jus' as well, an' all the Yankees I recollect was blue, was dressed in blue clothes, I can remember it, with blue junk right here, an' had a little pin on, on the coat right there. In fact I'm, an' course it was up here. You, yeah, I recollect jus' as well, day they come roun', an' they, black mules, have uh, maybe, oh I don' know how many black horses. Then they come along in with lot of these ol' gray mules, on it, hitched to them cannon, cannon. An' then they come back with horses, sorrell horses. Horses to [unintelligible]. That way for two days, they was going out through Jasper, two day. An' I remember an' the Yankees stop here, an' the Yankees stop right here on the courthouse square. I was a good size boy then. An' then what they call Freedmen's Bureau, you hear tell of it ain't you? An' they prosecuting people, you know, what they do, you know, an' all like that, an' I mean jus' as hard as they could I've seen two mens they had they were punishing for what they do. An' I see them jus' take them. I, uh, uh, uh, had [unintelligible] a big tent. We, we boys would go out an' see them, an' they'd take them, hang them up by his thumb. An' just let that tip [unintelligible] hang out so many men then let him down. That's the punishment they got. And the Yankees' come, an' after a while there'd be a whole troop of men come, they said they was Yankees. All walking, all walking. That crew of Yankees would go through. Next time you see, there come a whole troop of Yankees, all riding horses, big guns a-hanging on in there, an' all like that you know. Yeah. We all would stan' looking at them, all going home. An' I said, I ask them, I said, I ask them, I say, "Mama, where they, where they going?" Said, "They all going home now." An' old Col. McRae, that was our master, he was lookin' there, an' he say, "Well, Harriet, all of you niggers is all free now. Yankees all going home." I 'member that jus' as well.

TONEA STEWART: Alice Gaston, born 1853, was on a plantation in Alabama when she was recorded.

ALICE GASTON: I can remember when, uh, I can remember when the Yankees come through an', uh, they carried my father away an' carried away, my si, two sisters an' one brother. An', uh, they lef' me. An' I can remember when my missus use' to run in the garden, from the Yankees an' tell us if they come, don' tell them where they at. Tol', don' tell nobody where they at when they come. They all come an' they tol' me, don' get scared now an' tell them, where they is, where they is. I tol' them no, we tol' them no. An' uh, when they come an' ask for them I tol' them I didn' know there they was, an' they was in the woods. An' this was at the house. An' my father, when my father lef', he carried with the, he wen' away with the Yankees, an' carried two, carried two, two girls an' one son, the oldest one. Carried them with him. An' he with the Yankees. An' I can remember that.

TONEA STEWART: You are listening to "Remembering Slavery," from Smithsonian Productions and the Institute of Language and Culture.

[*music*]

TONEA STEWART: Tempie Cummings's master intended to keep word of freedom from his slaves. But Tempie's mother overheard his scheming and risked her life to spread the news. She said:

> Mother was workin' in the house, and she cooked, too.
> She say she used to hide in the chimney corner and listen
> to what the white folks say. When freedom was declared,
> marster wouldn't tell 'em, but mother, she hear him tellin
> missus that the slaves was free but they didn't know it and
> he's not gonna tell 'em till he makes another crop or two.
> When mother hear that she say she slip out the chimney
> corner and crack her heels together four times and
> shouts, "I's free!, I's free!" Then she run to the field,
> against marster's will and tol' all the other slaves and they

quit work. Then she run away and in the night, she slip into a big ravine near the house and have them bring me to her. Marster, he come out with his gun and shot at Mother, but she run down the ravine and gits away with me.

LAURA SMALLEY: Mama an' them didn' know where to go, you see, after freedom broke. Jus' turn, just, like you turn something out you know. Didn' know where to go. That jus' where we stayed.

INTERVIEWER: Uh huh. That's right.

LAURA SMALLEY: Didn' know where to go. Turn us out jus' like, you know, you turn out cattle. [*laughs*] I say.

TONEA STEWART: The voice of Laura Smalley.

An' I thought old master was dead, but he wasn'. He had been off to the war, an' uh, come back. But then I didn' know, you know, he went to the war I jus' know he was gone a long time. All the niggers gathered aroun' to see ol' master again. You know, an' ol' master didn' tell, you know, they was free.

INTERVIEWER: He didn't tell you that?

LAURA SMALLEY: No, he didn't tell. They worked there, I think now they say they worked them six months after that, six months. An' turn them loose on the nineteenth of June. Tha's why, you know, they celebrate that day. Colored folks.

INTERVIEWER: Is that right?

LAURA SMALLEY: On, on the nineteenth, you know, tha's 'cause they said they give them a big dinner, on the nineteenth. But now we didn' know, ourselves. I don' know how the other side of the folks know we was free, but we didn' know. We jus' thought, you know, jus' feeding us, you know. Just had a long table, an' jus' had, uh, jus' a little of everything you wan' to eat, you know, an' drink, you know. An' that was, an' they say that was on the nineteenth. An' everything you wan' to eat an' drink.

FOUNTAIN HUGHES: Now, there wasn', wasn' no schools. An' when they started a little school, why, the people that were slaves, there couldn' many of them go to school, 'cep' they had a father an' a mother. An' my father was dead, an' my mother was living, but she had three, four other little children, an' she had to put them all to work for to help take care of the others. We didn' have no property. We didn' have no home. We been slaves all our lives. My mother was a slave, my sisters was slaves, father was a slave.

TONEA STEWART: Robert Glenn decided to stay and work for his former master after his freedom came. He decided to wait until the time was right for him to be independent. James Earl Jones as Robert Glenn.

ROBERT GLENN: Marster told me to catch two horses and that we had to go to Dickenson, which was the county seat of Webster County. On the way to Dickenson he said to me, "Bob, did you know you are free and Lincoln has freed you? You are as free as I am." We went to the Freedmen's Bureau and went into the office. A Yankee officer looked me over and asked marster my name, and informed me I was free, and asked me whether or not I wanted to keep living with Moore. I did not know what to do, so I told him yes. A fixed price of seventy-five dollars and board was then set as the salary I should receive per year for my work. The

Yankees told me to let him know if I was not paid as agreed. I went back home and stayed a year. During the year I hunted a lot at night and thoroughly enjoyed being free. I took my freedom by degrees and remained obedient and respectful, but still wondering and thinking of what the future held for me. After I retired at night I made plan after plan and built air castles as to what I would do.

At this time I formed a great attachment for the white man, Mr. Atlas Chandler, with whom I hunted. He bought my part of the game we caught and favored me in other ways. Mr. Chandler had a friend, Mr. DeWitt Yarborough, who was an adventurer, and trader, and half-brother to my ex-marster, Mr. Moore, with whom I was staying. He is responsible for me taking myself into my own hands and getting out of feeling I was still under obligations to ask my marster and missus when I desired to leave the premises.

Mr. Yarborough's son went off at school at a place called Kilch, Kentucky, and he wanted to carry a horse to him and also take along some other animals for trading purposes. He offered me a new pair of pants to make the trip for him and I accepted the job. I delivered the horse to his son and started for home. On the way back I ran into Uncle Squire Yarborough who once belonged to DeWitt Yarborough. He persuaded me to go home with him and go with him to a wedding in Union County, Kentucky. The wedding was twenty miles away and we walked the entire distance.

I had been thinking for several days before I went back home as to just what I must tell Mr. Moore and as to how he felt about the matter, and what I will get when I got home. In my dilemma I almost forgot I was free.

I got home at night and my mind and heart was full but I was surprised at the way he treated me. He acted kind and asked me if I was going to stay with him next year. I was pleased. I told him, yes, sir, and then I lay down and went to sleep.

He had a boss man on his plantation then and next morning he called me, but I just couldn't wake. I seemed to be in a trance or something. I had recently lost so much sleep. He called me the second time and still I did not get up. Then he came in and spanked my head. I jumped up and went to work feeding the stock and splitting wood for the day's cooking and fires. I then went in and ate my breakfast.

Mr. Moore told me to hitch a team of horses to a wagon and go to a neighbor's five miles away for a load of hogs. I refused to do so. They called me into the house and asked me what I was going to do about it. I said I do not know. As I said that, I stepped out of the door and left. I went straight to the county seat and hired to Dr. George Rasby in Webster County for one hundred dollars per year.

[*music*]

TONEA STEWART: Isom Mosely was born in 1856 in Georgia. His 1941 interview took place in Gees Bend, Alabama.

ISOM MOSELEY: Well now, they tell me it was a, a year 'fore the folks knowed that, uh, they was free. An' when they foun' out they was free, they worked on shares, they tell me. Worked on shares, didn' rent no lan', they worked on shares. Now you know I was a boy, I'm about explaining to the best of my understanding. They say they worked on shares. I think they said it was, was it fourth, or third I think. They got the third, I think they say, what they made, after surrender.

TONEA STEWART: Most former slaves became sharecroppers, laborors who received as their year's pay a portion of the crop they produced. Families would also have to buy supplies from the land owners. Some were forced to stay there year after year to pay their debt. The voice of Laura Smalley.

LAURA SMALLEY: They'd let you go jus' as far in debt as you wan' to go you know. An' then see, uh, uh, they, they know your crop wasn' gonna, gonna clear it you know, an' then, then so next year you'd have to stay an' work out your debt. If you didn', you know, they'd take all your horses, cows an' everything away from you.

INTERVIEWER: And leave you with nothing.

LAURA SMALLEY: Yeah, leave you with nothing. You see, tha's why they, they keep them there, you know, that way. So they, you know, they could get everything they had if they didn' work. And wouldn' wait for some of them. They jus' take an' give everything they had up, and go on off. Give everything up. They see you is going, sure enough, they'd beg you to stay, you know. Another year, get anything you wanted, any kin' of money. But now you gonna stay there next year 'cause your crop ain' gonna clear it, you know, ain' gonna clear it. They'd let you stay. An' feed you to the highest. An' I have children like this girl here, jus' any kind of dress she wanted, they'd let you take it up. But now when the crop come, they take every bit of that crop. You wouldn' have nothing to live on, uh, uh, live on, you know, nex' year till, nex' year come. Well, they open account right there before Christmas, you know, get jus' what you wanted. Tha's the way they'd do.

[*music*]

TONEA STEWART: The Reconstruction Acts of 1867 promised voting rights to the newly freed people. These new Americans citizens wanted to vote and hold office. Some actually did. From the recorded interview of Harriet Smith:

INTERVIEWER: Was your husband Henry Smith, uh, much of a—

HARRIET SMITH: Jim Smith.

INTERVIEWER: Uh, oh, Jim Smith.

HARRIET SMITH: Hmmm.

INTERVIEWER: Was he a church man?

HARRIET SMITH: Yes, he was—

INTERVIEWER: What happened to him?

HARRIET SMITH: Church man, church man, an' a politic man too.

INTERVIEWER: Oh you were, y'all voted in those days.

HARRIET SMITH: Yes. My husban' was uh, he was known by white folks. He was well, uh, when he got kill them white folks was just crazy about him. That boy that killed my husban', I nursed him when he was a baby.

INTERVIEWER: How come him to kill your husband?

HARRIET SMITH: Well he just mean, just mean you know an' he, they didn' like people up to date you know. An' course there jus' thirteen months in the difference in my husban' kill and his brother. Stole—

INTERVIEWER: Killed your husband's brother?

HARRIET SMITH: Uh huh. He'd been to church. I think he went to gin that night to carry a bale of cotton. An' this Walter Beyer sat down on a seat an' a whole passel of them was settin' down talking. An' when the time to come to his cotton, they killed him an', an' they killed my brother, my husban' on the way from the cedar break. I could go right to the spot now nearly where he was killed at.

INTERVIEWER: Shot him or cut him—

HARRIET SMITH: Shot him, shot him on the way from the cedar, see, we have a cedar break at home.

INTERVIEWER: Well what kind of politicking did he do?

HARRIET SMITH: Well, he worked for white, white people when they want to be elected, you know, anything that time.

INTERVIEWER: He'd work amongst the colored folks.

HARRIET SMITH: Amongst the colored people. Then speak, an' white folks, you couldn' get in the house when he spoke hardly for white people. He had a good learning.

INTERVIEWER: And he's round up the votes, and that's how come them to kill him.

HARRIET SMITH: Uh huh. He roun', when he set the night for a speech, people from Austin, from San Marcos, from every which way, white an' colored, to hear him speak. He'd go to court house an' speak for them.

INTERVIEWER: Well, he uh, did the colored folks not like him?

HARRIET SMITH: No. The colored people all went too, but these white people, this boy that killed him, ol' Walter Beyer, I nursed him when he was a baby 'fore I was ever acquainted with my husban'.

INTERVIEWER: Well what I was, what I'm trying to, to find out is, how come him to kill your husband. Was it over politics?

HARRIET SMITH: Uh huh, politics and different things you know. Poor white people.

INTERVIEWER: Did the white folks have your husband killed or did uh, did he just, Walter Beyer just go shoot him—

HARRIET SMITH: No, my husban' went to cedar break that day, an' uh, an' on his way back from the cedar break, uh, he lay by the road an' killed him.

INTERVIEWER: What did they do to Walter Beyer?

HARRIET SMITH: Well, you know how that was. He lived up in there, you know. They would tell any kin' of tale. Didn' do nothing, didn' hang him up. But his brother-in-law killed him.

INTERVIEWER: Is that right?

HARRIET SMITH: Sure.

INTERVIEWER: They must have been a-shooting a lot of folk up in them days.

HARRIET SMITH: Oh yeah. Them peoples was poor peoples you know. Rich white people don' bother nobody.

INTERVIEWER: Oh, it was the poor white folks.

HARRIET SMITH: Y'all must have been kin folks in those days.

HARRIET SMITH: Which?

INTERVIEWER: Well all of you seem to have been—

HARRIET SMITH: White folks?

INTERVIEWER: . . . . and all.

HARRIET SMITH: No, they was white people.

INTERVIEWER: Oh Walter Beyer was a white man?

HARRIET SMITH: Was poor white persons. I know, I can go right to that place now where he was born.

INTERVIEWER: Oh, I didn't know he was a white man.

HARRIET SMITH: Yes, he was.

INTERVIEWER: Why do you reckon he want to shoot your—

HARRIET SMITH: Jus' 'cause he didn' like him. Because our boys was well learned, an' they'd have speakings, you know, at the school house, you know, for white folks would want to run for office or something.

TONEA STEWART: For the former slave, freedom came with a price. They had to pay with hard work, hardships, and sometimes their lives. Although the number of these recorded historical interviews are few, they illustrate a connection to contemporary American life. The Fountain Hughes interview was recorded in 1949.

FOUNTAIN HUGHES: Now, you all try to live like young people ought to live. Don' want everything somebody else has got. Whatever you get, it is yourn be satisfied. An' don' spen' your money till you get it. So many people get in debt. When you want something, wait until you get the money an' pay for it cash. Tha's the way I've done. If I've wanted anything, I'd wait until I got the money an' I paid for it cash. I never bought nothing on time in my life. I never done it. Now, I'm a hundred years ol' an' I don' owe nobody five cents, an' I ain't got no money either. An' I'm happy, jus' as happy as somebody that's oh, got million. Nothing worries me. I'm not, my head ain't even white.

INTERVIEWER: I don't believe it is —

FOUNTAIN HUGHES: I, nothing in the worl' worries me. I can sit here in this house at night, nobody can come an' say, "Mr. Hughes, you owe me a quarter, you owe me a dollar, you owe me five cents." No you can't. I don' owe you nothing.

TONEA STEWART: John Henry Faulk was one of the scholars who audio recorded his interviews with former slaves. His work was deposited in the Library of Congress and in the Center for American History at the University of Texas at Austin. In an interview forty years later, he described an event that made him think long and hard about prejudice.

JOHN HENRY FAULK: I remember sitting out on a wagon tongue with this old black man—completely illiterate—down here near Navasota a plantation there and I was telling him what a different kind of white man I was. I was really getting educated on blacks and their problems, except we called 'em colored folks. I said, "You know, you might not realize it but I'm not like the colored—the white folks you run into down here. I believe in giving you the right to go to school, to good schools. Now, I know you don't want to go with white people—I don't believe in going overboard on this thing—but I believe colored people ought to be given good schools. And I believe you ought to be given the right to go into whatever you qualify to go into, and I believe you ought to be given the right to vote."

And uh, I remember him looking at me, very sadly and kind of sweetly, and condescendingly and saying, "You know, you still got the disease, honey. I know you think you're cured, but you're not cured. You talking now you sitting there talking and I know it's nice and I know you a good man. Talking about giving me this, and giving me that right. You talking about giving me something I was born with just like you was born with it. You can't give me the right to be a human being. I was born with that right. Now you can keep me from having that if you've got all the policemen and all the jobs on your side, you can deprive me of it, but you can't give it to me, cause I was born with it just like you was."

My God it had a profound effect on me. I was furious with him. You try to be kind to these people, you see. 'You give them an inch and they'll take an ell." But the more I reflected on it, the more profound the effect. I realized this was where it really was. You couldn't give them something that they were born with just like I was born with. Entitled to it the same way I was entitled with it.

[*music*]

TONEA STEWART: Most former slaves gladly told their stories. For some, it was the first time anyone wanted to know about their lives as slaves. The society around them had given them the impression that being a former slave was something to be ashamed of, something not to be talked about. Today we need to hear their stories. For how can you know how far you have come if you don't know where you started?

Langston Hughes speaks so eloquently in his poem "Mother to Son" about what the experience of the elders means to their descendants.

> Life for me ain't been no crystal stair.
> It's had tacks in it,
> And splinters,
> And boards torn up,
> And places with no carpet on the floor—
> Bare.
> But all the time,
> I'se been a-climbin' on,
> And reachin' landin's,
> And turnin' corners,
> And sometimes goin' in the dark,
> Where there ain't been no light.
> So boy, don't you turn back.
> Don't you set down on the steps,
> 'Cause you finds it's kinder hard.
> Don't you fall now—
> For I'se still goin' honey,
> I'se still climbin',
> And life for me ain't been no crystal stair.

INTERVIEWER: When, when did you come to Baltimore?

FOUNTAIN HUGHES: You know when, you don' remember when Garfield died, do you? When they, when they shot Garfield? No, I don' think you was born.

INTERVIEWER: I don't think I was then.

FOUNTAIN HUGHES: No, you wasn't. Well I come to Baltimore that year anyhow. I work for a man by the name of Reed when I firs' came to Baltimore. I used to, I commence to haul manure for him. The old horses was here then. No 'lec, no 'lec, no, no 'lectric cars, an' no cable cars. They were all horse cars. An' I use' to haul manure, go aroun' to different stables, you know. Why people, everybody had horses.

INTERVIEWER: Did you ever think you'd live to see the automobile?

HARRIET SMITH: No. I never did think I'd ever live to see the automobile. An' the thing is, that I heard talk of them. I heard my husban' talk of them. He went North with a herd of beeves with some white folks an' he seen them up there. An' uh, an' then they put on a cable car, what they call cable car. Well they run them for a little while, or maybe a couple or three years or four years. Then somebody invented the 'lectric car. An' that firs' run on North Avenue. Well, uh, that run a while an' they kep' on inventing an' inventing till they got them all, different kinds of cars, you know. I jus' can't, I jus' can't think of, uh, what year it was.

Well I don' know how ol'. I don' know, to tell you the truth when I think of it today, I don' know how I'm living. None, none of the rest of them that I know of is living. I'm the oldes' one that I know tha's living. But, still, I'm thankful to the Lord.

Closing credits.

TONEA STEWART: *Remembering Slavery* was produced by Smithsonian Productions and the Institute of Language and Culture. Special thanks to the Library of Congress. Jacquie Gales Webb and Kathie Farnell, producers. Written by Judlyne Lilly and Jacquie Gales Webb. John Tyler, production manager. Todd Hulslander, production engineer. Martha Knouss, marketing manager. Wesley Horner, executive producer. Original music by Brian Pugh.. I'm Tonea Stewart.

APPENDIX 2

Recordings of Slave Narratives and Related Materials
in the Archive of Folk Culture, Library of Congress

Slave Narrative Reference Tapes

Tape Number	Reference Number	Description
1A	AFS 342 A3	Monolog on emancipation. Sung and spoken by Wallace Quarterman. Recorded at Frederica, Georgia, by Alan Lomax, Zora Neal Hurston, and Mary Elizabeth Barnicle, 1935.
	AFS 3975 A1	Slavery days. Spoken by Uncle Billy McCrea. Recorded at Jasper, Texas, by John A. and Ruby T. Lomax, 1940.
	AFS 3992 A	Monolog. Spoken by Uncle Bob Ledbetter. Recorded at Oil City, Louisiana, by John A. and Ruby T. Lomax, 1940.
	AFS 4011 A1	Monolog on plantation experiences. Spoken by Irene Williams. Recorded at Rome, Mississippi, by John A. and Ruby T. Lomax, 1940.

Tape Number	Reference Number	Description
1A	AFS 4016 A1	Monolog. Spoken by Irene Williams. Recorded at Rome, Mississippi, by John A. and Ruby T. Lomax, 1940.
1B	AFS 4033 B3	Monolog on White masters. Spoken by Joe McDonald. Recorded at Livingston, Alabama, by John A. and Ruby T. Lomax, 1940.
	AFS 4034 A3	Monolog on early days. Spoken by Joe McDonald. Recorded at Livingston, Alabama, by John A. and Ruby T. Lomax, 1940.
	AFS 4777 A & B	Talking with colored fellow about Jefferson Davis. Recorded in Mississippi by Alan and Elizabeth Lomax, 1942.
2A	AFS 4778 A & B	Same.
2B	AFS 4779 A & B	Same.
	AFS 5091 A	Talking about slavery days, etc. Spoken by Isom Moseley, age 85. Recorded at Gee's Bend, Alabama, by Robert Sonkin, 1941.
3A	AFS 5091 A (cont.)	Same.
	AFS 5091 B1	Talking about slavery days, etc. Spoken by Alice Gaston, age 88. Recorded at Gee's Bend, Alabama, by Robert Sonkin, 1941.
	AFS 5496 A & B	Interview with Mrs. Laura Smalley. Discusses slavery days, whipping slaves, recollections of Civil War. Recorded at Hempstead, Texas, by John Henry Faulk, 1941.
3A	AFS 5497 B2	Interview with Mrs. Laura Smalley. Discusses slave-breeding. Recorded at Hempstead, Texas, by John Henry Faulk, 1941.

Tape Number	Reference Number	Description
	AFS 5498 B2	Interview with Mrs. Laura Smalley. Working on a Brazos Bottom plantation. Recorded at Hempstead, Texas, by John Henry Faulk, 1941.
3B	AFS 5498 B2 (cont.)	Same.
	AFS 5499 A & B	Interview with Aunt Harriet Smith. Concerning slavery and Civil War days. Recorded at Hempstead, Texas, by John Henry Faulk, 1941.
	AFS 5500 A	Same.
4A	AFS 5500 A & B (cont.)	Same.
	AFS 8245 B	Narrative by Mrs. Williams, Norfolk ex-slave. Recorded by Roscoe Lewis of Hampton Institute, ca. 1937–1940.
	AFS 8256 A	Story of Cox's Snow. Spoken by Mrs. Annie Williams, Petersburg ex-slave. Recorded by Roscoe Lewis of Hampton Institute, ca. 1937–1940.
	AFS 8272 A & B	Names and Ages. Spoken by Petersburg ex-slaves. Recorded by Roscoe Lewis of Hampton Institute, ca. 1937–1940.
	AFS 8301 A	Personal Story. Spoken by Mrs. Annie Williams. Recorded by Roscoe Lewis of Hampton Institute, ca. 1937–1940.
	AFS 8301 B	Same.
4B	AFS 8301 B (cont.)	Same.

Recordings Not Included on Slave Narrative Reference Tapes

Reference Number	Description
AFS 341 B	Monolog on religious experiences. Spoken by Wallace Quarterman. Frederica, Georgia. Recorded by Alan Lomax, Zora Neal Hurston, and Mary Elizabeth Barnicle, June 1935.
AFS 342 A1	Monolog on his conversion. Spoken by Wallace Quarterman. Frederica, Georgia. Recorded by Alan Lomax, Zora Neal Hurston, and Mary Elizabeth Barnicle, June 1935.
AFS 342 A2	Monolog on his name and age. Spoken by Wallace Quarterman. Frederica, Georgia. Recorded by Alan Lomax, Zora Neal Hurston, and Mary Elizabeth Barnicle, June 1935.
AFS 342 B	Monolog on postbellum experiences. Sung and spoken by Wallace Quarterman. Frederica, Georgia. Recorded by Alan Lomax, Zora Neal Hurston, and Mary Elizabeth Barnicle, June 1935.
AFS 9990 A	Fountain Hughes, age 101, born in Charlottesville, Virginia, talks about family and slave boyhood. Recorded June 11, 1949, in Baltimore, Maryland, by Hermond Norwood.
AFS 17,476 LWO 8322	Mrs. Celia Black, 115 year old ex-slave, interviewed by Elmer Sparks at the Colonial Manor Nursing Home, Tyler, Texas, October 11, 1974.
AFS 17,510 LWO 8478	Interview with Charlie Smith, 130 year old African-born ex-slave and former cowboy, logger, etc., conducted by Elmer Sparks in Bartow, Florida, March 17, 1975.

SUGGESTIONS FOR FURTHER READING

The best short survey of slavery in the United States is Peter Kolchin, *American Slavery, 1619–1877* (New York, 1993). The origins and development of slavery in mainland North America are charted in Ira Berlin, *Many Thousands Gone: The First Two Centuries of Slavery in North America* (Cambridge, Mass., 1998) and Philip D. Morgan, *Slave Counterpoint: Black Culture in the Eighteenth-Century Chesapeake and Lowcountry* (Chapel Hill, N.C., 1998). Sylvia Frey, *Water from the Rock: Black Resistance in a Revolutionary Age* (Princeton, N.J., 1991) addresses the transformation of African-American slavery in the American Revolution. The starting point for understanding slavery in the period immediately preceding the American Civil War is Kenneth M. Stampp, *The Peculiar Institution: Slavery in the Ante-Bellum South* (New York, 1956). Stampp's study should be supplemented with three other books: Eugene D. Genovese, *Roll, Jordan, Roll: The World the Slaves Made* (New York, 1974), a brilliant and influential—if controversial—interpretation of the master–slave relationship; and John W. Blassingame, *The Slave Community: Plantation Life in the Antebellum South* (rev. ed., New York, 1979) and George Rawick, *From Sundown to Sunup: The Making of the Black Community* (Westport, Conn., 1972), both of which depict slave life from the vantage point of the quarter. Slave family and kinship relations receive extended treatment in Herbert G. Gutman, *The Black Family in Slavery and Freedom, 1750–1925* (New York, 1976), and the experience of slave children is considered in Wilma King, *Stolen Childhood: Slave Youth in Nineteenth-Century America* (Bloomington, Ind., 1995). On African-American expressive culture in slavery, see Lawrence Levine, *Black Culture and Black Consciousness: Afro-American Folk Thought from Slavery to Freedom* (New York, 1977) and Sterling Stuckey, *Slave Culture: Nationalist Theory and the Foundations of Black America* (New York, 1987). The best surveys of African-American Christianity during slavery are Albert J. Raboteau, *Slave Religion: The "Invisible Institution" in the Antebellum South* (New York, 1978) and Sylvia Frey and Betty Wood, *Come Shouting to Zion: African American Protestantism in the American South and the British Caribbean to 1830* (Chapel Hill, N.C., 1998). Education among slaves, broadly construed, is examined in Thomas L. Webber, *Deep Like the Rivers: Education in the Slave Quarter Community, 1831–1865* (New York, 1978) and Janet Duitsman Cornelius, *"When I Can Read My Title Clear": Literacy, Slavery, and Religion in the Antebellum South* (Columbia, S.C., 1991). On the slaves' passage to freedom during and after the Civil War see: Bell I. Wiley, *Southern Negroes, 1861–1865* (New Haven, Conn., 1938); Ira Berlin, Barbara J. Fields, Steven F. Miller, Joseph P. Reidy, and Leslie S. Rowland, *Slaves No More: Three Essays on Emancipation and the Civil War* (New York, 1992); and Leon F. Litwack, *Been in the Storm So Long: The Aftermath of Slavery* (New York, 1979).

Among the many collections of primary documents pertaining to American slavery, the most valuable include Willie Lee Rose, ed., *A Documentary History of Slavery in North America* (New York, 1976); John W. Blassingame, ed., *Slave Testimony: Two Centuries of Letters, Speeches, Interviews, and Autobiographies* (Baton Rouge, La., 1977); and Robert W. Starobin, *Blacks in Bondage: Letters of American Slaves* (1974; reprint, New York, 1988). For documents on emancipation and the experiences of slaves and ex-slaves during the Civil War, see Ira Berlin, Barbara J. Fields, Steven F. Miller, Joseph P. Reidy, and Leslie S. Rowland, *Free at Last: A Documentary History of Slavery, Freedom, and the Civil War* (New York, 1992).

The ex-slave narratives collected by the Federal Writers' Project have a substantial scholarly literature of their own. See Norman R. Yetman, "The Background of the Slave Narrative Collection," *American Quarterly* 19 (1967), pp. 534–52; C. Vann Woodward, "History from Slave Sources: A Review Article," *American Historical Review* 79 (1985), pp. 470–81; and Paul D. Escott, *Slavery Remembered: A Record of Twentieth-century Slave Narratives* (Chapel Hill, N.C., 1979). On the place of the ex-slave narratives in the larger African-American literary tradition, see Charles T. Davis and Henry Louis Gates, Jr., eds., *The Slave's Narrative* (New York, 1985).

Single-volume collections drawn from the Federal Writers' Project narratives include Benjamin A. Botkin, ed., *Lay My Burden Down: A Folk History of Slavery* (Chicago, 1945); Norman R. Yetman, ed., *Life under the "Peculiar Institution": Selections from the Slave Narrative Collection* (Huntington, N.Y., 1970); James Mellon, ed., *Bullwhip Days: The Slaves Remember* (New York, 1988); Charles L. Perdue, Jr., Thomas E. Barden, and Robert K. Phillips, eds., *Weevils in the Wheat: Interviews with Virginia Ex-Slaves* (Charlottesville, Va., 1976); and Ron Tyler and

Lawrence R. Murphy, eds., *The Slave Narratives of Texas* (Austin, Tex., 1997).

The recorded narratives get full consideration in Guy Bailey, Natalie Maynor, and Patricia Cukor-Avila, eds., *The Roots of Black English: Text and Commentary* (Amsterdam, 1991), which provides authoritative transcriptions of the narratives and important insights into African-American linguistic patterns.

SHORT TITLES USED IN NOTES

American Slave

George P. Rawick, gen. ed., *The American Slave: A Composite Autobiography*, 41 vols. (Westport, Conn., 1972–79).

Series 1
  Vol. 2 *South Carolina Narratives, Parts 1 and 2*
  Vol. 4 *Texas Narratives, Parts 1 and 2*
  Vol. 5 *Texas Narratives, Parts 3 and 4*
  Vol. 6 *Alabama and Indiana Narratives*
  Vol. 7 *Oklahoma and Mississippi Narratives*

Series 2
  Vol. 9 *Arkansas Narratives, Parts 3 and 4*
  Vol. 10 *Arkansas Narratives, Parts 5 and 6*
  Vol. 11 *Arkansas Narratives, Part 7, and Missouri Narratives*
  Vol. 12 *Georgia Narratives, Parts 1 and 2*
  Vol. 14 *North Carolina Narratives, Part 1*

Vol. 15 *North Carolina Narratives, Part 2*
Vol. 17 *Florida Narratives*

Supplement, Series 1
Vol. 2 *Arkansas, Colorado, Minnesota, Missouri, and Oregon and Washington Narratives*
Vol. 3 *Georgia Narratives, Part 1*
Vol. 4 *Georgia Narratives, Part 2*
Vol. 5 *Indiana and Ohio Narratives*
Vol. 6 *Mississippi Narratives, Part 1*
Vol. 7 *Mississippi Narratives, Part 2*
Vol. 8 *Mississippi Narratives, Part 3*
Vol. 11 *North Carolina and South Carolina Narratives*
Vol. 12 *Oklahoma Narratives*

Supplement, Series 2
Vol. 1 *Alabama, Arizona, Arkansas, District of Columbia, Florida, Georgia, Indiana, Kansas, Maryland, Nebraska, New York, North Carolina, Oklahoma, Rhode Island, South Carolina, Washington Narratives*
Vol. 3 *Texas Narratives, Part 2*
Vol. 4 *Texas Narratives, Part 3*
Vol. 6 *Texas Narratives, Part 5*
Vol. 7 *Texas Narratives, Part 6*
Vol. 8 *Texas Narratives, Part 7*

NOTE: Many volumes of *American Slave* are composed of distinct parts, each with its own pagination. In citations to such volumes, the relevant part is indicated in parentheses, for example: *American Slave*, ser. 1, vol. 4 (Tex., pt. 2), pp. 158–69.

Weevils in the Wheat

Charles L. Perdue, Jr., Thomas E. Barden, and Robert K. Phillips, eds., *Weevils in the Wheat: Interviews with Virginia Ex-Slaves*. (Charlottesville, Va., 1976).

NOTES

CHAPTER 1

1. Harriet Smith, interviewed Hempstead, Tex., 1941, Archive of Folk Culture, Library of Congress.

2. Delia Garlic, interviewed Montgomery, Ala., n.d., *American Slave*, ser. 1, vol. 6 (Ala.), pp. 129–32.

3. August Messersmith, interviewed Rolla, Mo., n.d., *American Slave*, supp. ser. 1, vol. 2 (Mo.), pp. 240–65.

4. Vinnie Busby, interviewed Rankin Co., Miss., n.d., *American Slave*, supp. ser. 1, vol. 6, pp. 308–311.

5. Laura Smalley, interviewed Hempstead, Tex., 1941, Archive of Folk Culture, Library of Congress.

6. Henrietta King, interviewed West Point, Va., n.d., *Weevils in the Wheat*, pp. 190–92.

7. Leah Garrett, interviewed Richmond Co., Ga., n.d.,

American Slave, ser. 2, vol. 12 (Ga., pt. 2), pp. 11–16.

8. William Colbert, interviewed Ala. [1937], *American Slave*, ser. 1, vol. 6 (Ala.), pp. 81–82.

9. Sarah Ford, interviewed Houston, Tex., n.d., *American Slave*, ser. 1, vol. 4 (Tex., pt. 2), pp. 41–46.

10. Jenny Proctor, interviewed Tex., n.d., *American Slave*, ser. 1, vol. 5 (Tex., pt. 3), pp. 208–217.

11. Sam Kilgore, interviewed Fort Worth, Tex., 12 Sept. 1937, *American Slave*, supp. ser. 2, vol. 6, pp. 2181–92.

12. Georgia Baker, interviewed Athens, Ga. [1938], *American Slave*, ser. 2, vol. 12 (Ga., pt. 1), pp. 37–57.

13. Manda Boggan, interviewed Weathersby, Miss., n.d., *American Slave*, supp. ser. 1, vol. 6, pp. 155–59.

14. Delicia Patterson,

interviewed St. Louis, Mo., n.d., *American Slave*, ser. 2, vol. 11 (Mo.), pp. 269–76.

15. Betty Simmons, interviewed Tex., n.d., *American Slave*, ser. 1, vol. 5 (Tex., pt. 4), pp. 19–23.

16. Salomon Oliver, interviewed Tulsa, Okla., n.d., *American Slave*, ser. 1, vol. 7 (Okla.), pp. 233–35.

17. Anna Baker, interviewed Aberdeen, Miss., n.d., *American Slave*, ser. 1, vol. 7 (Miss.), pp. 11–17.

18. William I. Johnson, Jr., interviewed Richmond, Va., 28 May 1937, *Weevils in the Wheat*, pp. 165–70.

19. Adelaide Vaughn, interviewed Little Rock, Ark., n.d., *American Slave*, ser. 2, vol. 11 (Ark., pt. 7), pp. 7–12.

20. Daniel Dowdy, interviewed Oklahoma City, Okla., n.d.,

American Slave, ser. 1, vol. 7 (Okla.), pp. 76–80.

21. W. B. Allen, interviewed Columbus, Ga., 10 May 1937, *American Slave*, supp. ser. 1, vol. 3, pp. 4–22.

22. Fannie Berry, interviewed Petersburg, Va., 26 Feb. 1937, *Weevils in the Wheat*, pp. 30–50.

23. W. P. Jacobs, interviewed Phoebus, Va., n.d., *Weevils in the Wheat*, pp. 155–58.

24. Frank Bell, interviewed Vienna, Va., n.d., *Weevils in the Wheat*, pp. 25–28.

25. Lorenzo L. Ivy, interviewed Danville, Va., 28 Apr. 1937, *Weevils in the Wheat*, pp. 151–54.

26. Ishrael Massie, interviewed Petersburg, Va., 23 Apr. 1937, *Weevils in the Wheat*, pp. 205–211.

27. Morris Hillyer, interviewed Anderson, Okla., n.d., *American Slave*, ser. 1, vol. 7 (Okla.), pp. 138–44.

28. Arnold Gragston, interviewed Eatonville, Fla., n.d., *American Slave*, ser. 2, vol. 17, pp. 146–55.

CHAPTER 2

1. Sarah Gudger, interviewed Asheville, N.C., 5 May 1937, *American Slave*, ser. 2, vol. 14, pp. 350–58.

2. Wes Brady, interviewed Harrison Co., Tex., n.d., *American Slave*, ser. 1, vol. 4 (Tex., pt. 1), pp. 133–36.

3. W. P. Jacobs, interviewed Phoebus, Va., n.d., *Weevils in the Wheat*, pp. 155–58.

4. George Fleming, interviewed Spartanburg, S.C., 28 Oct. 1937, *American Slave*, supp. ser. 1, vol. 11 (S.C.), pp. 126–39.

5. Cora Carroll Gillam, interviewed Little Rock, Ark., n.d., *American Slave*,

supp. ser. 2, vol. 1 (Ark.,), pp. 76–93.

6. Charley Williams, interviewed Tulsa, Okla., n.d., *American Slave*, ser. 1, vol. 7 (Okla.), pp. 330–43.

7. Gabe Hunt, interviewed Rustburg, Va., n.d., *Weevils in the Wheat*, p. 148.

8. Katie Darling, interviewed Marshall, Tex., 2 Aug. 1937, *American Slave*, supp. ser. 2, vol. 4, pp. 1047–51.

9. Mother Anne Clark, interviewed El Paso, Tex., n.d., *American Slave*, ser. 1, vol. 4 (Tex., pt. 1), pp. 223–24.

10. Emma Knight, interviewed Hannibal, Mo., n.d., *American Slave*, supp. ser. 1, vol. 2 (Mo.), pp. 202–204.

11. Ebenezer Brown, interviewed Amite Co., Miss. n.d., *American Slave*, supp. ser. 1, vol. 6, pp. 239–54.

12. Mary Island, interviewed El Dorado, Ark., n.d., *American Slave*, ser. 1, vol. 9 (Ark., pt. 3), pp. 389–90.

13. Marie Askin Simpson, interviewed Rolla, Mo., n.d., *American Slave*, supp. ser. 1, vol. 2 (Mo.), pp. 230–34.

14. Isom Moseley, interviewed Gee's Bend, Ala., 1941, Archive of Folk Culture, Library of Congress.

15. Ella Wilson, interviewed Little Rock, Ark., n.d., *American Slave*, ser. 1, vol. 11 (Ark., pt. 7), pp. 201–206.

16. Mildred Graves, interviewed Richmond, Va., 23 Apr. 1937, *Weevils in the Wheat*, pp. 120–21.

17. Sarah Wilson, interviewed Fort Gibson, Okla., n.d., *American Slave*, ser. 1, vol. 7 (Okla.), pp. 344–53.

18. Emanuel Elmore, interviewed Spartanburg, S.C., 23 Dec. 1937, *American Slave*, ser. 1, vol. 2 (S.C., pt. 2,), pp. 6–10.

19. Octavia George, interviewed Oklahoma City, Okla., n.d., *American Slave*, ser. 1, vol. 7 (Okla.), pp. 111–14.

20. Henry C. Pettus, interviewed Marianna, Ark., n.d., *American Slave*, ser. 2, vol. 10 (Ark., pt. 5), pp. 338–43.

21. Laura Thornton, interviewed Little Rock, Ark., n.d., *American Slave*, ser. 2, vol. 10 (Ark., pt. 6), pp. 322–29.

CHAPTER 3

1. Tempie Herndon Durham, interviewed Durham, N.C., n.d., *American Slave*, ser. 2, vol. 14, pp. 284–90.

2. Matthew Jarrett, interviewed Petersburg, Va., n.d., *Weevils in the Wheat*, p. 158.

3. Caroline Johnson Harris, interviewed Caroline Co., Va., n.d., *Weevils in the Wheat*, p. 129.

4. Andrew Jackson Gill, interviewed Lincoln Co., Miss., n.d., *American Slave*, supp. ser. 1, vol. 8, pp. 839–47.

5. Rose Williams, n.p., n.d., *American Slave*, ser. 1, vol. 5 (Tex., pt. 4), pp. 174–78.

6. Frank Bell, interviewed Vienna, Va., n.d., *Weevils in the Wheat*, pp. 25–28.

7. Fannie Moore, interviewed Asheville, N.C., 21 Sept. 1937, *American Slave*, ser. 2, vol. 15, pp. 128–37.

8. Laura Smalley, interviewed Hempstead, Tex., 1941, Archive of Folk Culture, Library of Congress.

9. Maria Smith and "Grammaw," interviewed Augusta, Ga., n.d., *American Slave*, supp. ser. 1, vol. 4, pp. 571–74.

10. Caroline Hunter, interviewed Portsmouth, Va., 8 Jan. 1937, *Weevils in the Wheat*, pp. 149–51.

11. Jordan Johnson, interviewed Lynchburg, Va., n.d., *Weevils in the Wheat*, p. 160.

12. Martha Spence Bunton, interviewed Austin, Tex., 16 Sept. 1937, *American Slave*, supp. ser. 2, vol. 3, pp. 519–26.

13. Hannah Chapman, interviewed Simpson Co., Miss., n.d., *American Slave*, supp. ser. 1, vol. 7, pp. 379–85.

14. Vinnie Busby, interviewed Rankin Co., Miss., n.d., *American Slave*, supp. ser. 1, vol. 6, pp. 308–312.

15. Anna Lee, interviewed Madisonville, Tex., 16 Sept. 1937, *American Slave*, supp. ser. 2, vol. 6, pp. 2272–90.

16. Henry Ferry, n.p., n.d., *Weevils in the Wheat*, p. 91.

17. J. W. Terrill, interviewed Madisonville, Tex., n.d., *American Slave*, ser. 1, vol. 5 (Tex., pt. 4), pp. 80–82.

18. Robert Glenn, interviewed Raleigh, N.C., n.d., *American Slave*, ser. 2, vol. 14, pp. 328–39.

19. Mattie Dillworth, interviewed Lafayette Co., Miss., n.d., *American Slave*, supp. ser. 1, vol. 7, pp. 612–17.

20. Mary Ferguson, interviewed Columbus, Ga., 18 Dec. 1936, *American Slave*, ser. 2, vol. 12 (Ga., pt. 1), pp. 326–31.

21. Maggie Pinkard, interviewed Muskogee, Okla., n.d., *American Slave*, supp. ser. 1, vol. 12, pp. 254–59.

22. Josephine Howard, interviewed Houston, Tex., n.d., *American Slave*, ser. 1, vol. 4 (Tex., pt. 2), pp. 163–65.

23. Caleb Craig, interviewed Winnsboro, S.C., n.d., *American Slave*, ser. 1, vol. 2 (S.C., pt. 1), pp. 229–33.

24. Mingo White, interviewed Burleson, Ala., n.d., *American Slave*, ser. 1, vol. 6 (Ala.), pp. 413–22.

CHAPTER 4

1. Rachel Cruze, interviewed Cleveland, Ohio, n.d., *American Slave*, supp. ser. 1, vol. 5 (Ohio), pp. 290–323.

2. Prince Johnson, interviewed Coahoma Co., Miss., n.d., *American Slave*, supp. ser. 1, vol. 8, pp. 1167–80.

3. James Bolton, interviewed Athens, Ga., n.d., *American Slave*, ser. 1, vol. 12, pp. 91–104.

4. Tom Holland, interviewed Madisonville, Tex., n.d., *American Slave*, ser. 1, vol. 4 (Tex., pt. 2), pp. 144–47.

5. Green Cumby, interviewed Abilene, Tex., n.d., *American Slave*, ser. 1, vol. 4 (Tex., pt. 1), pp. 260–62.

6. Harriet Jones, n.p., n.d., *American Slave*, ser. 1, vol. 4 (Tex., pt. 2), pp. 231–36.

7. Fannie Berry, interviewed Petersburg, Va., 26 Feb. 1937, *Weevils in the Wheat*, pp. 30–50.

8. Uncle Bob Ledbetter, interviewed Oil City, La., 1940, Archive of Folk Culture, Library of Congress.

9. Vinnie Brunson, interviewed McLennan Co., Tex., 1 Dec. 1937, *American Slave*, supp. ser. 2, vol. 3, pp. 512–18.

10. James Bolton, interviewed Athens, Ga., n.d., *American Slave*, supp. ser. 1, vol. 3, pp. 76–90.

11. Charley Roberts, interviewed Perrine, Fla., 30 June 1938, *American Slave*, ser. 2, vol. 17, pp. 364–65.

12. Julia Henderson, interviewed Augusta, Ga., 16 Sept. 1937, *American Slave*, supp. ser. 1, vol. 3, pp. 319–28.

13. Clara Young, interviewed Monroe Co., Miss., n.d., *American Slave*, ser. 1, vol. 7 (Miss.), pp. 169–74.

14. Beverly Jones, interviewed Gloucester Court House, Va., n.d., *Weevils in the Wheat*, pp. 181–85.

15. Richard Carruthers, interviewed Houston, Tex., n.d., *American Slave*, ser. 1, vol. 4 (Tex., pt. 1), pp. 197–201.

16. Jeff Calhoun, interviewed Tex., n.d., *American Slave*, ser. 1, vol. 4 (Tex., pt. 1), pp. 188–90.

17. Shang Harris, interviewed Toccoa, Ga., n.d., *American Slave*, ser. 1, vol. 12 (Ga., pt. 2), pp. 117–25.

18. Silvia King, interviewed Falls Co., Tex., n.d., *American Slave*, supp. ser. 2, vol. 6, pp. 224–39.

19. Richard Carruthers, interviewed Houston, Tex., n.d., *American Slave*, ser. 1, vol. 4 (Tex., pt. 1), pp. 197–201.

20. Fountain Hughes, interviewed Baltimore, Md., 1941, Archive of Folk Culture, Library of Congress.

21. Ishrael Massie, interviewed Petersburg, Va., 23 Apr. 1937, *Weevils in the Wheat*, pp. 205–211.

22. Laura Smalley, interviewed Hempstead, Tex., 1941, Archive of Folk Culture, Library of Congress.

23. Alice Sewell, interviewed St. Louis, Mo., n.d., *American Slave*, ser. 2, vol. 11 (Mo.), pp. 301–307.

24. Mandy Jones, interviewed Lyman, Miss, n.d., *American Slave*, supp. ser. 1, vol. 8, pp. 1226–42.

CHAPTER 5

1. Barney Alford, interviewed Pike Co., Miss., n.d., *American Slave*, supp. ser. 1, vol. 6, pp. 23–49.

2. William H. Adams, interviewed Fort Worth, Tex., n.d., *American Slave,* ser. 1, vol. 4 (Tex., pt. 1), pp. 9–11.

3. Katie Phoenix, interviewed San Antonio, Tex., n.d., *American Slave,* supp. ser. 2, vol. 8, pp. 3082–86.

4. Susan Snow, interviewed Meridian, Miss., n.d., *American Slave,* ser. 1, vol. 7 (Miss.), pp. 135–42.

5. Andy Anderson, interviewed Fort Worth, Tex., n.d., *American Slave,* ser. 1, vol. 4 (Tex., pt. 1), pp. 14–16.

6. John Finnely, interviewed Fort Worth, Tex., n.d., *American Slave,* ser. 1, vol. 4 (Tex., pt. 2), pp. 35–40.

7. Thomas Cole, interviewed Corsicana, Tex., n.d., *American Slave,* ser. 1, vol. 4 (Tex., pt. 1), pp. 225–35.

8. George Johnson, interviewed Minn., n.d., *American Slave,* supp. ser. 1, vol. 2 (Minn.), pp. 115–17.

9. Jack and Rosa Maddox, interviewed Dallas, Tex., 3 Mar. 1938, *American Slave,* supp. ser. 2, vol. 7, pp. 2521–50.

10. George Kye, interviewed Fort Gibson, Okla., n.d., *American Slave,* ser. 1, vol. 7 (Okla.), pp. 172–75.

11. Isaac Adams, interviewed Tulsa, Okla., n.d., *American Slave,* ser. 1, vol. 7 (Okla.), pp. 1–5.

12. Mary Anderson, interviewed N.C., n.d., *American Slave,* ser. 2, vol. 14, pp. 19–26.

13. Katie Rowe, interviewed Tulsa, Okla., n.d., *American Slave,* ser. 1, vol. 7 (Okla.), pp. 275–84.

14. Fountain Hughes, interviewed Baltimore, Md., 1941, Archive of Folk Culture, Library of Congress.

15. Mary Barbour, interviewed Raleigh, N.C., n.d., *American Slave,* ser. 2, vol. 14, pp. 78–81.

16. George Conrad, Jr., interviewed Oklahoma City, Okla., n.d., *American Slave,* ser. 1, vol. 7 (Okla.), pp. 39–44.

17. Julius Jones, interviewed Coahoma Co., Miss., n.d., *American Slave,* supp. ser. 1, vol. 8, pp. 1215–25.

18. Mary A. Bell, interviewed St. Louis Co., Mo., n.d., *American Slave,* ser. 2, vol. 11 (Mo.), pp. 25–31.

19. Rachel Cruze, interviewed Cleveland, Ohio, n.d., *American Slave,* supp. ser. 1, vol. 5 (Ohio), pp. 290–323.

20. Lorenza Ezell, interviewed Beaumont, Tex., n.d., *American Slave,* ser. 1, vol. 4 (Tex., pt. 2), pp. 25–32.

21. Cato Carter, interviewed Dallas, Tex., 6 Dec. 1937, *American Slave,* supp. ser. 2, vol. 3, pp. 639–52.

22. Felix Haywood, interviewed San Antonio, Tex., n.d., *American Slave,* ser. 1, vol. 4 (Tex., pt. 2), pp. 130–34.

23. Charlotte Brown, interviewed Woods Crossing, Va., n.d., *Weevils in the Wheat,* pp. 58–59.

24. Wallace Quarterman, interviewed Frederica, Ga., 1935, Archive of Folk Culture, Library of Congress.

25. Susan Merritt, interviewed Marshall, Tex., 6 July 1938, *American Slave,* supp. ser. 2, vol. 7, pp. 2639–45.

26. Tempie Cummins, interviewed Jasper, Tex., n.d., *American Slave,* ser. 1, vol. 4 (Tex., pt. 1), pp. 263–65.

27. Robert Glenn, interviewed Raleigh, N.C., n.d., *American Slave,* ser. 2, vol. 14, pp. 328–39.

28. Tom Robinson, interviewed Hot Springs, Ark., n.d., *American Slave,* ser. 2, vol. 10 (Ark., pt. 6), pp. 64–68.

AFTERWORD

For more than one hundred years the Library of Congress has been collecting materials by and about African Americans. The pioneering builder of the Library's unparalleled African American collections was Daniel Alexander Payne Murray, who began his long career in the Library in 1871 as assistant to Librarian of Congress Ainsworth R. Spofford. Murray devoted a large part of his career at the Library to building the Library's African American holdings, believing that "the true test of the progress of a people is to be found in their literature."

For Daniel Murray, "literature" meant primarily print materials. But as the twentieth century unfolded, "literature" came to encompass "oral literature" preserved in an array of documentary materials in every medium, and the Library's holdings reflecting the African American experience expanded exponentially in all these media. The sound recordings, manuscript interviews, and photographs featured in *Remembering Slavery* are a small but powerful sampling. The recordings of former slaves in this volume are in the collections of the Library's American Folklife Center. Made in the 1930s and early 1940s by John A. and Ruby T. Lomax, Alan Lomax, Zora Neale Hurston, Mary Elizabeth Barnicle, John Henry Faulk, Roscoe Lewis, and others, they provide first-hand oral accounts of the institution of slavery by individuals who had been held in bondage three generations earlier. The narratives from manuscript sources are held by the Library's Manuscript Division, which has extensive collections made under the auspices of the United States Works Progress Administration (WPA), including the ex-slave narrative collection. The WPA ex-slave narrative collection also includes the photographs used throughout *Remembering Slavery*.

The sound recordings, manuscript materials, and photographs may be regarded as windows through which we are vouchsafed glimpses of the experience of slaves in the mid-19th century. At the same time, they are evidence of an extraordinary period in the 1930s, when the federal government, as part of its response to the Great Depression, organized a number of national initiatives documenting the lives, experiences, and cultural traditions of ordinary Americans. The ex-slave narratives, as documents of the 1930s, reveal the birth of our modern concept of "oral history," which was invented by folklorists, writers, and other cultural documentarians under the aegis of the Library of Congress and various WPA offices—especially the Federal Writers' Project—during the 1930s. "Oral history" has subsequently become both a new tool for the discipline of history and a new cultural idea undertaken in homes, schools, and communities by Americans from all walks of life. The monumental ex-slave narrative project, in both recorded and manuscript form, stands as our first national exploration of the idea of oral history.

More than 130 years have elapsed since the ratification of the Thirteenth Amendment to the U.S. Constitution declared slavery illegal in the United States, yet America is still wrestling with the legacy of slavery. Through the introduction and the commentary that accompanies the narratives, Ira Berlin, Marc Favreau, and Steven F. Miller help us to understand slavery through the stories of the people who survived it. Listening to their voices and reading their stories will enrich our common memory and widen our horizons as Americans.

James H. Billington
Librarian of Congress

INDEX